AN INFORMATIVE, PRACTICAL GUIDE TO

PALMS
OF THE WORLD
THEIR CULTIVATION, CARE & LANDSCAPE USE

AN INFORMATIVE, PRACTICAL GUIDE TO
PALMS
OF THE WORLD
THEIR CULTIVATION, CARE & LANDSCAPE USE

Alec Blombery & Tony Rodd

ANGUS
& ROBERTSON
PUBLISHERS

ANGUS & ROBERTSON PUBLISHERS

Unit 4, Eden Park, 31 Waterloo Road,
North Ryde, NSW, Australia 2113, and
16 Golden Square, London W1R 4BN,
United Kingdom

First published in Australia
by Angus & Robertson Publishers in 1982
First published in the United Kingdom
by Angus & Robertson (UK) in 1983
Reprinted 1984, 1985
Reprinted with corrections 1988

Copyright © Alec Blombery 1982
Tony Rodd 1982

National Library of Australia
Cataloguing-in-publication data.

Blombery, Alec M. (Alexander Morris)
    Palms.

    Includes index.
    ISBN 0 207 14848 1.

    1. Palms — Identification. I. Rodd, A.N.
    (Anthony Norman). II. Title.

584. '5

Typeset in 10pt Garamond by Setrite Typesetters
Printed in Singapore

CONTENTS

FOREWORD

The cultivation of palms dates back to antiquity with the number of different species grown escalating in comparatively modern times, following exploration and opening up of areas where palms occur naturally, particularly in tropical areas. Since the Victorian era, interest in palms has continued to grow, particularly in the warmer parts of the world where many different kinds of palms can be grown out of doors. In colder areas, palms have been cultivated in heated glasshouses. Fashion has resulted in surges of interest and at the time of writing there is a resurgence in growing palms, particularly as potted specimens; specialist nurserymen have responded by producing numbers of different palms for sale.

For the person interested in palms, there has frequently been difficulty in obtaining information about the various species, as most published literature is contained in Floras of different countries and in specialized scientific journals, a number of which are classics in their own right, but unfortunately are generally not available to the public, being in scientific and botanical libraries. The Palm Society (based in the U.S.A.), through their journal *Principes*, is an excellent source of information and this is available to the public for a modest subscription.

The object of this book is to present to the reader a general outline of the palm family with advice on cultivation and uses, followed by a detailed description of some of the better known genera, with a photographic representation of at least one species of each genus. The presentation has naturally been limited by the palms the authors have been able to photograph over a number of years in different countries. Some palms have been photographed in their natural habitats but most are cultivated specimens, mainly in botanical gardens. We are indebted to the directors and staffs of botanical gardens who maintain and add to their collections both for scientific purpose and for the public to appreciate. The following are the botanical gardens where photographs have been taken: Fairchild Tropical Gardens, Miami; Bogor Botanical Gardens, Indonesia; Foster Botanical Gardens, Honolulu; Royal Botanic Gardens, Sydney; Cairns Botanic Gardens, Queensland; Rockhampton Botanic Gardens, Queensland. All photographs are by the authors, unless otherwise acknowledged.

In preparing the text many works have been freely consulted, and all of these are listed in the bibliography.

Although the number of genera and species discussed represent only a minor proportion of the 2800 palm species, we hope that those presented will serve to encourage the reader to pursue a further interest into this fascinating group of plants.

We wish to acknowledge the assistance which has been provided by different people and organizations. Thanks are due particularly to Garuda Airlines for their generosity, to Betty Maloney for her artwork and finally to our respective spouses Marie and Margaret for their tolerance and assistance, particularly in producing a legible manuscript.

opposite:
Areca catechu.

1

INTRODUCTION

The term "palm" is commonly given to those plants which carry a cluster of large leaves at the top of an unbranched stem or trunk, often referred to as a crown or head.

This book deals with those plants belonging to the true palm family, Palmae (alternatively, Arecaceae). The palm family has over 200 genera and about 2800 species found in nearly all warm parts of the world. They are most abundant in the wettest parts of the equatorial tropics; however, in tropical Africa, the number of species is few compared with the American and Asian tropics. The areas richest in palms are peninsular Malaysia, Sumatra and Borneo, rivalled only by Central America and the upper Amazon region of South America. A number of tropical oceanic islands, although not large, have rich palm floras, particularly Madagascar, the Mascarene and Seychelles Islands, New Caledonia, and islands of the West Indies such as Cuba and Hispaniola. The number of palm species reduces considerably further away from the equator; for example, there are fewer palm species occurring in Australia than are recorded from the small island of Singapore, and in Europe there is only one species, *Chamaerops humilis*. In the large area of the United States of America, excluding the Florida Peninsula, there are only 5 species of palms. Although Australia has approximately 50 species, 40 of these are found only north of the Tropic of Capricorn.

Palms appear to have originated and are still most abundant where warm, perpetually wet conditions prevail, ideal for the growth of many plants. Under such conditions palms have evolved into many forms which have become adapted to specialized places in the ecosystem, e.g. the deep shade of the rainforest floor, poorly drained areas such as swamps and edges of streams, or climbing amongst larger woody forest trees. A much smaller number of palms have become adapted to harsher environments, such as areas of low rainfall, or cooler regions where the minimum temperatures would cause tissue damage to most tropical palms. Hardly any palms which occur in dry regions are adapted to survive a complete absence of soil moisture; their adaptation is that of having a leaf structure which will tolerate very low humidity and fierce heat for long periods and a root system which can penetrate the soil to considerable depths. Many of the palms from arid areas are also resistant to frost damage.

A large number of palms grow beneath the forest canopy under low light conditions, but they are usually smaller, more delicate plants. Most larger palms require a higher light level and, as a result, exploit situations in the rainforest such as stream banks, sides of steep hills, cliff edges, and newly

PALM HABITATS

opposite:
Palms in natural habitat — a recently discovered species of Livistona *on cliff above the Victoria River in northern Australia.*

3

created gaps in the forest canopy which permit the entry of additional light (though palms are generally not amongst the earliest pioneer species). Another common strategy by which palms obtain sufficient light is by the development of climbing mechanisms, such as hooks, combined with a very rapid stem growth, in order that the leaves may be carried up to the level of the highest tree tops; other palms may grow sufficiently tall to enable them to emerge through the forest canopy.

Many palm species grow in tropical savannah woodland, a characteristic vegetation-type of tropical regions with highly seasonal rainfall, often with frequent fires in the dry season. Most of the species in such communities are well adapted to survive fires and this applies to the palms equally. A common feature of these palms is the trunks' being covered with layers of fibres from the leaf sheaths or a corky outer layer from the dead remains of the leaf bases and leaf stalks, which serve to insulate the living tissue from excessive heat. Palms which grow in these regions are generally deep rooted in order to have access to deep subsoil moisture throughout the dry season. They also generally show other morphological features of palms from arid environments.

Another significant palm habitat is in poorly drained or swampy ground, either in rainforests or elsewhere. Palms under these conditions seem to have a competitive advantage over other large plants, often forming pure stands in such situations. A number of palms, though only in the tropics, have adapted to a saline environment, mainly in coastal regions. The extreme adaptation to salt water is represented by the palm *Nypa* which is a true mangrove species, occurring on mudbanks only exposed at low tide. Quite a few other species are found in brackish water, e.g. the Sago Palm, *Metroxylon sagu*, and others, like the Coconut Palm, are adapted to grow near the ocean shores and are able to tolerate salt spray.

Tropical swamp forest with dominating palms of Hydriastele *and* Licuala. *Tropical north-eastern Australia.*

Palms in undisturbed rainforest in steep gully. Tropical eastern Australia.

Washingtonia filifera *in soak of permanent water. Mohave Desert, California.*

ECONOMIC IMPORTANCE

The importance of the role which palms play in tropical areas of the world is not generally realized. While palms are used extensively for ornamental purposes, they are also of significant economic value, particularly in the less industrialized countries.

Local Uses

In some regions almost all parts of some species are made use of. Leaves are commonly used for thatching both roofs and walls of houses; leaflets and leaf stalks are used for weaving into numerous articles, such as mats, baskets and bags of many types, for hats and even as material on which to write. The trunks of palms are used in many different ways, for example as building material, as irrigation pipes, and for making implements such as spears, bows and arrows. The inner fibrous part of the stem in species of the genus *Metroxylon* yields large quantities of carbohydrate in the form of sago, which is pure starch; the sugary sap from the cut stems and inflorescences of some palms is used for producing palm sugar, or jaggery, and fermented into alcoholic beverages such as toddy or palm wine, or spirits like arrack. The long flexible stems of climbing palms such as *Calamus* and allied genera, commonly known as rattan cane or rotangs, as well as being used for building and structural purposes and as a tying material, are extensively used for cane furniture of various types and for weaving into baskets, woven seats of chairs and various other cane articles.

The apical buds or young shoots of many species are edible and are known as "palm cabbage" or "palm hearts". As the removal of the growing tip results in the death of the palm, the term "millionaire's salad" is sometimes applied, particularly to valuable species such as the Coconut Palm. The fruits of a number of palms are used as food — Date Palms and Coconut Palms provide examples. Many fruits also yield oil, which may be used for cooking purposes. The fibres from the leaf sheaths of a number of palms are used for various purposes such as brooms, ropes and thatching.

Commercial Uses

The fruit of the Date Palm, *Phoenix dactylifera*, is widely cultivated both for local use and export in many parts of the hot, dry Middle East and North Africa, and also in the low rainfall areas of southern California.

Copra from the Coconut Palm, *Cocos nucifera*, is produced in large quantities in tropical areas such as New Guinea, the Pacific Islands and the Malay Archipelago. The copra is the dried endosperm of the seed and is exported from its place of origin to more industrialized areas, where oil is extracted for food, soap and many other products. The dried endosperm is also grated to form the well-known desiccated coconut, widely used for confectionery and cake making.

In more recent times the oil from copra is tending to be replaced by the oil extracted from the fruit of the African Oil Palm, *Elaeis guineensis*, which is being widely grown in plantations in tropical areas. This palm bears fruit at an earlier age than the Coconut Palm and gives a higher yield of oil.

A lesser-known product but one of considerable economic importance is carnauba wax, which is obtained from the thick surface layer of wax found on the leaves of the palm *Copernicia prunifera*. This palm forms large natural stands in north-eastern Brazil and is the basis of an industry in that area. Carnauba wax is used extensively in automobile and furniture polishes.

The fibres from palms are also used for many commercial purposes, the best known being coir from the outer layer or husk of the coconut, used for making mats and rope as well as other products. The leaf sheaths of several species, particularly *Leopoldinia piassaba*, provide a strong, tough fibre known as "piassava fibre". This dark brown to black fibre is widely used in the manufacture of brooms of various types and is made into tough, strong ropes. Fibres from the leaflets of the palm *Raphia ruffia* from Madagascar provide the material known as "raffia", used as a tying material and for basket and hat making.

The Betel Palm, *Areca catechu*, provides a fruit which is chewed with lime and leaves of a species of *Piper*. It has mildly stimulant properties and somewhat narcotic effects when chewed to excess. Considerable use is made of betel nut in southern Asia, the Pacific Islands and parts of Africa. In India alone the production of betel nut has exceeded 140 000 tonnes per annum.

GENERAL CHARACTER-ISTICS OF PALMS

Palms have a number of characteristics which differ from those of other plants. The following summary of these characteristics should lead to a better understanding of palms' growth habits and thereby assist with propagation and cultivation.

The palm plant may be divided into several parts:

1 Stem or trunk
2 Roots
3 Leaves
4 Inflorescence and flowers
5 Fruits

Stem or Trunk

The stem or trunk may be single or multiple. In the latter case branching occurs below or near the ground; only a very few species of palms branch from the upper part of the trunk. In some palms the stem may be completely below the ground level; for example in the genus *Nypa* only the leaves and inflorescences emerge above the surface.

The trunk varies considerably in different species. It may be short to very long, robust to very slender, and sometimes swollen to various degrees; the surface may be smooth, finely to distinctly ringed, rough to very rough with the old leaf bases remaining attached at all times as in most species of *Phoenix*. The surface may be covered with fibres from the old leaf sheaths or there may be sharp spines or short roots projecting from the old leaf scars. The distance between the rings or scars from the old leaves varies considerably and depends largely upon how quickly the trunk grows in height. This varies with the different species and the conditions available for growth. Climbing palms hold the record, however. They may have a distance of a metre or more between leaf scars, and a stem up to 150 metres in length. More commonly palms have a solitary trunk with the leaves fairly close together and restricted to the trunk apex. Those palms which shed their leaves immediately they age usually leave a neat scar or ring on the trunk, while those species which retain their leaves for an indefinite period usually have a rough, uneven scar or ring or persistent leaf bases.

Palms do not form rings of wood as trees do; their new tissues are laid down only by the massive growing tip or apical bud. The conducting and supporting tissues of the trunk are formed of long, parallel fibres (fibro-vascular bundles) scattered in a ground tissue of thin-walled cells, which are stiffened and made rigid by the pressure of sap. While a number of palms increase their trunk diameter, particularly in the lower part, this occurs by the cells of the ground tissues swelling and forming air spaces between them. Unlike trees, which can repair damage to their stems, in palms any damage which occurs to the trunk remains for all time. It is important therefore that care should be exercised with the trunks of cultivated palms to ensure that damage does not occur.

1

2

3

4

5

6

7

8

9

SOME EXAMPLES
OF PALM TRUNKS

1. Smooth and ringed.

2. Distinctly ringed and stepped.

3. Rough and ringed.

4. Rough and indistinctly ringed.

5. Indistinctly ringed and patterned
with petiole scars.

6. Rough with projecting petiole bases.

7. Persistent leaf bases with fibrous
leaf sheaths.

8. Persistent split leaf bases.

9. Ringed, spiny between rings.

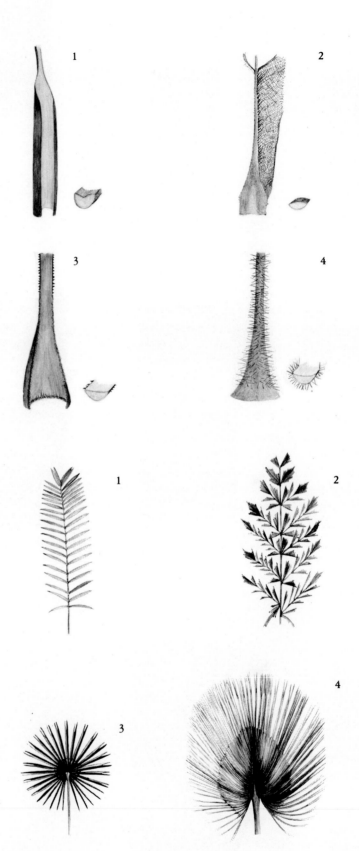

LEAF BASES WITH SECTIONS OF PETIOLE

1. Completely encircling tubular leaf base from a palm with crownshaft, showing also part of the petiole.

2. Leaf base showing persistent fibrous leaf sheath cut down one side, unrolled, with the other side attached to the base and petiole, and showing part of the petiole.

3. Flanged leaf base with rough margins where fibres of sheath have been attached, showing part of the spiny-margined petiole and the petiole cross-section.

4. Flanged leaf base and petiole with spines on the under side and margins, showing also a section of the petiole.

TYPES OF LEAVES

1. Pinnate blade or feather leaf.

2. Bipinnate blade.

3. Palmate or fan-shaped blade, circular in outline, divided into segments to about 2/3rds its depth, each segment forked at apex.

4. Costapalmate or fan-shaped blade with costa, almost circular in outline, undulate, divided to about half its depth into segments, each forked at apex.

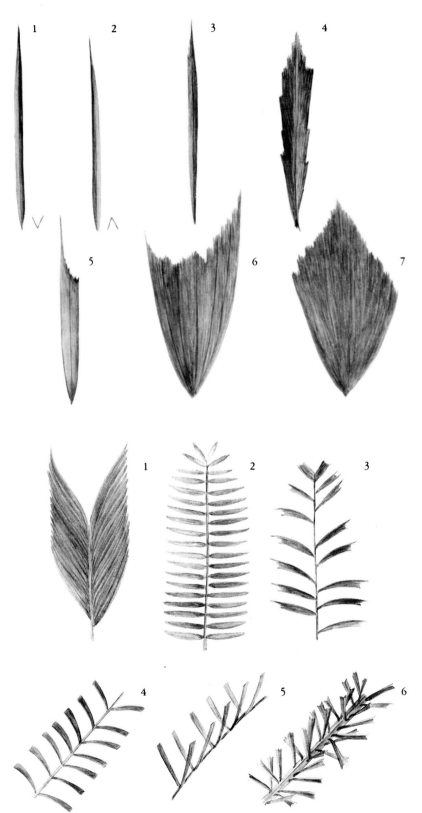

LEAFLET SHAPES

1. Leaflet linear, tapered to a pointed apex and folded upwards at the base (induplicate).

2. Leaflet linear, tapered to a pointed apex and folded downwards at the base (reduplicate).

3. Leaflet linear and tapered to a point with toothing on the lower margin near apex.

4. Leaflet oblong-wedge-shaped, with notching and toothing on margins and apex.

5. Leaflet oblong, truncate, oblique, with apex notched and toothed, one margin extended into a point.

6. Leaflet wedge-shaped with several veins, oblique, notched and toothed at the apex with both margins extended into points.

7. Leaflet rhomboid, notched and toothed on the upper margins.

LEAFLET ARRANGEMENTS

1. Leaf simple and pinnately ribbed with toothed margins and V notch at apex.

2. Leaflets closely and evenly spaced along rhachis.

3. Leaflets irregularly spaced along rhachis.

4. Lower part of both ranks of leaflets, arising from the rhachis in more or less the one plane.

5. Lower parts of both ranks of leaflets arising in the one plane but with the 2 ranks directed upwards forming a V.

6. Lower parts of leaflets arising from the rhachis in a number of different planes, giving the leaf a plumose appearance.

Roots

The roots of palms, like those of other monocotyledonous plants, do not thicken with age and have a limited branching capacity. As the palm develops, new roots emerge from the stem base between the existing roots and progressively from the lower outer part of the trunk. In older palms there is usually a mass of roots of equal thickness growing from the trunk base, frequently emerging above the ground surface and growing outwards and downwards into the soil. In some species, and particularly in palms in shallower soils, the continued growth of roots may lift the base of the trunk above the ground. This frequently occurs with palms grown in containers. Some species of palms produce roots from the trunk, from up to about 1 to 2 metres above the ground. These roots grow downwards at an angle and form stilt roots.

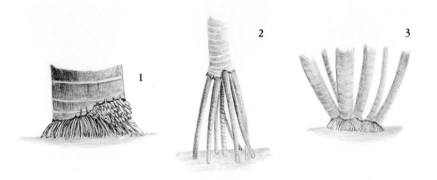

TRUNK BASES SHOWING ROOTS

1. Base of mature palm with new roots developing from trunk above ground.
2. Trunk with stilt roots.
3. A cluster palm with a number of stems arising at ground level and additional roots developing from their bases.

Leaves

Palm leaves or ''fronds'' are found in two main shapes — hand- or fan-shaped (palmate), and feather-shaped (pinnate). A few species with basically pinnate leaves have the leaflets further subdivided. These leaves are called bipinnate. Different palm species show great variation in the number and size of leaves, from a few to several hundred and from small and delicate to massive, sometimes reaching 20 metres in length. Generally the leaves are crowded closely together in a spiral manner at the top of the trunk, forming a crown or head, with some species such as climbing palms and others like *Rhapis* having the leaves spaced more widely along the stem.

The leaves or fronds consist of three main parts: the sheathing base, the leaf stalk (petiole) and the blade (lamina).

Sheathing Base

The base of the leaf forms a sheathing cylinder. All subsequently developing leaves must grow up through the sheathing cylinder, there being considerable differences in the manner in which the base develops in different groups of palms.

Crownshaft   At one extreme, the base remains as an outer, distinctly sheathing cylinder of fairly even thickness, merging into the thickened leaf stalk at its apex. In this form of base, the whole of the sheathing cylinder remains as live conducting tissue until the whole leaf is about to fall, when it finally splits on the side opposite the leaf stalk and with the other parts of the leaf falls off, leaving a distinct ring or scar around the trunk. Palms which have this characteristic are said to have a crownshaft, a term suggested 60 years ago by L. H. Bailey. Palms with a crownshaft usually have a smooth trunk, although in some species both crownshaft and trunk may be armed with sharp spines.

Other Types of Sheathing Bases   In many species of palms, although the sheathing base forms an encircling cylinder in the early stages of growth, it is very thin, except for the thickened flanged base of the leaf stalk. As later-formed leaves expand within it, the surrounding cylindrical base is extended and the softer tissues disintegrate, leaving only fibre bundles forming a network of fine to thick, tough, coarse fibres surrounding the trunk, with the only solid, live parts being the thickened leaf stalk base attached to the trunk. The fibrous network of the sheathing cylinder varies considerably in different species, some having a fine and woven appearance, others being tough and matted or even spiny. Palms with this form of sheathing base commonly retain the old leaves, and usually matted fibres, for indefinite periods, particularly in younger plants, or they may be retained immediately below the crown in older mature specimens. When the leaves fall, they leave scars on the trunk of different patterns and from smooth to rough, depending upon the shape of the junction between sheathing base and trunk, and the manner in which dead leaves are shed. In some genera, such as *Phoenix*, sections of the thickened leaf stalk base remain attached to the trunk indefinitely.

Between those species with a distinct crownshaft and those with narrow, flanged leaf bases, there are many species which have leaf bases between the two extremes, sometimes carried close against the trunk and almost forming a crownshaft.

Leaf Stalk

The leaf stalk or petiole is the connecting section between the sheathing base and the blade; often there is no sharp distinction between it and the sheathing base. The leaf stalk may be very short (the leaves being then termed subsessile or sessile) to long. Generally the leaf stalk is stiff and tough to support the large leaves, although in some palms it is thin and flexible. In some species, particularly in fan palms, the edges of the leaf stalk, especially towards the base, are armed with stiff, sharp teeth, or the margins are sharp and razor-like. Some species have sharp spines on the surface of the leaf stalk as well as on the sheathing leaf base. This spiny character is no doubt an adaptation to discourage animals from eating the tender new growth.

Blade

Leaf blades are found in 3 basic shapes: palmate, pinnate and bipinnate. In its early stages of growth, the blade is folded in a fan-like manner and, as it elongates, the leaflets or segments split along predetermined lines. The leaflets or segments are always folded shallowly or deeply into a V-shape where they join the midrib (rhachis) or leaf stalk apex. In the majority of

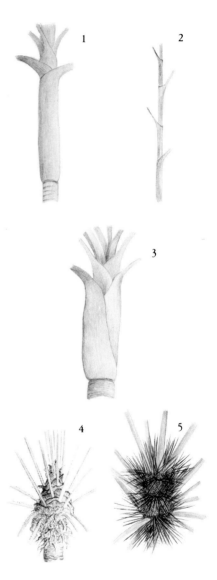

SOME ARRANGEMENTS OF LEAF BASES AT TOP OF TRUNK

1. Bases remaining completely encircling and not breaking down into fibres, forming a crownshaft.
2. As for 1, but stem elongated and a crownshaft not formed.
3. Bases broad but not completely encircling for their whole length, hence not forming a crownshaft.
4. Leaf bases covered with fibres of old leaf sheaths.
5. Leaf bases covered with fibres and marginal spines of old leaf sheaths.

feather palms, the opening of the V faces downwards, the leaves then being termed reduplicate; an exception among feather palms is the genus *Phoenix* where the V is upright and termed induplicate.

Some palms, chiefly from protected rainforest areas, have a simple leaf blade, not divided into leaflets or segments. In these simple blades, however, the arrangement of the major ribs or veins determines whether they are classified as fan palms or feather palms.

Palmate and Costapalmate Leaves   Palms with leaves of this type are commonly known as fan palms, having a blade which is more or less semi-circular to circular in outline, unfolding into a fan shape. The surface, as well as being pleated, may also be wavy or undulate, often with the two halves directed upwards and inwards, or sometimes almost flat.

When all the ribs or veins arise from the leaf stalk apex and all radiate outwards from this central point, the blade is said to be palmate. At this central point there is frequently a raised projection from the leaf stalk apex on the upper side which is known as a hastula. Frequently, though, the leaf stalk is extended into a stout midrib or rhachis, from which some of the ribs arise. The form of leaf blade which results is termed costapalmate. Close examination will reveal that the majority of fan palms are costapalmate to some degree. The more extreme costapalmate blades have an appearance which is intermediate between a fan palm and feather palm.

The blade in fan palms is usually divided or lobed to varying depths into segments, each of which may be further divided at the apex into 2 points or lobes. In some cases the blade may be divided right to the base into segments. The ends of the segments of some species hang in a pendulous manner, whilst in others they are stiff and radiating. In some species fine, thread-like fibres may be present on the margins of the blade.

Pinnate Leaves   Palms with pinnate leaves are commonly known as feather palms and have the blade divided or partly divided into leaflets which are arranged along either side of the midrib in the manner of a feather, the midrib being a continuation of the leaf stalk. The leaflets are linear to lance-shaped, elliptical, wedge-shaped or rhomboid and tapering to a pointed or raggedly toothed apex or notched in a fishtail-like outline. The leaflets vary greatly in number and may be closely to widely and evenly to unevenly spaced along the midrib. The two rows or ranks of leaflets may arise in the same plane, be inward directed, arched or drooping; sometimes the leaflets may arise in a number of different planes and give the whole blade a plume-like appearance, it then being termed plumose. Leaflets commonly have a single midrib or vein, but in some species there are several major veins.

Bipinnate   This form of leaf is limited to the small genus *Caryota*. In a basically pinnate leaf, each leaflet is further divided into a number of broad, fishtail-shaped leaflets or pinnules, each with a ragged, cut-off, toothed apex. These palms are commonly known as fishtail palms. Some other feather palms have the leaflets divided to the base into a number of segments, resulting in a blade type somewhat intermediate between pinnate and bipinnate.

Inflorescence

The inflorescence is a specialized flower-bearing branch and, in most palms, is the only form of branching which the stem undergoes above ground level. It always arises in the early bud stage amongst the leaf bases, but sometimes its expansion may be delayed until the leaf enclosing the inflorescence has fallen. This gives it the appearance that the inflorescence arises from the trunk below the leaves. All palms with a crownshaft display this pattern of development, as also do some palms without a crownshaft. Inflorescences of this type are said to be infrafoliar (meaning below the leaves). Where the inflorescence develops to flowering stage while still amongst the leaves, it is said to be interfoliar.

Inflorescence, Bracts and Flowers

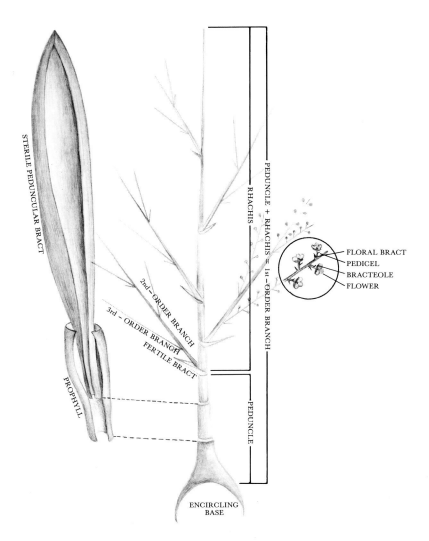

STERILE PEDUNCULAR BRACT

PEDUNCLE + RHACHIS = 1st – ORDER BRANCH

RHACHIS

2nd – ORDER BRANCH

3rd – ORDER BRANCH

FERTILE BRACT

FLORAL BRACT
PEDICEL
BRACTEOLE
FLOWER

PROPHYLL

PEDUNCLE

ENCIRCLING BASE

Diagrammatic representation of a typical palm inflorescence, showing enclosing bracts separated from peduncle.

The inflorescence consists basically of three parts: the stalk or peduncle, which is that portion below where the inflorescence first branches or where the first flower arises; the central stem or rhachis, from which side branches may arise (in some palms there are no side branches, in which case the inflorescence is called a spike); and the flower-bearing branches or branchlets. After the first branching from the rhachis, further branching may occur. All branches and branchlets terminate in a flower-bearing portion, even the central stem.

Bracts

A significant and conspicuous feature of palm inflorescences is the presence of large, tough bracts, or modified leaves, which usually enclose the whole inflorescence in bud up to an advanced stage of development. These bracts are necessary to protect the young, extremely succulent inflorescence, which has a high sugar content, from animals.

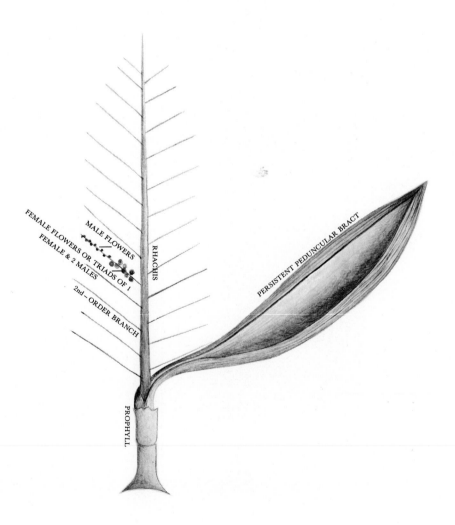

Diagrammatic inflorescence with many branches of second order only, and persistent, large, sterile, peduncular bract, enclosing the whole in bud, as found in most palms of the Cocosoid group.

Prophyll and Peduncular Bracts   There is always one lowermost bract on the inflorescence stalk known as the prophyll, which subtends no branches, and hence is called sterile. Between this and the lowermost branch, there may be one or more additional sterile bracts, called peduncular bracts. Often one of these bracts is very large and encloses the whole inflorescence, though sometimes the prophyll is equally large and encloses the peduncular bract. Mostly these sterile bracts completely encircle the peduncle. They may be cylindrical, spindle or club-shaped, boat-shaped to flattened and 2-edged. They may be from thin and papery to thick and woody, sometimes falling off by abscission at the base, usually just before the flowers open, or frequently persisting for long periods after they have split open on one side to release the flowers.

Fertile Bracts and Bracteoles   A fertile bract subtends a flower-bearing branch or flower. In many palms the fertile bracts on the midrib are large and tubular and, together with any peduncular bracts, are arranged in an overlapping series which encloses the inflorescence in bud, the flower-bearing branches being finally freed by rapid elongation of the rhachis. In many other palms the fertile bracts are greatly reduced in size, or so small as to be considered absent, and have no significant function, all the protecting function being left to the peduncular bracts. In some palms each flower or small group of flowers is subtended and protected by one or several bracts, sometimes fused together into elaborate structures. Others carry additionally small bracts called bracteoles which are positioned immediately beneath the flowers, but do not subtend them as do the floral bracts.

Flowers

The flowers of palms are usually quite small, but generally make up for their size in the large number produced. Their colour varies from white to cream, bright yellow, orange or pink to purplish, often with a strong, sweet, fruity perfume. Most flowers are adapted to insect and animal pollination, whilst others, for example *Phoenix*, are wind pollinated.

As with other monocotyledonous plants, the flower parts are in multiples of 3 with a basic pattern of 3 sepals, 3 petals, 6 stamens, and an ovary with 3 carpels with 3 ovules, 3 styles and 3 stigmas. Evolutionary changes have brought about modification of the above arrangement with various degrees of fusion and reduction of sepals and petals, multiplication in the number of stamens and so on.

In many groups of palms the flowers have evolved into separate male and female flowers, this being achieved by the degeneration of the carpels or stamens into sterile organs accompanied by reduction in size or virtual disappearance.

The majority of palms have separate male and female flowers on the one plant (monoecious), whilst others have male and female flowers on separate plants (dioecious), or both sexes in the one flower (hermaphrodite). Where there are separate male and female flowers, it is a common pattern for the male flowers to open and fall off before the female flowers open.

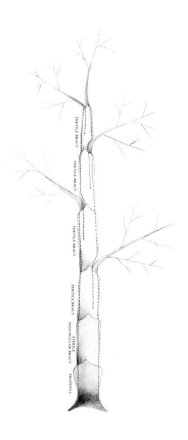

Diagrammatic inflorescence with elongated rhachis sheathed in persistent tubular bracts, as found in many palms of the Coryphoid group.

There may be great variation in the way individual flowers are grouped on the flower-bearing branches of the inflorescences of different palms. The most basic or primitive arrangement is that in which the flowers are spirally arranged on the branchlets, each with a distinct flower stalk or pedicel. Sometimes the flowers may be in small clusters or rows. When flowers are of different sexes these are often segregated on the inflorescence, there being a general tendency for the female flowers to be at the bases of the branchlets and the male flowers towards the ends. A common arrangement is a group of 3 flowers, termed a triad, consisting of 1 female flower flanked by 2 male. In some palms the flowers or groups of flowers are situated in sunken pits on the thickened floral branchlets.

Fruits

The palm fruit develops from the fertilized ovary of a female or hermaphrodite flower. Enclosed in the fruit are one or more seeds. The technical distinction between fruit and seed is that the former is derived from the ovary wall and the latter from the ovule. Most palm fruits are classed as drupes, meaning fruits with a fleshy outer layer or mesocarp (in addition to the outer skin or exocarp) and an inner layer of different texture and hardness, the endocarp. This endocarp encloses the underlying seed coat (testa) and may persist as its covering after the softer outer layer is removed; it then appears to be part of the seed but botanically is a layer of the fruit, for example the hard stone of *Butia*.

In some drupes the endocarp encloses more than one seed, or there may be separate envelopes of endocarp enclosing separate seeds. A variant of the drupe is the nut, which has dry rather than fleshy mesocarp. If the fruit is fleshy but has no distinct endocarp enclosing the seed or seeds, it is classed as a berry. Some palm fruits fall into this category.

Different palm fruits have many characteristics which aid in classification and identification. Overall shape and size are of obvious importance. Also useful are presence and position of the scar, or remains, of the stigma or style, which in the flower are attached to the ovary. Where the style is attached low down on one side of the ovary, it remains in this position in the fruit. One-sided growth of the ovary after fertilization can result in the remains of a style which was apical in flower being in a lateral position on the fruit.

The petals, or petals and sepals, sometimes persist on the fruit, clinging closely to its base and accompanying it when it falls. Often they increase in size as the fruit develops.

The wall of the fruit is particularly rich in characters; the surface texture, thickness, toughness and colour of the outer skin vary greatly; the mesocarp in the majority of palms contains fibres, the size, density and arrangement of which vary widely. Instead of, or as well as, fibres, there may be small woody bodies, or sclerosomes (as in the flesh of a pear), which may be disc- or star-shaped. The endocarp is likewise variable in thickness, hardness and colour. Sometimes it is remarkably sculptured, with folds

FLOWERS

1. Separate male and female flowers (in bud) in groups of 3 (triads) with a female flanked by 2 longer male flowers, the groups spirally arranged on the branchlets.

2. Bisexual flowers (in bud) in groups, the groups spirally arranged on branchlet.

3. Unspecialized bisexual flower (hermaphrodite) with 3 sepals joined at base, 3 petals, 6 stamens and ovary with 3-lobed stigma.

18

penetrating deeply into the seed. In the cocosoid palms (related to the coconut) it is thick and woody and has 3 pores which may vary in position.

The function of the fruit is to assist in dispersal of the seed (or seeds) contained in it. In palms this is achieved in two main ways. Fleshy fruits, usually with a high sugar or fat content, present a rich energy source to birds and animals, who often eat the fruit whole, in which case the seeds remain undigested and are passed through, usually being carried some distance in the meantime. This process usually aids germination by removing inhibiting substances present in the fruit wall. Larger fleshy fruits are often picked by tree-dwelling animals such as monkeys, who then carry them a little way through the tree tops, eat the flesh and discard the seed.

A smaller number of palms have fruits with dry, fibrous walls — the coconut is an example. This is considered to be an adaptation for dispersal by floating in water. Many palm fruits adapted for dispersal by animals are also effectively dispersed by floodwaters.

Seeds

Palm seeds vary greatly in size, shape and structure, but have some common features. All are of the endospermic type, the main food storage being in the form of a tissue called endosperm (or albumen), as in the wheat or maize grain, rather than enlarged cotyledons, as in beans. Most palms have a hard, horny, white endosperm, rich in oil, starch and other carbohydrates. A peculiarity of the coconut is that, while the outer layer of endosperm is of the above type, in the centre the endosperm is liquid in form.

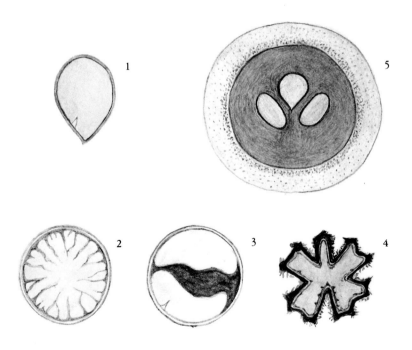

FRUIT SECTIONS

1. Longitudinal section of fruit showing thin mesocarp, thin endocarp, seed coat and non-ruminate endosperm with small embryo at the lower left.

2. Transverse section of fruit showing thin mesocarp, thin endocarp, seed coat and ruminate endosperm.

3. Longitudinal section through fruit showing thin mesocarp, thin endocarp, and seed with a plug of the seed coat tissue penetrating from one side through the non-ruminate endosperm, and with a small embryo at lower left.

4. Transverse section through endocarp and seed showing hard woody endocarp deeply penetrating the slightly ruminate endosperm.

5. Transverse section through fruit showing thick fibrous mesocarp, thick, very dense, hard endocarp with 3 seed cavities and 3 seeds, each seed with a very thin coat and the endosperm non-ruminate.

1. Globose fruit with remains of stigma at apex and persistent sepals and petals at the base.

2. Ovoid fruit with remains of stigma at the apex.

3. Ellipsoid fruit with remains of stigma at apex.

4. Ovoid-conical fruit with remains of stigma at apex.

4a. Fruit with mesocarp removed showing woody endocarp with 3 pores, typical of Cocosoid palms.

4b. Longitudinal section through fruit with fibrous mesocarp, thick woody endocarp, seed coat and hollow, non-ruminate endosperm.

Enclosing the endosperm is the seed coat or testa. This may be extremely thin, appearing merely as a layer of contrasting colour, or quite thick and sometimes of flint-like hardness. A peculiarity of the seed coat of many palms is that it intrudes into the endosperm in a variety of patterns. One of the most distinctive, and the most common, is where the intrusions take the form of numerous flanges, which in cross section appear as darker coloured, somewhat irregular "spokes", radiating inwards through the white endosperm; where this occurs, the endosperm is called ruminate. The other common type of intrusion is in the form of a plug of darker seed coat tissue, penetrating in towards the centre of the endosperm from the base or from one side. In many seeds, however, the seed coat does not penetrate the endosperm which is then termed homogeneous.

In a few palms (e.g. *Salacca*), the seed has an additional layer outside the seed coat, which originates as an outgrowth of the seed stalk or funicle. This layer is white and fleshy, and functions as a substitute for a fleshy layer in the fruit wall, usually absent in such palms. This fleshy part of the seed is called an aril. The fruit of the Lychee (not a palm) also has an aril as its edible part.

The most important part of the seed is the embryo, representing the beginning of the new plant. In all palms the embryo is a relatively small plug of tissue which fits neatly into a cavity in the surface of the endosperm. In different genera, the position of the embryo varies, being either basal (near the fruit stalk), lateral (at one side), or apical (at opposite end to stalk).

Germination of palm seed is a gradual process, occurring over a period of weeks or even months. The first leaf (plumule) arising from the shoot is very short and tubular. Successively larger seedling leaves grow up through its centre. These seedling leaves have a shape characteristic for the genus and most of the major groups have a consistent type of seed leaf; although in most fan palm genera the seed leaf is undivided and strap-like, in some genera it is palmate in shape. A further example of variation is in the Arecoid feather palms where most of the seedling leaves are 2-lobed, however in some they are pinnate and a few are undivided.

TYPES OF GERMINATION AND SEED LEAVES, ALSO SHOWING DEVELOPING ROOTS

1. Seed with adjacent germination, showing early stages of growth.

2. Seed with adjacent germination and first seedling-leaf pinnate.

3. Seed with adjacent germination and first seedling-leaf bifid or V-notched.

4. Seed with remote germination and first seedling-leaf wedge-shaped and toothed.

5. Seed with remote germination and first seedling-leaf fan-shaped.

CULTIVATION

Palms differ from many other plants in their particular habit of growth, and for a better understanding of these characters a recapitulation of some of the points discussed under General Characteristics (p.8) should be found helpful for the gardener wanting to cultivate palms successfully:

Those palms which have a solitary trunk cannot be generally induced to develop additional trunks. Although the trunk is strong, tough and fibrous, any damage which occurs is permanent, as palms are unable to produce new tissues to repair the damage.

When the growing apex or bud is removed from the top of the trunk, the stem will die and, if the palm has only a solitary trunk, this means the end of the life of that plant. Palms which have multiple trunks are able to produce new growths from the base of the trunk at or below ground level; the rate at which new growths are produced is chiefly governed by conditions available for growth.

The roots are tough and strong and fairly even in width. They branch to a limited degree, and do not increase in diameter in the manner of woody plants. Roots are continually being replaced and in older established palms frequently develop from the trunk slightly above the ground, growing outwards and downwards into the soil. When grown in containers, the roots of strong-growing species tend to lift the plant above the ground.

The leaves pass through a juvenile stage and may differ in appearance from the mature leaves; the length of time between the first juvenile leaves and appearance of the mature type varies with the species — in some cases it may be many years.

Most palms when mature develop a fixed number of leaves in the crown, with a new leaf expanding at the apex only as the oldest leaf dies. In many large palms it may take quite a number of years for a new leaf to reach maturity and die.

If the older leaves are cut while still green and alive, the growth of the palm can be affected, particularly when a number are removed at the one time. The removal of old spent leaves from those species which retain their dead leaves for indefinite periods is a matter of personal choice.

The strong, tough, flexible nature of the trunk, the tough tenacious roots and the flexible leaflets make palms very resistant to damage and uprooting by strong winds.

IMPORTANT FACTS ABOUT PALMS

opposite:
An avenue of Royal Palms creates an imposing landscape. Java.

CONDITIONS FOR GROWTH

While some palms, Date Palms, for example, will grow under hot, dry conditions, and others such as the Coconut Palm will grow adjoining the sea in warm areas subject to strong winds, most palms will grow more successfully in protected positions, with ample moisture and deep soil. When exposed to drying conditions, the leaflets of palms from rainforest and moist areas usually become burnt and dried at the tips. The leaflets of many palms suffer in the same manner when exposed to frosts. For growing rainforest type palms, the soil should be enriched with leaf mould and peat moss to hold moisture. This should be renewed at regular intervals as it breaks down over a period.

While some palms will grow better in well drained soils, many are tolerant of very wet conditions. It is important that a plentiful supply of moisture be provided for all developing palms, particularly during the early stages of development. Most species from rainforests prefer acid soils, but most species from dry areas will grow successfully in a wide range of soils, both acid and alkaline.

Palms are chiefly surface feeders and nutrient materials should be added to the upper layer of the soil.

Palms from hot humid tropical areas will not grow successfully in dry or cooler areas unless the correct environment is provided, for example container cultivation in a heated glasshouse, or in suitable heated indoor conditions. In a similar manner, those palms which come from temperate regions do not grow successfully in tropical lowland areas.

There are a large number of different palms which may be cultivated under a wide range of conditions and many may be grown as potted specimens, permitting suitable conditions to be provided artificially.

Palms grown under unsuitable conditions, such as too warm or cool a climate, excessive dryness or heavy shade, may not flower successfully or set or hold fruit.

See Appendix III (p.185) which lists palms suitable for cultivation in different climatic zones and in different conditions.

The large numbers of different kinds of palms provide quite a wide scope for their use as landscape subjects and for decorative use as pot plants, for both outdoor and indoor use.

LANDSCAPING WITH PALMS

Selection is limited by factors such as temperature and moisture availability and in many areas by the small range of species stocked by most nurseries. This limited range of palms often results in palm enthusiasts increasing their collection by personally raising the less common species from seed.

When planning for the use of palms as a major element in landscaping, it is important to carefully consider the possible effects which will be produced as the palms mature, and the length of time required to achieve the results. Incorrect selection of species may result, in the long term, in aesthetic effects being lost with a resultant crowded jumble of many different sizes and heights; where rapid growing species may grow up through the crowns of slow growing, sun-loving types, such as *Butia* and *Chamaerops*, the latter then being overshadowed and not showing to advantage.

A most important consideration for the attractive use of palms in landscaping, even where the climate is suitable, is the area available for planting and the effects it is desired to achieve; for example it should be remembered that a collection of larger-growing palms will require an extensive area for their effective display. By correct planning, it is possible, even in a small garden, to use a number of palms from genera such as *Chamaedorea* and *Rhapis* or to use, for example, only a single specimen of species such as *Howea*, *Trachycarpus*, *Archontophoenix*, *Phoenix roebelenii*.

Palms often grow better with one another than with competition from other surface feeding plants.

The effect resulting from planting palms with other plants should be given careful consideration, as they blend more effectively with bold-leaved tropical and subtropical plants such as *Pandanus*, *Cordyline*, *Dracaena*, *Monstera*, *Philodendron*, and the like, than with more sombre or fine-leaved or deciduous trees and shrubs: consider, for example, the sight of a massive-leaved palm mingling its fronds in winter with the delicate tracery of bare twigs of a deciduous tree such as a poplar, a sight which in our opinion would be rather incongruous. As a general rule, being guided by what one would expect to find in nature is a sure way to avoid lack of harmony in plantings.

When extensive grounds are available, attractive contrasts may be obtained by bordering grassed areas with stands of tall, solitary-trunked species, interplanted with clumps of lower-growing, multistemmed types; making use of foliage texture, colour and glossiness, to achieve maximum contrasting effects. Further complementary effects are achieved when sunlight illuminates translucent leaves, particularly those of a thin texture, from rainforest areas. The strong reflection of light from shiny leaf surfaces also adds to contrast. Palms should be thoughtfully positioned to take full advantage of their various characters.

top:
Group plantings of the one species,
Archontophoenix cunninghamiana, *provide
an imposing feature in this garden
landscape. Los Angeles.*

right:
*Palms make an elegant setting for this
modern open air restaurant. Sydney.*

opposite top:
Old specimen of Phoenix canariensis
*complements this period architecture.
Sydney.*

opposite bottom:
*Foundation planting of palms blends with
modern buildings in tropical eastern
Australia. Cairns, northern Australia.*

In open areas, the grouping of a number of similar types of palms, such as *Roystonea, Archontophoenix, Phoenix*, in a central position may create an imposing feature; similarly a large clumping palm such as *Phoenix reclinata* makes a striking lawn contrast.

Around the edges of pools and streams (the natural habitat of many palms), groups of palms may be shown to advantage, e.g. fringing stands of robust fan palms such as *Sabal* and *Livistona* and feather palms such as *Roystonea* and *Arecastrum*. The Coconut Palm with its leaning trunk is a natural feature adjoining tropical seashores.

With smaller protected ponds or streams, the edges may be bordered by lower-growing species such as *Sabal minor*, which are especially useful where separation is required between a path and the water without interrupting the vista at eye level. In the tropics, palms with crowded stems, such as *Ptychosperma macarthurii* or *Cyrtostachys renda*, are appropriate subjects.

Where palms are to be the major element in a swimming pool surround, a relatively few ornamental species are best used so as not to shade the water of the pool, or create a nuisance by dropping debris such as leaf fragments, fruit and the like. With smaller pools, the use of well-established potted specimens may be more appropriate, particularly as they can be moved when required. In tropical areas, *Cyrtostachys renda, Licuala grandis, Ptychosperma elegans, P. macarthurii* and *Chrysalidocarpus lutescens* are appropriate suggestions, while in warm-temperate areas, *Howea, Archontophoenix, Rhapis* and *Chamaedorea* are amongst those which may be used.

Where it is proposed to use tall-trunked species for avenue planting, thought should be given to interplanting smaller plants between the tall-trunked species to soften the regular, pole-like appearance which develops. However, a curved or straight avenue of tall palms may serve to effectively delineate areas of different functions or to direct attention to some focal point.

Palms may be used to advantage to complement buildings and their surrounds. The bare appearance of walls may be softened by "foundation plantings" of clumping species like *Rhapis, Chamaedorea, Chrysalidocarpus* and the like, which are also useful for creating screens to sections of the building and grounds. In courtyards and plazas, small groups of palms or advanced, larger, clump-forming types, such as *Phoenix reclinata* or *Chamaerops humilis*, make attractive centrepieces. When restoring old, historic buildings which have included palms as part of the master plan, provision should be made to ensure that this character is preserved.

The hardiness of palms such as *Phoenix* in withstanding adverse factors, such as harsh sun, strong winds and shading, make them particularly suited to built-up areas.

The complementary use of well-established palms in suitable containers can add to any setting, particularly as they can be moved as required. It must be remembered, however, that potted specimens require continued watering and maintenance.

Well-grown potted palms in containers or planter boxes have almost un-limited use for complementing landscape subjects, for they can be moved and rearranged as required and individual specimens may be changed to provide a different effect. They provide attractive accents around pools, in courtyards, on entrance porches and in other selected garden positions. In selecting the species to be used for outdoor purposes it is important to remember that climate is the chief governing factor in the use of particular species. Attempting to grow palms from moist tropical areas in cold or dry areas only produces struggling, unattractive specimens. (See Appendix III (p.185) listing palms suitable for different climates.) There is considerable scope for indoor use of potted palms in both domestic and commercial buildings, the latter, with air-conditioning and artificial lighting, often providing suitable conditions for species from more tropical climates. (See listing of palms suitable for indoor use on p.188.) It must be remembered that potted specimens require continual watering and maintenance, and unless this can be provided one will ultimately be left with dried-out, unattractive plants which may take years to recover or even die.

Landscaping with palms in containers

*A Victorian-style conservatory in this hotel shows the manner in which palms (*Howea forsterana*) were formerly used for decoration. Victoria, British Columbia, Canada.*

PLANTING IN THE GARDEN

Soil Preparation

Although palms will grow in various types of soil, often with poor drainage, it will be generally found that better results are obtained, particularly in the establishment stage of the plant, if simple preparation of the soil is carried out where the palm is to be planted. The addition of humus material and peat moss to the soil where the palm is to grow assists with moisture retention and establishment; as these materials break down, additional materials should be added to the surface of the soil. Heavy soils may be improved by the addition of coarse river sand in addition to the peat moss and humus. In poorly drained areas, the raising of the planting area above the surrounding ground assists in establishment. As palms are chiefly surface feeders, the soil improvement should be carried out in the upper 30 cm of the soil. When the plant is well established, surface mulching with leaves or other organic material is usually sufficient to provide good soil conditions. Except when undesirable for landscape purposes, the fallen palm leaves make an excellent mulch and where possible should be left in position. A mild organic fertilizer, such as blood and bone, may be added to the soil during preparation and periodically during the season of maximum growth.

Planting

Where the palm is to be planted, an area of soil approximately 1 metre square should be prepared as above; a hole is then made in the soil, slightly larger than the container in which the palm is growing, and the hole filled with water which is allowed to drain away. It is most important in heavy clay soils that a deep hole is *not* made in the ground and filled with improved soil, as the hole then merely acts as a sump retaining water, and this may lead to root rot. The potted plant should be immersed in water and allowed to soak until bubbles cease to come from the soil, when the container and plant are then removed from the water and allowed to drain. A large knife may be slipped around between the container and plant, to facilitate removal. The palm is knocked from the container and, if roots are densely matted on the outer surface, they should be gently loosened before planting. The plant is then placed in position in the prepared hole at a depth which will bring the base of the stem level with the surrounding ground surface. Soil is filled around the plant and firmed with the hands or feet, after which the soil is thoroughly saturated with water.

Planting is best carried out during late spring, or in tropical areas the beginning of the wet season. It is most important during the first 12 months of establishment that watering is not neglected, particularly during hot, dry periods. Newly planted palms should be protected from drying winds and excessive sunlight by the use of screens of sacking, shade cloth, or similar material. With delicate species, it can be helpful to provide a plastic covering to provide the necessary humidity, ensuring that adequate shade and ventilation are available to prevent overheating.

Transplanting Palms

Palms of reasonable size may be successfully transplanted from one position to another, provided proper care is taken during the process and the plant in its new position in not allowed to dry out at any time during the first 12 months, or 2 years for larger specimens.

When the palm is to be transplanted, it should be prepared in advance, otherwise losses can readily occur.

With a small plant (under about 1 metre), the soil in which the palm is growing should be saturated 2 to 3 days before removal occurs. To remove the plant, a spade is pushed into the ground to its full depth a number of times around the plant, which is then removed with the soil attached. To transfer the plant from one position to another, the palm should be placed on strong sheeting which is used to lift the plant and soil. The transplanted palm is removed to the required site and placed in position in a prepared hole in the manner as described under Planting (p.30).

Larger palms (2 metres or more) require much more preparation and may take months before they are ready to move. Mechanical equipment is also required to lift the palm with the large ball of soil and roots necessary for satisfactory results. Having decided on the ball of soil required, which may be up to 2 metres across for larger specimens, preparatory work should begin at the commencement of the growing season, if possible 12 months before the palm is to be moved.

During the week before work commences, the plant should be thoroughly watered. The roots are cut around the perimeter of the soil which is to be removed later; this may entail digging a trench to approximately 60 cm depth around the perimeter, carefully cutting the roots vertically as work progresses and ensuring that the soil in the area to be removed later is not disturbed. The trench is filled in sections as work proceeds to prevent drying of the roots (some prefer to only cut the roots from half the perimeter at one time, to prevent a setback to the palm). During the next 12 months, the area of soil where the roots have been cut should be watered regularly to ensure new root growth, and to prevent them growing into the adjoining trench an implement such as a spade should periodically be pushed into the soil around the perimeter of the palm.

When the palm is growing well, preferably at the beginning of the next growing season, preparations should be made for its removal by freely watering for 1 week. The trench previously excavated is reopened and made approximately 1 metre deep when the soil and roots are undercut, making the soil mass in the shape of a hemisphere. Using a mobile crane, or similar mobile equipment, the trunk is pulled sideways, and at the same time any remaining roots are cut. The fronds are then tied together to prevent damage and loss of moisture during removal. Tough plastic sheeting, large enough to completely surround the ball of soil, is spread on the ground adjoining the palm, which is then removed by the crane. The plastic sheeting is then tied around the trunk. The palm is transferred to its new position in a hole previously prepared and thoroughly saturated with water, as described under Planting (p.30).

The palm must not be neglected for the next two years, as re-establishment may be slow and losses may easily occur.

In areas of higher rainfall, perhaps less preparation may be necessary; nevertheless, adequate preparation ensures that the palm will not suffer a long-term setback, which may not be apparent for several years.

The elegant form of this large Phoenix reclinata *provides an imposing feature in this landscape. Sydney.*

GROWING PALMS IN CONTAINERS

When palms are to be grown in containers as specimen plants, it is important that the pot used should not be larger than required, as overpotting may lead to poor drainage and, with good soil, encourages the palm to grow rapidly. This usually defeats the object of keeping the plant as a potted specimen for an indefinite period and, further, when frequent repottings are carried out, the palm rapidly outgrows its usefulness. Deeper containers are best used for strong-growing species as there is a tendency for the roots to lift the stem above the soil in the pot. In order to regulate the rate of growth, smaller species such as *Chamaedorea elegans* should be first potted in, say, a 100 mm pot, and larger-growing plants such as *Phoenix canariensis* may be commenced in a 200 mm container. When repotting is required, the next sized pot only should be used. Where it is desired that the palm should be grown as rapidly as possible, larger sized pots and a good, rich, well drained potting mixture, may be made use of. When roots grow through the drainage holes they should be cut off when first noticed, as they may make removal of the plant difficult at repotting and even lead to the loss of the palm.

Potting Soils

Soils used for potting should be friable, permit free drainage, and retain moisture. For seedlings and small plants, the potting soil should contain a higher percentage of well rotted humus material and peat. The addition of materials such as charcoal or pieces of foamed polystyrene added to any mixture opens up the soil and permits better drainage.

Mixtures of 1 part friable loam, 1 part peat, humus, ricehulls or the like and 1 part coarse river sand are very satisfactory for seedlings and small plants. For long-term pot cultivation, the mixture may consist of 2 parts loamy soil, 1 part coarse river sand, 1 part charcoal, polystyrene or perlite and 1 part peat moss. The addition of ground limestone in the proportion of 20 grams per 9 litre bucket (2 gallons) of the mix is recommended when plants from alkaline areas are to be grown.

When peat or humus are to be used in potting mix it is important that they be thoroughly wetted before adding to the mixture.

Sterilizing of the potting soil at a temperature of 60°C for 30 minutes will ensure that diseases are not transmitted to the plant.

Where watering of palms will not be neglected, they may be successfully cultivated in potting materials such as gravel, coarse sand, perlite or similar substances with a regular addition of slow-release fertilizer. This form of cultivation may result in rapid growth, but it may produce palms less suitable for later planting into the ground; the soft growth produced may be more prone to disease.

Potting the Palm

As plants will be kept in the container for an indefinite period, it is most important that extra care be given to ensure that drainage holes are free from

An interior view of the famous Palm House at Kew, which houses probably the world's oldest major palm collection. Kew, England.

An indoor planting box with palms and other plants growing with artificial light and airconditioning makes an oasis of greenery in this office building. Vancouver, Canada.

This border of potted palms makes a beautiful surround for diners in this glassed, airconditioned restaurant in a large department store. Toronto, Canada.

This old specimen of Rhopalostylis baueri *in a large (75 cm) wooden tub in Palm House, Kew, shows how palms can be grown for many years in a container. Kew, England.*

obstructions. To further assist with drainage, coarse material such as gravel, clinker ash, stones or pieces of foam plastic should be placed in the bottom of the container, to a depth of approximately 2 centimetres for small pots, or 6 centimetres for tubs.

When the drainage material is in position, the container should be filled to approximately one-third its depth with potting soil which is then watered. The plant to be potted is held in the pot at a level which will bring the base of the stem slightly below the top of the container. Soil is then carefully filled around the roots until the pot is full and the container is then bumped once or twice on the bench or floor to consolidate the soil, additional soil being added as required. The plant is then watered well and placed in a protected position for several weeks to allow it to become established.

Watering must not be neglected as palms use a considerable amount of water and, if allowed to dry out, the plant suffers a setback and may take some time to recover; in addition, drying of leaflets may occur, leaving damage which remains until the leaf is replaced, which may take some time.

During the process of potting, it is important that the roots of the plant should not be allowed to dry out at any time. When a number of small plants are being handled, they should be kept with the roots in water whilst potting is in progress. Bare-rooted plants should be handled with care to prevent damage of the delicate root tips.

The addition of a layer of pebbles on the top of the pot, as well as improving the appearance, assists in preventing the surface soil from drying out.

Repotting

When plants are to be repotted, which is best carried out during spring when growth has commenced, the plant and container should be immersed in water and allowed to soak for about one hour. The next sized container to be used for repotting is prepared in the manner as discussed under Potting the Palm (p.33). When the plant in the container is removed from the water, it should first be allowed to drain before the plant is removed from the pot. Where the roots of the palm have grown through the drainage holes so that it is not possible to remove it without damage, the pot should be cut as necessary to allow for the palm's easy removal. When the plant is removed from the container, the matted roots around the outside of the soil are gently loosened and pieces of drainage material, which may be between the lower roots, should be removed. The plant is then potted as described on p.33.

Fertilizing Potted Palms

While the palm is growing satisfactorily, it is not necessary to use fertilizers, for they speed up the growth of the plant, making repotting more frequent. The application of a slow release fertilizer such as ''Osmocote'' once a year will be found adequate for long-term nutrition of the plant or a periodic spray with a diluted soluble fertilizer may be carried out. Heavy fertilizing of potted plants forces growth and, as well as making the plant soft and liable to attack by disease, defeats the object of controlling the size of the palm as a potted subject.

Watering

It is important when watering is carried out that the soil should be thoroughly saturated, as light, frequent watering only wets the upper surface, inducing most root growth towards this moist zone near the surface. During hot dry periods this results in drying of the shallow roots. For many palms standing the container in water for about 2 hours once a week during summer and once every 3 weeks during winter is adequate, except during hot periods, but other palms from more humid environments prefer more frequent and copious watering, so that the soil remains constantly moist throughout, and preferably the leaves also wetted by frequent mist spraying (except during cold weather).

Growing Palms Indoors

Palms are very suitable and attractive plants for indoor use, providing proper conditions are available for growth. Positions in a room which are subject to drying air movement, particularly where heaters are used, may cause burning of the ends of the leaflets. When such positions cannot be avoided, spraying the foliage with a fine mist from a small hand spray several times a day assists in preventing damage. Standing the plant in a large tray filled with coarse sand or gravel which is kept wet helps to make the atmosphere around the plant more humid; however, it is important that the palm should not stand in a tray of water.

Many palms will grow under low light conditions; however, darker parts of rooms should be avoided. Where adequate natural light is not available, the use of twin standard 40-watt fluorescent lights at 45 cm above the foliage of the palm makes a good substitute.

As palms collect dust and grime, the leaves should be periodically gently sponged with lukewarm water, using a sponge or suitable cloth for the purpose. Where the leaflets are very dirty, a weak solution of soap and water should be first used which is then sponged off with clean water. The periodic removal of palms from indoors to a glasshouse or suitable shadehouse for several weeks will allow plants to recover from unsuitable conditions of growth. Where possible, having several plants which may be rotated from the glass or shadehouse to indoors ensures more attractive specimens.

Palms, like other plants, are attacked by pests such as chewing insects which may cause considerable damage. Some chewing insects often bunch the leaflets of growing leaves together with web and chew out the centre of the leaf. Plants may become heavily infested with mealy bug, particularly potted specimens. Scale Insects and Red Spider may also attack plants. In some tropical and subtropical areas various beetles can do considerable damage to the growing tip of the expanding leaf, which may even result in the death of the palm.

In some parts of the world there are serious diseases which affect palms with fatal results and which do not respond to control measures, and it is most important that plants and seed from areas subject to such diseases should not be taken into disease-free areas, if the spread of these diseases is to be prevented. One of the best known of these diseases, thought to be caused by a virus, is "Lethal Yellowing", which has become established in Florida and has caused the death of many palms, especially Coconuts.

PESTS AND DISEASES

The control of various pests is carried out in a similar manner to that adapted for other plants, a spray attached to a hose being used for taller specimens.

Chewing insects may be physically removed in smaller plants. Gloves should be worn when pulling off caterpillars as these may cause skin irritation. Spraying plants with chemicals, such as Maldison (Malathion), Carbamates (Carbaryl) and similar substances, when the attack is first noticed, with a follow-up spray 10 days later, generally gives effective control. Other sprays such as Pyrethrum and naturally prepared bacterial toxins and similar substances less toxic to humans can also be used. It is most important that chemicals should be used strictly in accordance with the manufacturer's recommendations and that considerable care is exercised to prevent inhalation of the spray and to avoid contact with the skin. This applies to animals as well as to humans.

Small plants attacked by scale and mealy bug may be treated by using a toothbrush and soapy water. As mealy bugs also attack the roots of plants, particularly potted specimens, the soil may be treated by first watering well, then drenching with a solution of Malathion at half the strength of that recommended by the manufacturer. Treatment may be followed up 2 weeks after the first application of the insecticide.

Pest Control

PROPAGATION

Except for clump-forming palms which produce additional stems from the base and may be increased vegetatively by division, all other types with a solitary trunk cannot be reproduced by vegetative means and new plants must be raised from seed.

Raising Palms from Seed

Collecting Fruit

The fruit of palm usually take some months or even years to develop, from the time of fertilization until they have ripened. Ripening of fruit is usually indicated by changing colour, for example from green to white or yellow, orange or red to black, depending upon the particular species. When ripe, the fruit falls from the palm over a period. Fruit may be collected from the ground, but old fruit from a previous year's crop which have been on the ground for some time should be avoided, as they are usually not viable. If the fruit has all changed colour, the whole fruiting inflorescence may be collected. With many species of well established palms there may be several fruiting inflorescences at different stages of development. If in doubt about the maturity of fruit, a simple test is to cut into the seed endosperm, which, when mature, is white to greyish and, in most palms, very hard.

The Seed

The viability of most palm seed after collection is usually very short-lived, particularly when stored under dry conditions.

Remember that what is commonly called the seed is often the whole fruit. The outer coat (mesocarp) of many species contains substances which inhibit germination and, until it has broken down, most seeds will not germinate. Where a quantity of seeds is being dealt with, the removal of the fleshy coat by hand is often slow and difficult. One method of removing the outer layer is to place the fruit in a bag and then gently beat with a stick to bruise and damage the fleshy layer, after which the fruit can be placed under running water and the surface scrubbed off. Alternatively, the fruit may be allowed to stand in water in the sun for several days to bring about fermentation, after which the outer coat is scrubbed off. It is most important that the water is not allowed to evaporate away during the period of fermentation. The fruit is finally washed and is ready for sowing. If the whole fruit is sown without any treatment, the germination period may be extended. The period required for germination varies considerably with different species, from approximately 4 weeks to 2 or 3 years. Most species will germinate in 2 to 3 months if seed is mature and fresh and conditions favourable.

Sowing the Seed

The medium in which seed is sown may consist of various substances which will hold moisture, at the same time allowing good aeration, such as peat-moss and sand, perlite, vermiculite, or sterilized humus and sand. The sowing material should be placed in well-drained pots, trays, troughs, single tubes or similar containers, depending upon the number of seeds to be sown. The mixture should be first lightly settled by gently bumping the tray or pot once or twice on the bench. The seed is placed in position and then covered to approximately a depth equal to its own thickness. Alternatively seed may be pressed into the surface of the soil. With large fruits, such as the Coconut, the whole fruit is buried to approximately half its depth. After sowing, the seed box should be placed in a protected position to prevent drying of the soil. The use of bottom heat for the seed box at temperatures of approximately 24° to 30°C, depending upon the species, helps to shorten germination time. During germination and subsequent seedling growth, the medium should not be allowed to dry out at any time.

Potting Seedlings

Seedlings should be potted when the seedling leaf appears and before the root system has penetrated too deeply and spread too widely through the soil. In potting the seedling, the container in which the plant is to be potted should be filled with potting soil (see p.33) and lightly settled by bumping the container once or twice on the potting bench. A hole is made in the soil sufficiently large to accommodate the roots of the seedling to be potted; the hole is then watered. A seedling is pricked out of the seed box (a kitchen fork makes an excellent implement for pricking out seedlings) and held in position in the hole previously prepared, at a level which will bring the base of the small stem slightly below the top of the soil. The soil is then firmed around the roots with a dibbler or piece of stick, additional soil being added as required. The plant is watered well and the container is then placed in a protected position. The seedling should be allowed to grow on in the container until well established before being repotted into a larger container.

It is of the utmost importance that the attached seed should not be removed from the seedling as its presence has considerable influence on the growth of the seedling and its removal may result in the seedling's ultimately dying.

While multistemmed palms may be reproduced from seed, species such as *Rhapis*, *Chrysalidocarpus* and similar clump-forming types may be reproduced from sections of an existing plant. When the plant is growing in the ground a section of the clump may be divided from the main palm with a spade at the beginning of the growing season but allowed to remain in position until new growth has developed. The larger stems may then be cut off and the divided section carefully removed from the ground, disturbing the soil and ball of roots as little as possible. The section removed is best potted in a large container and kept in a shaded position, and allowed to grow on for 12 months until well established, when it can be planted out in the ground if so desired.

Plants growing in containers lend themselves more readily to division, as a section of the plant can be cut from the main growth when it is removed from the container for repotting. The divided section and existing plant should be repotted and grown on as above.

It is important that for the first 12 months after division the plant is freely watered, as re-establishment is often slow.

Vegetative Reproduction of Multistemmed Palms

THE PALMS

Acoelorrhaphe (syn. *Paurotis*)

This handsome, clump-forming palm with compact crowns of silvery foliage occurs in southern Florida, parts of Central America, Cuba and the Bahamas. The genus contains only 1 species and is often known by its synonym *Paurotis*. It is a multistemmed fan palm with numerous slender trunks 3 to 8 m high and 6 to 10 m in diameter growing closely together at the base and covered in leaf bases and dark grey fibres, or in older stems free of leaf bases and marked with leaf scars. The crown is compact, without a crownshaft; the leaves are about 1 to 2 m long; the very slender leaf stalks 60 to 120 cm long have coarse, brown, incurved teeth along the margins. The blade is circular in outline, about 60 to 100 cm broad, palmate, and deeply divided into narrow, pointed segments, each of which is further divided at the apex. The leaves are light green and somewhat silvery above, and silvery greyish-green beneath.

The inflorescences arise among the leaf bases and are slender, about 1 m long, with several branches, each with numerous small branchlets. The stalk and branches are sheathed by tubular, persistent bracts. The small white flowers are bisexual and grouped in slightly raised clusters of usually 3, sometimes 2. Occasionally flowers are solitary. The 3 sepals are joined near the base and the 3 petals have the edges touching in bud. There are 6 stamens; the 3 single-celled ovaries are slightly joined at the base and the 3 short styles are joined near the apex into a conical stigma. The fruit is small and round to oval in shape, ripening to black, with a thin, fleshy mesocarp and a thin endocarp; there is no intrusion by the seed coat into the endosperm.

HABITAT, USES, CULTIVATION   This tropical palm is an inhabitant of moist or wet forests, savannahs, or swampy areas and stream banks in lower regions, occurring up to about 200 m altitude. It is occasionally grown as an ornamental in warm areas. It needs a plentiful supply of water, preferably in full sunlight, and ample room for its full spread, its effect being similar to that of *Chamaerops*. Growth is slow if plants are grown in drier areas. Propagation is from seed which germinates within 2 to 3 months; young plants retain entire leaves for a number of years.

A. *wrightii* (syn. *Paurotis wrightii*)

For description see above under genus.

opposite:
Acoelorrhaphe wrightii

41

Acrocomia

Distinctive, strongly spiny feather palms make up this genus of about 25 species, widely distributed through central and South America and the West Indies. They are medium to large. Their trunks are solitary, with some species clothed in the remains of the old, spiny sheathing leaf-bases, or smooth and regularly ringed with needle-like spines at the rings. On older parts of a trunk, the spines may be weathered away. The leaf bases do not form a crownshaft; these and the leaf stalks are very spiny and often hairy as well. The leaves are large, generally plumose, with very numerous, crowded, long, narrow leaflets, which often droop gracefully. The leaflets are glossy above, whitish and sometimes finely hairy beneath. In some species they are crowded into groups along the midrib.

The numerous inflorescences arise amongst leaf bases. They are much shorter than the leaves and are enclosed in bud by two bracts, clothed with various combinations (depending on species) of spines and hairs. The lower outer bract is short and tubular, and falls when no longer needed. The inner bract is long, club- or spindle-shaped, and tough to woody; it splits on one side to release the flowers. It does not fall, but remains hanging below the leaves. The inflorescence stalks are thick and spiny and the rhachises (central stems) have numerous wiry branchlets, each of which has a bract at its base. The flowers are separate male or female on the same inflorescence, with several large widely spaced female flowers on the lower part of the branchlets and the upper part covered in small male flowers, the bases of which fit in pits on the branchlet. Male flowers are oblong and angular in bud, with 3 tiny sepals and 3 obtuse petals with the edges touching in bud; there are 6 stamens and the sterile pistil is prominent. Female flowers have 3 overlapping sepals and 3 larger overlapping petals; sterile stamens are united into a 6-toothed cup. The ovary is 3-celled, each with one ovule; stigma is sessile and 3-lobed. The fruits are round and smooth to slightly spiny, with the remains of the flower attached to the base and a small protrusion at the apex. The mesocarp is fleshy and sticky with scattered fibres; the endocarp is thick and hard with 3 pores at or about the middle; the endosperm of the seed is non-ruminate and has a central cavity.

HABITAT, USES, CULTIVATION   Acrocomias are characteristically palms of relatively dry, well drained country, often on hill slopes or ridges in poor sandy or stony soil, but sometimes on grassy plains or in savannah woodlands or dry scrubs. They are rarely, if ever, found at altitudes higher than 1000 m and seem to reach their greatest abundance and diversity in coastal lowland regions. The local inhabitants make many uses of these palms. The starchy pith from the split trunks is fed to livestock in drought periods, as are the leaves. Starch is also prepared for human consumption from this pith, and from roots of young plants. The pith is also frequently fermented to give an alcoholic drink. The leaves yield a useful twine, made by tearing strips of the desired width from the leaflets. The fruits, mostly oily and sometimes quite bitter, are used for human food (boiled with sugar in Mexico and Guatemala), or to feed livestock. The seed kernels are a source of high quality oil, while the very hard endocarp enclosing the seeds is cut into rings or carved and pierced for rosary beads.

These palms with their striking spiny trunks make interesting landscape subjects, as long as ample space is available so that they are shown to advantage and their spines are not a nuisance. Warm-temperate to tropical conditions are required for satisfactory results. Propagation is from seed which is frequently difficult to germinate, and so procedures such as reducing the thickness of the hard endocarp and soaking for weeks in water have been used to assist with germination.

A. media
A tall palm with a trunk to about 15 m high, 30 cm diameter below, swelling to about 50 cm in the enlarged upper part and closely ringed with long black spines directed upwards or downwards. The crown carries a number of erect to arched or drooping plume-like leaves, 1 to 2 m long. The leaf stalks are short and heavily armed with spines. The numerous narrow leaflets are crowded on the spiny midrib, glossy above and bluish-grey on the undersurface with a dense covering of short hairs. The inflorescences are about 1.5 m long with woolly sheathing bracts which are often spineless, and crowded pale yellow flowers. The round yellow fruits are about 4 cm diameter. Distribution: Puerto Rico.

A. totai
The trunk of this tall palm is closely ringed and spiny, and is of even diameter. The palm is about 15 m high and 20 to 40 cm diameter, with a dense crown of erect to arched, drooping leaves, 2.5 to 3 m long. The leaf stalks are short and armed with strong spines; the leaflets are numerous, green above and below, crowded along the spiny midribs, arising in different planes and presenting a plume-like appearance. The inflorescences are about 1 m long, with numerous yellow flowers; the sheathing bracts carry reddish woolly hairs and a few spines at the apex. The round fruits are 20 to 30 mm in diameter.
Distribution: Argentina, Paraguay, Bolivia.

Aiphanes (syn. *Martinezia*)
This genus consists of about 38 distinctive, small to medium-sized spiny palms, the majority of them native to northern and western South America, but with a few also occuring in the West Indies and Central America. Most have solitary trunks, but there are some with multiple stems; a few have no above-ground stem. Trunks are armed with long needle-like spines, grouped in rings, alternating with unarmed rings. The spines extend over most parts of the plant, including sheathing leaf bases, leaf stalks, midribs, leaflets, inflorescence stalks and larger bracts. There is no crownshaft, and the sheathing bases of the leaves narrow fairly abruptly from a clasping basal part to the prominent, erect leaf stalks. Leaves are pinnate, varying greatly in number, shape and arrangement of leaflets. Most species are characterized by truncate to jagged-tipped leaflets, but some have pointed leaflets with only obscure apical teeth. Leaflets may be regularly and often closely spaced along the midrib or gathered into groups.

Inflorescences arise among the leaf bases, and have an erect, spiny stalk and long, straight or slightly arching rhachis, once-branched only with numerous weak, slender branchlets. Each inflorescence is enclosed in bud in a long, slender, thin-textured cylindrical bract which splits down one side to release the flowers and persists as a dried, parchment-like strip hanging below the inflorescence. Flowers are of different sexes, usually both on the one inflorescence, often with solitary females towards bases of branchlets and groups

Acrocomia totai

of 2 male and 1 female on upper parts. Male flowers have 3 small sepals, 3 petals joined at base with edges of free parts touching in bud, 6 short stamens, and a minute sterile pistil. Female flowers are larger, with petals much longer than sepals, joined at base, the upper parts with edges touching or slightly overlapping in bud. The sterile stamens are fused into an urn-like structure, its top truncate or 6-toothed, surrounding the ovary which is 3-celled but with only 1 functional ovule and terminated by a 3-lobed stigma.

Fruits are spherical, small to medium, with fleshy mesocarp layer and woody endocarp. The endocarp has 3 pores midway between base and apex and small projections over its inner surface. The surface of the small seed is pitted to correspond with these projections.

Aiphanes caryotifolia

HABITAT, USES, CULTIVATION   *Aiphanes* species inhabit high-rainfall tropical regions, occurring in rainforest, woodland, swampy areas, or on steep rocky hillsides, from sea-level to about 2000 m altitude, in a variety of soil types, often on limestone in the West Indies.

As ornamentals they make striking subjects, though only suitable for tropical climates with high rainfall. Under suitably moist, sheltered conditions in fertile soil they can make fast growth. They require shade at least when young and should not be planted in positions where passers-by can readily brush against the trunks or leaf bases, as these are viciously spiny. Propagation is by seed, which takes 2 to 3 months or more to germinate, requiring ample warmth and moisture.

Aiphanes erosa

A. caryotifolia (syn. *Martinezia caryotifolia*)

A medium-sized, elegant palm with solitary, smooth, pale brown, straight trunk to 10 or 12 m tall and 8-12 cm diameter, strongly armed with very sharp blackish spines of mixed length, the longest about 10 cm. The crown is rather open, with leaves arching and later drooping, and about 2-2.5 m long. The narrow, whitish-felty, spiny leaf stalks press close against the trunk in the lower part, abruptly bending away from it above. The leaflets are carried in compact groups of 4-10 along the whitish, spiny midribs. They are wedge-shaped, clear green, very broad at the end and strongly frilled with 2 or 3 longer points, and with scattered needle-like spines on both surfaces. The inflorescences are about 1.5 m long, very slender and erect. They have short, flattened spines on stalk, rhachis and bracts. Flowers are yellow and fruits bright red, 15-20 mm diameter.

Distribution: Colombia, Venezuela, Ecuador.

A. erosa (syn. *Martinezia erosa*) Macaw Palm

The densely crowded cream flowers of this striking palm give way to clusters of red fruit, about 15 mm diameter. It is a medium-sized palm, with a solitary, densely-spined trunk, about 4-6 m tall and about 10 cm diameter, with a compact, fairly dense crown of spreading to drooping flat leaves about 2 m long. The short leaf stalks and midribs are thickly covered in black spines. Leaflets are closely and regularly arranged along the midribs, narrowly wedge-shaped, truncate (cut off squarely) at the apexes, and have scattered spines on their lower sides. The inflorescences are about 1 m long, the narrow whitish bract persisting and hanging after flowers open. Flowers are cream, densely crowded; fruits are red, about 15 mm diameter.

Distribution: Barbados (West Indies).

Allagoptera (syn. *Diplothemium*)

Small, clustering feather palms, which usually have stems below ground or short trunks covered with leaf bases and fibres. The 5 species of the genus occur in South America. Individual crowns are usually small, with several forming a dense head; leaf stalks are slender with bases covered by fibres. The leaf blades have a number of tapered pointed leaflets, each with a prominent midvein and arranged in very regular, radiating groups along the midribs, except toward the leaf apexes where they are evenly spaced.

The inflorescences are amongst the leaf bases. Each consists of an unbranched, erect, dense spike of flowers on a longer, erect stalk, and is enclosed in bud by 2 bracts. The lower outer bract is short and tubular and the inner one is large with longitudinal grooves, woody and club-shaped, tapering to a pointed apex. It splits down one side to expose the flowers, spreads and hangs below the inflorescence. Flowers are separate male or female, in the lower part of the spike in groups of 1 female flower between 2 male, but with male flowers becoming dominant on the upper part of the spike. Male flowers have 3 lance-shaped sepals united near the base, 3 egg-shaped, overlapping petals, 6 to 20 or more stamens, and a small sterile pistil. Female flowers have 3 small sepals and 3 petals which are egg-shaped and sometimes finely toothed, and sterile stamens united in a small cup. The ovary has 3 cells, 3 ovules and 3-lobed stigma. Fruits are ovoid. Each has the old stigma attached at the apex, and has a fleshy, thinly fibrous mesocarp and hard woody endocarp which is 3-pored at the base. The seed has a non-ruminate endosperm (not intruded by the seed coat). There is sometimes a small central cavity in it.

HABITAT, USES, CULTIVATION   These feather palms grow in poorer soils and the species *A. arenaria* occurs in sandy saline dunes adjoining the sea where it frequently forms dense thickets.

To date these palms, apart from their representation in botanic gardens, have received little attention in general cultivation and would be useful small cluster palms for warm sunny positions near the sea. Propagation is from seed which takes about 3 months to germinate.

A. arenaria (syn. *Diplothemium maritimum*)

A small clustering palm with stem beneath the ground and several crowns of erect to arched leaves about 1 m long. The leaf stalks are slender and about 30 cm long, the blades are arching, with a number of long linear leaflets, each tapered to a pointed apex and with prominent midrib. The leaflets are dark green above and whitish beneath, arranged in clusters of 2 to 3 along the midrib and arising in different planes, giving the leaf a plumose appearance, with upper leaflets often single. The inflorescences arising among the leaf bases, are about 60 cm long, enclosed in bud in a large, woody, club-shaped pointed bract which remains on the plant after opening. Flowers are yellow on a dense, erect spike. Fruit are greenish-yellow, egg-shaped, slightly angular and about 12 mm long.

Distribution: Brazil, east coast, in the region of Bahia.

Archontophoenix

Graceful feather palms, forming a genus of 2 species, with solitary, greenish to grey, smooth, tall, slender, ringed trunks. The rings may be distinct or indistinct and closely to widely spaced, the trunk is also swollen to varying degrees at the base and is surmounted by a distinct crownshaft formed from the basal sheaths of the leaves. The crown is moderately compact, with the leaves erect to spreading, often twisted from the base to the apex; the leaf stalks are short and without spines; the blades have numerous leaflets evenly but closely spaced along the midrib, each tapering to a pointed apex. On the undersides of the leaflets there are scattered coarse, chaffy scales on the midrib, or fine silvery scales all over, or both.

The inflorescences, borne below the crownshaft, are much branched, pendulous to slightly drooping, enclosed in the bud stage by two large, thin papery bracts each pointed at the apex and falling shortly before the flowers open. The flowers are separate male or female on the same inflorescence, spirally arranged on branchlets in groups of 3, with 1 female between 2 male, or pairs of males only towards the end of the branchlets. Male flowers are asymmetrical with 3 angled sepals and 3 petals with edges touching in bud; there are 8 to 24 stamens and the sterile pistile is slender and as long as the stamens. Female flowers have 3 sepals, 3 overlapping petals and 3 tiny sterile stamens. The ovary is 1-celled with 1 ovule and a 3-lobed stigma. Fruits are ellipsoid to almost globular, with remains of stigma at the apex, pink to red, with a thin, soft, fleshy mesocarp through which run flattened, longitudinal fibres which are conspicuously branched and

interlocked; the seeds are ellipsoid to globular, and the endosperm distinctly ruminate.

HABITAT, USES, CULTIVATION   *Archontophoenix* species grow in moist rainforests from sea level to elevations of about 1200 m in warm-temperate to tropical regions with high rainfall, often in wet gullies, on banks of streams, or edges of swamps, in a variety of soils.

These graceful feather palms have been widely cultivated in many warm-temperate and tropical parts of the world, where they have been used for landscaping as single specimens or for group planting in various situations. In their younger stages of growth and in dry areas, the leaves tend to burn if exposed to full sun or drying winds. They will not tolerate heavy frosts, though *A. cunninghamiana* is the more cold hardy. For best results a plentiful supply of water should always be provided. When used for indoor decoration, unless a humid atmosphere is maintained, the leaves rapidly become brown at the tips; they are less tolerant of very low light than a number of other palms. Propagation is from seed which germinates readily when fresh and usually requires from about 6 weeks to 3 months to germinate, depending upon temperature; growth is fairly rapid.

A. cunninghamiana (syn. *"Seaforthia elegans"* of nurseries) Bangalow or Piccabeen Palm
This tall palm has a trunk 20 to 22 m high, 10 to 20 cm diameter and slightly swollen at the base. The crown is of medium density, the leaves erect to spreading with a distinct green to rusty brown or dull purplish crownshaft; the leaves are 2 to 3.5 m long, with short leaf stalks; the blades have numerous broad leaflets, green above and below, with a few large brown scales on the undersides of the mid-veins near their bases. The inflorescences are 60 to 90 cm long, densely branched, with long pendulous branchlets; the flowers are pale lavender to purplish and the pink to red fruits almost globular, 10 to 15 mm in diameter.
Distribution: eastern Australia: southern coast of New South Wales to central coast of Queensland.

A. alexandrae Alexandra Palm
The Alexandra Palm has a number of different geographical forms some of which eventually may be separated as distinct species or subspecies. They have trunks to 25 m or more high and 10 to 20 cm in diameter, usually prominently ringed and strongly swollen just above ground level. The crown is of medium density and the leaves erect to spreading, 2 to 3.5 m long; the crownshafts are prominent, very smooth and pale green to purplish or brownish-red; the leaves are often not twisted and the leaf stalks are short; the blades have numerous broad leaflets, pale to dark green above, greyish beneath due to being clothed with silvery appressed scales. The inflorescences are 40 to 80 cm long, much branched, outward-directed to pendulous; and the flowers cream to yellow. The red fruits are ellipsoid to almost globular, 15 to 25 mm in diameter.
Distribution: eastern Australia: northern and central east coast of Queensland, from near Cape York to a little south of the Tropic of Capricorn.

Areca

These are most attractive, decorative feather palms, for moist, protected tropical areas. *Areca* is a genus of about 50 species occurring from eastern India and Sri Lanka, through South-East Asia and the Malay Archipelago to the Solomon Islands. Its members are slender, small to tall feather palms with ringed, solitary or multiple trunks, sometimes with stilt roots. The trunks are surmounted by smooth crownshafts formed from the leaf bases. The crowns are light and open with relatively few, usually arching, leaves with short leaf stalks; the leaf blades have few to relatively numerous leaflets which may be very broad or narrow or both on the same leaf, and single or multi-ribbed. The leaflet apexes may be either truncate and toothed or pointed, the two leaflets at the apex of a blade usually united in a fishtail shape.

The inflorescences are below the crownshaft, usually small, branched or reduced to a spike, covered in bud by a single bract which is cast off as the inflorescence expands. There are separate male and female flowers, usually arranged in groups of 3 with 1 female between 2 males, but generally on the slender outer parts of the branches there are males only, in twos. These flower-groups are arranged spirally or in one or two rows on the branches, or there may be a change from 1-rowed near the bases to 2-rowed on the outer parts of branches. Male flowers are very small with 3 tiny sepals, free or joined at the base, and 3 petals with edges touching in bud; the stamens number from 3 to 24. The female flowers are larger with 3 sepals and 3 petals which overlap in bud, minute sterile stamens, and an ovary which is 1-celled with 1 ovule and a 3-lobed stigma. Fruits are oblong to egg-shaped with the remains of the stigma attached; they have a thin,

smooth skin and a fleshy fibrous mesocarp; the seed has a flattened base and ruminate endosperm.

HABITAT, USES, CULTIVATION   These palms are inhabitants of tropical high-rainfall forests. Some of the taller species reach among the forest canopy and are exposed to full light, but most are understorey plants. They range from sea level to altitudes of 1500 m or more in mountain areas.

In their native areas the leaves of these palms are sometimes used for thatching and the trunks for arrows, bows or spears. However by far the most economically important and well known product from this genus is the inner part of the seed (endosperm) of *Areca catechu*, the betel nut. This is usually chewed with the leaves of a pepper plant, a gum, and often lime. It is a narcotic, and when chewed with lime turns the mouth, teeth and saliva red. The use of betel nut in Asia goes back many centuries and has spread from there out into the Pacific Islands. In some countries there is quite an industry producing and marketing the nuts.

This group of feather palms will not tolerate cold conditions. Propagation is from seed which must be fresh and take from about 6 weeks to 3 months to germinate.

A. catechu Betel Palm

A tall slender feather palm with solitary green to greyish distinctly ringed trunk, the Betel Palm stands about 10 to 20 m or more high and is 15 to 20 cm in diameter. The crown consists of a number of arched leaves about 1.5 to 2 m long and greenish to greyish-green smooth crownshafts. The leaf stalks are short and the blades have a number of broad, several-ribbed leaflets with truncated toothed apexes crowded along the midrib, the two terminal ones forming a fishtail shape. Inflorescences are below the crownshaft, about 60 cm long, much branched into very straight slender branchlets bearing small, pale yellow flowers. Fruits are ovoid to oblong, narrowed at the apex, 4 to 5 cm long, smooth and yellow to orange or scarlet.
Distribution: original habitat unknown but widely cultivated from India and South-East Asia to the Pacific Islands.

A. triandra

This is a clump-forming feather palm with a number of slender, smooth, green to greyish, distinctly ringed stems about 3 to 7 m high and 4 to 5 cm diameter, sometimes with stilt roots. The crownshafts are smooth green; and the crowns light, with several arched leaves 1 to 2 m long. The leaf stalks are slender, 20 to 30 cm long; the blades have a number of broad truncated leaflets toothed at apexes and crowded along the midrib; terminal leaflets are fishtailed; inflorescences small, with many stiff slender branchlets below crownshafts; flowers are tiny, greenish. Fruits are olive-shaped 2 to 2.5 cm long, brownish to orange red.
Distribution: eastern India to Indo-China, Sumatra, Borneo, Philippines.

A. vestiaria (syn. A. langloisiana)

Attractive compact clump-forming or sometimes solitary feather palm with several distinctly ringed brownish trunks with stilt roots, about 5 to 10 m tall and 5 to 10 cm diameter. The crowns are open and spreading with arched leaves 2 m or more long. The swollen crownshafts are a striking reddish-orange. The leaf stalks are very short, and the blades have a

Areca catechu

number of broad leaflets obliquely truncate at the apexes which are deeply and unevenly toothed. Inflorescences are below the crownshafts, short and branched, with stalks becoming a similar colour to the crownshaft; flowers are cream. The reddish-orange fruit are oblong-ovoid, about 20 mm long and 10 mm broad.

Distribution: Celebes, Moluccas (eastern Indonesia).

Arecastrum *

Tall, robust feather palms, commonly known as Queen Palms, form this genus of 1 variable species, which occurs in South America from Brazil to Paraguay, Uruguay and northern Argentina. The solitary trunks, 20 to 25 m high and 20 to 35 cm (occasionally 45 cm) in diameter, are smooth, grey, and distinctly or indistinctly ringed, and sometimes swollen towards the middle, or less frequently near the top or bottom. There is no crownshaft and the crown is open to moderately dense with erect to spreading, arching to rather drooping leaves 3 to 5 m long; on young vigorous plants these are widely spaced and extend a considerable way back down the trunk. The margins of the sheathing leaf bases break down into coarse fibres which wrap closely around the trunk apex, becoming shredded and fuzzy on the margins of older leaf stalks. The leaf stalks are about 1 m long, stout and strong, very broad at the base and pressed close against the trunk for much of their length. The blades carry numerous long, narrow, acute-tipped leaflets crowded along the midrib, often in small groups and directed outwards in different planes giving the leaf a strongly plume-like appearance.

The inflorescences arise among the leaf bases and are up to 2 m long. Each has a short stalk and a long stout erect rhachis (central axis or stem) from which arise numerous slender, sinuous branchlets almost at right angles to it. The inflorescences are erect in flower but become drooping as fruits develop. In bud stage each inflorescence is enclosed by 2 bracts: a lower, outer short tubular one and a much longer inner spindle-shaped pointed green woody bract with distinct vertical grooving, which splits down one side to release the flowers and remains on the plant for some time. The numerous flowers are deep yellow, the male and female separate, borne in the bends of the sinuous branchlets, with groups of 3 (1 female between 2 males) in the central part of each branchlet. The solitary female flowers are towards the base, and pairs of male flowers are on the upper part. Male flowers are angular in bud, with 3 minute sepals, 3 narrow petals and 6 stamens. The female flowers are conical in bud, with 3 sepals and 3 petals enclosing the woolly-surfaced 3-celled ovary which bears at its apex a 3-lobed stigma. Only 1 ovule usually develops into a seed.

The fruits, which ripen to yellow and orange, are variable in shape and size, broadly ovoid to oblong-ovoid, with the outer mesocarp layer fleshy but densely fibrous and the endocarp hard and woody with 3 pores at the base and irregularly ridged on the inner surface. These ridges penetrate quite deeply into the non-ruminate seed endosperm, giving the seed also an irregular shape.

Within the species 2 varieties are generally recognized, distinguished mainly on size and shape of fruits. They are:

*See Appendix IV (p. 189)

52

var. *romanzoffianum* — fruits broadly ovoid to somewhat conical, 25 mm or less
long

var. *australe* — fruits elliptic to oblong, about 30 mm
long

HABITAT, USES, CULTIVATION   This palm grows in forest
areas, commonly along river banks and sea coasts, sometimes
extending to more elevated regions, often occurring in very
large stands.

In parts of Brazil it is often cut down in times of
drought to provide fodder for cattle. The unexpanded leaves
in the apical bud are eaten by humans, as are the fruits in
some regions. The palms are sometimes planted to provide
food for pigs, which thrive on the fallen fruits. Their trunks
are used for various constructional purposes and are frequently hollowed out to make water pipes or aqueducts for
irrigation.

Arecastrum in its various forms is widely cultivated as
an attractive landscape subject or as a large decorative tub
plant in warm-temperate or subtropical areas where a plentiful
supply of water is available. The plant thrives in full sun,
except in the earlier stages of growth. It is a fast-growing and
adaptable palm which will tolerate a wide range of conditions
providing it is not too cold and there is an adequate supply of
moisture to the roots. A notable feature is its ease of transplanting at virtually any size, making it popular commercially
for "instant" landscaping. Nurserymen sell it under the long-
superseded name *Cocos plumosa* which can now virtually be
regarded as a common name.

Propagation is from seed, which requires about 2
months for germination. Early seedling growth is rapid if
adequate room is provided for the deep-running roots. A striking feature of young plants is the size of the undivided
juvenile leaves, which, given adequate shade and high nutrient
levels, may reach 1.5 m long and 15 cm wide before giving
way to pinnate leaves.

A. romanzoffianum (syn. *Cocos plumosa, C. roman-
zoffiana, C. botryophora*) Queen Palm
For description see above under genus.

Arenga (including *Didymosperma*)

This interesting genus of about 17 species consists of large to
small feather palms. They occur in India, South-East Asia to
South China, the Malay Archipelago, western Pacific Islands
and northern Australia. They have solitary or multiple
trunks, commonly covered with old leaf bases and tough,
spiny, long, black to dark brown fibres from old leaf sheaths.
In older specimens some species have a bare, ringed trunk.
The crowns may be dense with numerous large leaves, to
small and sparse with very few leaves. The leaf stalks are stout
to slender with the sheathing leaf bases edged with black to
dark brown, stiff, spiny fibres. The blades have leaflets from
almost linear to broad and wedge-shaped or they are sometimes entire. The leaflets are irregularly notched in the upper
part, the notching extending back down the margins, their
apexes are toothed and frequently have a ragged appearance;

Arecastrum romanzoffianum, fruit

the terminal leaflets are often broader and fan-shaped. The bases of the leaflets are shallowly folded upwards (induplicate), and their lower edges at the junction with the midrib frequently form a projection or auricle.

There are one to several inflorescences at each node, in most species appearing first in the upper leaf axils, then progressively occurring down the stem at the old leaf base scars with the trunk ultimately dying after the lowest is produced. This spent stem is replaced by suckers in multiple-stemmed species, but in solitary-stemmed species the whole plant dies. The inflorescence is branched or reduced to a spike; its peduncle is covered with several tubular, papery bracts which enclose flowers in early bud. The flowers are separate male or female and usually occur in groups of 3, with 1 female between 2 male; sometimes the inflorescence may be all male or female flowers but with the sexes rarely occurring on separate plants. The male flowers have 3 overlapping sepals and 3 much larger petals with edges touching in bud, 6 to many stems, and no sterile pistil. The female flowers have 3 sepals and 3 petals joined in the lower part and with edges touching in bud, with or without sterile stamens, each female flower has 2 to 3-celled ovary, each cell with 1 ovule, and 3-lobed stigma. Fruits are globular to oblong, their flesh having an irritant juice and 1 to 3 embedded seeds; the seed coat is very hard and the endosperm is not ruminate.

HABITAT, USES, CULTIVATION   This group of palms grows in tropical regions chiefly in moist rainforest from lowlands to elevated areas, mostly in deeper soils.

Arenga engleri

Arenga obtusifolia

The Sugar Palm, *Arenga pinnata*, has been widely cultivated for centuries in India and regions further east as a source of palm sugar. The sugar is obtained by beating and bruising the developing inflorescence which is then cut and juice obtained from the cut end over a period. The juice is boiled and concentrated and set in moulds. An alcoholic beverage is also made by fermenting the sugary juice. Fibres collected from around the leaf bases were at one time extensively used for making tough rope, but with the introduction of synthetic fibres the demand for this material is greatly reduced; the fibres are also used for making brooms and for thatching roofs. In some areas the old trunks of dead plants are allowed to rot and become hollow and are then used as pipes for conducting water in farm areas. The leaves are also used as a source of thatching material and the new shoots are sometimes used for food.

These palms may grow fairly rapidly, and require warm conditions for satisfactory results. The fact that the stem dies after a period of flowering is a disadvantage to their use, although with multiple-stemmed species the dead stems are obscured by the new growth.

Propagation is from seed; the time taken for germination varies from 2 months to 12 months or more.

A. engleri

A cluster-forming palm from about 2 to 6 m high with several to many fibre-covered stems. Crowns are slender, with several leaves 1.5 to 3 m long, with a number of crowns forming a dense mass of leaves. The leaf stalk is sometimes quite long, almost equalling the blade, and circular in cross section; the blade has a number of leaflets, narrow except for the apical ones, variably notched along the margins and the apex and evenly spaced along the midrib, except for the lowermost leaflets which are usually clustered. The inflorescences are fairly short and arise among the leaf bases. They bear large orange, strongly sweet-smelling flowers. The fruits are globular, about 15 mm in diameter, dark purplish-red, and 2 to 3-seeded.

Distribution: Taiwan, Ryukyu Islands.

A. obtusifolia

A large palm with solitary, or several, trunks, about 6 to 12 m high and 17 to 30 cm diameter, covered with old leaf bases and blackish fibres, or smooth and ringed in the lower part. The crowns are dense with a number of large leaves, 3.5 to 5 m long. The leaf stalks are stout, about 90 cm long, and the blades have numerous linear leaflets with an obtuse to forked, toothed apex, shiny green above, greyish beneath, arranged evenly along the midrib and arising in the one plane. The inflorescences, progressing up the trunk, are branched and 1.2 to 1.5 m long. They bear yellowish-brown flowers with numerous stamens. Fruits are red, oblong, often broader than long, somewhat angular, 3 to 5 cm long.

Distribution: Malay Peninsula, Sumatra, Java.

A. pinnata (syn. A. saccharifera) Sugar or Gomuti Palm

This large palm has a solitary trunk to about 20 m high and 40 to 60 cm diameter, covered with old leaf bases with numerous, long, projecting, black, spiny fibres. The crown is dense with numerous large leaves to about 10 m long, at first erect, sometimes becoming spreading. The leaf stalks are very stout, about 1 to 1.5 m long, and the blades have numerous

Arenga pinnata

long, strap-like leaflets crowded along the midrib strongly
auricled at the base and arising in different planes, presenting
a distinctly plumose appearance. The plant has huge, pendulous inflorescences, 2 m or more long, arising from among or
below the leaves. It bears numerous, greenish to bronzy
flowers. Fruits are globular to oblong, 5 to 6 cm long, yellow-
brown to blackish.

Distribution: widely cultivated in India, South-East Asia and
Malaysia. Wild origin uncertain but probably western
Indonesia.

A. porphyrocarpa (syn. *Didymosperma porphyrocarpum*)

A small cluster-forming palm with a number of slender stems
about 2 m high and about 25 mm diameter, rough with leaf
bases and fibres. The crowns bear a number of leaves 1.5 to

Arenga porphyrocarpa

2.5 m long with slender leaf stalks, 30 cm to 1 m long. The blades have a few, light green, distinctly lobed leaflets, broadly wedge-shaped at the base, the upper part being lyrate, and widely spaced along the midrib. The inflorescences are among the leaf bases, slender, few-branched with cream to greenish flowers. Fruits are ovoid, purplish, 16 to 18 mm long with 1 to 2 seeds.
Distribution: Java; Sumatra.

A. undulatifolia

A cluster-forming palm to about 10 m high, the trunks covered with leaf bases and fibres, or bare and ringed in the lower part. The crowns are dense with a number of erect, long, arched leaves; the leaf stalks are short and stiff and the blades have numerous, broad, distinctly lobed and undulate, notched leaflets, evenly distributed along the midrib. The inflorescences are among the leaf bases, short and branched. Fruits are small and globular.
Distribution: Borneo.

Astrocaryum

Medium to tall, particularly spiny feather palms make up this genus of 47 species, occurring chiefly in tropical South America to Central America and Mexico. *Astrocaryum* is closely related to *Bactris* and *Acrocomia*. They usually have solitary trunks, but sometimes have multiple stems or they may be stemless. The trunks are densely armed with long, sharp spines between the old leaf scars. On older palms these spines may later be shed to varying degrees on the lower part of the trunk. The crown of large, erect to arching leaves does not have a crownshaft; the leaf sheaths, leaf stalks and midribs are densely armed with sharp spines; the blades have numerous leaflets which are evenly arranged along the midrib or in clusters and may arise in different planes, giving the leaf a plumose appearance. The leaflets, with a distinct midrib and lateral ribs, are often armed with spines, particularly along the margins; their apexes are obliquely pointed or sometimes raggedly toothed; their lower surfaces are covered with a greyish bloom or with close, short, woolly hairs.

The inflorescences arise among the lower leaf bases and are simply branched with a number of floral branchlets. In the bud stage they are sheathed with 2 bracts which are not shed when the flowers open. The lower, outer bract is hidden among the leaf bases, the larger one is spindle-shaped, armed with spines and inserted on the upper part of the spiny inflorescence stalk. The flowers are separate male and female on the same inflorescence, with the small, stalked male flowers arranged in pits on the upper part of the branchlets, sometimes with only one female flower at the base of each branchlet between 2 males or with several such groups present. The male flowers have 3 small sepals and 3 petals, the latter being united at the base with the filaments of the 6 to 12 stamens; there is usually a sterile pistil present. The female flowers have 3 sepals, and 3 petals united into a tube and sterile stamens united in a ring. The ovary is 3-celled, each cell with 1 ovule; the style is extended into a long, 3-lobed stigma. The fruits are of variable shape, oblong to ovoid, obovate, or almost globular, with the remains of the stigma attached at the apex, forming a distinct beak; the mesocarp is either pulpy with fibres or dry and fibrous; the hard bony endocarp has 3 pores near the apex with lines radiating from

Arenga undulatifolia (photograph: Julie Seur)

the pores; the outer surface is smooth or spiny; the endosperm of the single seed is non-ruminate with a central cavity.

HABITAT, USES, CULTIVATION *Astrocaryum* species occupy a variety of natural habitats, from disturbed ground around villages to river banks, floodplains, rainforest undergrowth or dry sandy ridges. Species such as *A. aculeatum* and *A. vulgare* are long associated with human settlement and are put to many uses by native peoples of the Amazonian region. The hard, strong and durable wood is used in houses, and the leaves yield a fine, soft fibre for weaving and cordage. The fruits are eaten by humans, cattle and pigs, and a useful oil is also extracted from them. Cultivation of these palms as ornamentals has been attempted mainly in the larger tropical botanical gardens, and, given the right conditions, growth can be quite fast, producing long internodes in some species. A sheltered position with plenty of sun and an abundant supply of water to the roots is recommended. As in other Cocosoid palms having seeds enclosed in a hard endocarp, germination may be slow or at least very erratic.

A. aculeatum

A tall palm with a solitary trunk to about 25 m high and 20 to 30 cm diameter, densely armed with very long black spines, of unequal length, and with broad, unarmed leaf scars. The crown carries large, erect leaves about 5 to 6 m long; the leaf stalks are about 2 m long, densely armed with black, somewhat flattened spines; the leaf blades have numerous leaflets arranged closely in groups along the spiny midrib arising in different planes and giving the leaf a plumose appearance. The inflorescences are about 2 m long with numerous branchlets. Flowers are cream; fruits are subglobular to ovoid, 4 to 5 cm diameter, with a long pointed beak, yellowish-orange when ripe.

This palm has sometimes been included with *A. vulgare*, a cluster-forming palm to which it is closely allied. Distribution: northern South America, Trinidad.

A. vulgare

A cluster-forming palm with a few to many trunks, about 4 to 10 m high and 15 to 20 cm diameter; densely armed with black, flattened spines, with narrow unarmed leaf scars. The crowns have a number of leaves 5 to 6 m long; the leaf stalks are about 2 m long, armed, but not densely, with long, unequal, flattened, shiny black spines. The leaf blades have numerous, linear, drooping leaflets, arranged in groups along the midrib and arising at different angles giving the leaf a plumose appearance. The leaflets are shiny green above, greyish below. Their apexes are obliquely pointed and somewhat bifid, the midveins sometimes with scattered spines on the upper surface, and the margins have black prickles. The inflorescences are about 2 m long with numerous branchlets. Flowers are cream, fruits are ovoid to subglobular, about 3.5 cm diameter, with a short pointed beak at the apex, orange when ripe.

A. vulgare closely resembles *A. aculeatum* and is sometimes included in the same species. Distribution: northern South America.

Astrocaryum aculeatum

Astrocaryum vulgare

Bactris (Syn. *Guilielma, Pyrenoglyphis*)

Bactris species are small to medium-sized tropical feather palms. The large genus of about 200 to 250 species is second only to *Calamus* in the number of species and occurs chiefly in tropical South America, with about 35 species being found in Central America and the West Indies. It belongs to the Cocosoid Group of palms and is one of the 6 closely allied genera — *Acrocomia, Acanthococos, Astrocaryum, Aiphanes, Bactris* and *Desmoncus*, which are included in the *Bactris* Alliance, all of which have a spiny habit and the seed enclosed in a hard woody endocarp, with 3 pores positioned at or above the middle. The stems in *Bactris* may be solitary or in clusters or arising from a creeping underground rhizome, or sometimes without any stem above the ground. The trunks are ringed, usually armed with black spines arising from the rings, in more robust types often having alternating spiny and smooth zones on the trunk. The crowns are without a crownshaft and the leaf stalks and sheathing bases have a covering of brownish, scurfy scales and are densely armed with black, needle-like spines. The leaf blades may be small to large, sometimes undivided and 2-lobed at the apex, or commonly with numerous, narrow, linear leaflets, uniformly arranged along the scaly, prickly midrib. The midvein of the leaflets is distinct and there are several prominent additional veins; the margins have fine prickles and the apex is obliquely pointed or sometimes divided or truncate. The inflorescences arise amongst the leaf bases, usually with a spiny stalk and frequently a short rhachis with several slender branchlets; in bud the inflorescence is sheathed with 2 thin-textured to woody, persistent bracts, which have a covering of brownish, scurfy scales. The lower, outer bract is cylindrical and prickly in the upper part, and the inner bract, which is inserted well above the lower one, is large and cylindrical in the lower part and spindle-shaped in the upper section and densely armed with black spines. The flowers are separate male and female on the same inflorescence, the floral branchlets being densely covered with male flowers intermingled with female flowers. The male flowers have 3 sepals and 3 petals, the latter joined to about the middle, with the pointed lobes having edges touching in bud; there are 6 stamens with the filaments united, and no sterile pistil; the female flowers have 3 sepals, and 3 petals united into a fleshy tube; the sterile stamens are united into a shallow ring. The ovary is 3-celled but with 2 cells non-functional, and has a 3-lobed sessile stigma. Fruits are variable in shape, ovoid to almost globular, oval or compressed, with the remains of the stigma at the apex, and in colour ranging from greenish-yellow to orange, red, purple to black. The mesocarp is fleshy and fibrous and is edible in some species; the endocarp is hard and bony with 3 pores at or above the middle; the endosperm is non-ruminate, solid or with a central cavity.

HABITAT, USES, CULTIVATION   These palms are found in a variety of natural habitats. Some species grow in the open on alluvial soils, while others occur among river bank vegetation, which may be subject to prolonged seasonal inundation. There are other species which grow in the undergrowth of forests or scrub in well drained soils, often of a poor sandy nature. The majority of *Bactris* species grow at low altitudes, for example *B. major* is found on the edges of estuaries where the fresh water meets the sea water; there are also other types which are found in mountain rainforests at elevations of 1000 m or more.

A few *Bactris* species are of value to the inhabitants of the regions in which they occur, the leaves and stems being used for various purposes, and the fruits used as a source of food for both humans and animals.

The fruits of most species are edible but not highly palatable, but an exception is the Peach Palm, *B. gasipaes*, widely cultivated in tropical America. Its fruits, although inedible when raw, after boiling in salt water are floury-textured, oily and pleasant tasting with good nutritive qualities. They are also ground into flour for baking and sometimes fermented into an alcoholic drink. The wood of the outer trunk is exceptionally hard and strong and is put to many uses.

Bactris maraja

This group of tropical palms, apart from *B. gasipaes*, has received limited attention in cultivation. For successful results, moist protected tropical conditions are required. Propagation is from seed which should be fresh as it deteriorates fairly rapidly and takes about 2 months or more to germinate. No doubt the cluster-forming species could be reproduced vegetatively.

B. gasipaes (syn. *Guilielma gasipaes*) Peach Palm, Pejibaye
A tall palm with a slender, clustered, or sometimes solitary trunk, to about 10 to 20 m high and 10 to 15 cm diameter, with rings of sharp spines. The crown carries spreading, arched leaves about 3 m long; the leaf stalks are up to about 1 m long, armed with spines; the leaf blades have numerous light green leaflets, crowded along a spiny midrib, arising in different planes and giving the leaf a slightly plumose appearance with drooping tips. The inflorescences are among the lower leaves, becoming pendulous; and the stalks have no spines. Fruits are densely massed, orange-red, ovoid, large, but of variable size (mostly 4 to 6 cm long), in the cultivated forms usually without seeds, but with an occasional larger fruit containing a seed.
Distribution: Widely cultivated in central and northern South America: exact origin unknown, now found only in cultivation throughout the Central and South American tropics.

B. maraja (syn. *B. pallidispina*)
A clump-forming palm with an underground, creeping rhizome, with trunks 4 to 8 m high and 3 to 5 cm diameter, densely armed with rings of somewhat flattened black spines. Each crown has several leaves 1.5 to 3 m long, a number of crowns forming a dense head; the leaf stalks are 40 to 60 cm long and both they and the leaf sheaths are densely armed with pale brownish spines and prickles; the leaf blades have numerous, shiny, mid-green, drooping, forward-directed leaflets, crowded along the spiny midrib. The margins of leaflets have black prickles. The inflorescences are 30 to 50 cm long; the inner bract is armed sparsely with flattened spines, and the rhachis is short with simple branches. The inflorescence stalk has long spines and the flowers are yellowish. Fruits are purplish-black, globular, depressed and about 1.5 cm diameter.
Distribution: Widespread in tropical South America.

Borassodendron

These attractive tall fan palms form a genus of 2 species, closely allied to *Borassus*. They occur in the Malay Peninsula and Borneo. They have solitary trunks marked with leaf scars, or covered with old leaf bases in younger plants. The dense spreading crowns without a crownshaft have numerous, very large leaves; the leaf stalks are long with the edges smooth, sharp and razor-like, and the base split where it joins the trunk; the large leaf blades are almost circular in outline, palmate, and divided to the base into a number of long wedge-shaped segments, each of which is further divided in the upper part into a number of segments to various depths, each of these ultimate segments rounded to forked at its apex and sometimes drooping.

The inflorescences, which arise among the leaf bases, are male or female on separate plants. The pendulous male inflorescence is branched into a number of thick spikes, in groups of 2 to 5 surrounded by a large bract which becomes fibrous with age. The male flowers are crowded on the spikes in groups of 2 to 6 with an enclosing bract, each flower having a small bracteole; the sepals are joined into a tube which is 2 or 3-lobed at the apex. The petals are also joined into a narrow tube with 3 much expanded lobes; the stamens number 6 to 15, and are attached to the petals and partly joined at the base. The female inflorescence is unbranched and pendulous with deciduous bracts; the flowers are very large and occur mainly crowded towards the apex, each being subtended by a bract. There are 3 tough sepals, 3 spreading petals, and sterile stamens united into a ring. The ovary is 3-celled, each cell with one ovule, and from 3 to 4 warty stigmas.

Fruits are large, roundish, with a flattened top and somewhat angular, and have a hard shiny skin covering a fleshy, fibrous mesocarp layer in which are embedded 3 seeds, each in a hard, bony case of endocarp which has from 8 to 12 shallow wings on its inner surface, projecting inwards and pushing the thin seed coat into the hard endosperm, which is not ruminate but has a central cavity.

HABITAT, USES, CULTIVATION   These palms grow in tropical forest areas with a high rainfall, sometimes on limestone hills with a plentiful supply of moisture; they are becoming rare in the wild state.

The new shoots of the crown and also the fruit are sometimes eaten.

These large fan palms have been grown in such hot tropical places as Malaysia, where, with a plentiful supply of water, they make most attractive specimens. Propagation is by seed which requires heat for satisfactory results.

B. machadonis

A tall palm with trunk to almost 20 m high and 30 cm diameter. The dense crown carries numerous spreading, large leaves to about 6 m long; the leaf stalks are about 4 m long with a split base and smooth razor-sharp edges; the leaf blades are strongly undulate, 3 to 4 m in diameter, shiny mid-green, divided almost to the leaf stalk into a number of long wedge-shaped segments, each further divided to various depths into segments with a rounded to forked apex, drooping at the top.

Inflorescences arise between leaf bases on separate palms; male inflorescences are about 2 m long, branched, the thick floral branches with numerous bracts and cream flowers; female inflorescences are unbranched, pendulous, about 60 cm long with large cream flowers about 3.5 cm in diameter and crowded towards the end of the spike.

Fruits are large, roundish, about 10 cm in diameter, with a flattened top and somewhat angular with a shiny, hard outer purplish-green to brownish surface, with the old stigma at the apex.

Distribution: Malay Peninsula, Thailand.

Borassus

These are massive, striking fan palms with dark grey trunks and stiff crowns of greyish-green leaves. Depending on how broadly its species are defined, this genus has been regarded as consisting of a single widespread and variable species, or several (4 to 7) closely related species occurring in Africa, Madagascar, India, Sri Lanka, South-East Asia, and the Malay Archipelago as far east as New Guinea.

Borassodendron machadonis

The ringed trunks, which may be smooth or rough, sometimes have the split leaf bases remaining attached. The crown is dense, broad, with numerous large, stiff leaves; the leaf stalks are stout and stiff, armed with small, irregularly spaced spines along the margins; the leaf bases are divided where they adjoin the trunk. The blades are costapalmate, broadly wedge-shaped to almost circular, large, stiff, bluish to greyish-green, distinctly pleated, divided to almost half their depth into spreading, tapered, pointed segments, each sometimes divided at the apex.

Inflorescences, which are all male or all female on separate plants, arise among the leaf bases. They are long and much branched, becoming drooping as they develop, and sheathed with overlapping bracts which persist when the flowers open. Male flowers are tiny, numerous, in two rows, sunken in pits in the thick spikes with many closely arranged bracts. Each has 3 sepals, 3 petals, 6 stamens and a small sterile pistil. Female flowers are less numerous than male. They are single, large, about 25 mm across, with 3 sepals, 3 petals, and 6 sterile stamens united into a ring. The ovary is 3-celled with 3 erect ovules, all developing into seeds.

Fruits are very large, roundish, depressed at the top, yellow to brown, with the stigma remaining attached; there are usually 3 seeds, each enclosed in a separate woody case of endocarp, all surrounded by thick fibrous mesocarp; the endosperm is not ruminate and there is a large central cavity in each seed.

HABITAT, USES, CULTIVATION

These palms occur in dry, hot, monsoonal areas in both forested and open country and often form very large stands in soils of varying type, but chiefly well drained and frequently alluvial.

The better known species, *B. flabellifer*, the Palmyra Palm (it is believed by some that all plants in the genus are varieties of this species), is a very important, economically valuable palm, its cultivation dating back to early history. In some communities it is of equal importance to the Coconut Palm, *Cocos nucifera*. In areas where it grows naturally, particularly India, the uses are untold and an early Tamil poem gives 801 different uses for the palm. The leaves are used for many purposes, such as thatching for houses, weaving into baskets, mats and innumerable other articles; they provide fibres for string and rope, fencing and the like. Very early Hindu writings of some thousands of years ago are recorded on the dried leaflets.

The fruit is used as food, raw or roasted; juice rich in sugar is also obtained from the inflorescences. To obtain the juice, the developing inflorescence is first tied together to prevent opening; it is then beaten daily for several days using a wooden implement, such as a mallet. After a few days a slice is cut daily from the end of the inflorescence and almost a week later a clear juice begins to flow which will continue for several months, provided the inflorescence is tapped daily by the removal of a slice. Large palms will yield up to 20 litres of juice per day. The juice is used for many purposes, often being fermented into an alcoholic drink such as toddy, and also evaporated into palm sugar known as jaggery. The flowers serve as a source of honey for bees.

Borassus species are widely cultivated, particularly in Asia, and make arresting specimen palms with the large broad

crown attracting attention. Seed is difficult to germinate, taking maybe 12 months or more; when germination occurs the massive cotyledon grows several metres down into the ground before the roots and leaves appear; seeds should thus be planted in deep containers, or into a permanent position in the ground when the growth begins to appear.

B. flabellifer Palmyra or Lontar Palm.

A large palm with a rough to smooth, ringed trunk, 20 m or more tall and 60 cm or more in diameter, enlarged at the base and sometimes swollen in the middle, sometimes with old split leaf bases attached. The crown is very dense and it has numerous large leaves. The leaf stalks are stout, stiff, 1 to 1.5 m long, and toothed along the margins. The costapalmate leaf blades are 2.5 to 3 m broad, bluish to greyish-green, broadly wedge-shaped to almost circular and distinctly pleated. The inflorescences are 1.5 to 2 m long, and much-branched. The tiny, numerous male flowers are on thick dense branches; female flowers are large, cream, 25 mm across. Fruits are globular, yellow to brown, 15 to 20 cm in diameter.

Distribution: Sri Lanka, India, South-East Asia, Malay Archipelago to New Guinea.

Brahea (syn. *Erythea*)

Brahea palms are medium-sized, usually solitary-trunked fan palms with striking bluish or pale green foliage which makes them attractive ornamental plants. There are about 12 species, including those species which were formerly regarded as comprising the genus *Erythea*. They occur mainly in Mexico, with 2 species extending into Guatemala. The trunk may be closely ringed, particularly on the lower part, or may be covered with remains of old leaf bases. The sparse to dense crown consists of erect leaves with stiff leaf stalks, with or without spines along their margins, and with brown fibres from the leaf sheaths sometimes persisting around their bases. The blades are shortly costapalmate, fan-shaped to circular in outline, cupped inwards and somewhat undulating, divided to about half their depth into stiff, tapered segments each of which is further subdivided into two finely pointed lobes.

The long inflorescences arise among the leaf bases; in early growth the stalks and branches are completely enclosed in tubular bracts which persist after the flowers open. Flowers are arranged singly or in groups of three; they are all bisexual, small, cream to yellow, with 3 sepals and 3 petals which are free or slightly joined at the base. The ovary is divided into three one-celled segments, united above into a single style. Only one cell usually develops into a fruit. Fruits are egg-shaped to spherical, often flattened on one side, with a thin, fleshy mesocarp and with remains of the stigma persisting at the apex. The seed coat intrudes into the non-ruminate endosperm on one side.

HABITAT, USES, CULTIVATION   These palms occur in dry areas in low woodland, or on rocky limestone soils, often on the sides of hills, or in steep gullies.

Brahea species are very slow growing and prefer areas of lower rainfall with poorer, often alkaline soils. Some species do not grow very successfully in richer acid soils in areas of higher rainfall, and although they are attractive plants, their slow growth may be a deterrent to their use. Propagation is from seed which takes from 2 to 3 months to germinate.

B. armata (syn. *Erythea armata; E. roezlii*) Blue Hesper Palm

A palm with a stout solitary trunk 15 m or more high and about 45 cm diameter, ringed in the lower part or covered with stubs of old leaf stalks. The crown is moderately dense with stiff leaves and the leaf stalks are 1 to 1.5 m long with coarse, downward-pointing spines on the margins. The bluish-grey costapalmate blades have a waxy coating and are divided to about half their depth into stiff tapered segments. Inflorescences are about 4 m long and extend beyond the leaves; the flowers are yellow, in groups of 3 on the hairy branchlets. The yellow to brownish fruits are ovoid to globose, about 20 mm long.

Distribution: north-western Mexico.

Brahea edulis

B. edulis Guadalupe Palm

A robust palm with a solitary, brown, ringed trunk to about 10 m high and 30 to 50 cm in diameter. The Guadalupe Palm has a fairly dense crown and the leaf stalks are about 1.5 m long with short spines along the margins. The mid-green, costapalmate leaf blades are undulate, about 1.5 to 2 m broad, and divided to approximately half their depth into tapered segments, each further shortly subdivided. The inflorescences are long and slender, arising among the leaf bases, and the yellow flowers are in groups of 3 on the hairy branchlets. Fruits are globular, about 25 mm in diameter, brown to black in colour.

Distribution: Guadalupe Island (off western Mexico).

B. brandegeei San Jose Hesper Palm

The San Jose Hesper Palm is tall, 10 to 12 m high, and less than 60 cm in diameter, with an indistinctly ringed, sometimes bent trunk. Old leaves sometimes hang under the crown; younger plants are often covered with old leaf bases. The crown is rather open and the leaf stalks 1 m or more long, with woolly brown hairs towards the base, their margins armed with strong spines. The fan-shaped, palmate leaf blades are a dull green above, greyish beneath, about 1 m broad, and are divided to almost half their depth into tapered segments, each of these further divided at the apex. The inflorescences are much branched, shorter than the leaves, with numerous cream flowers. The oblong to globular fruits are variable in size, 15 to 22 mm long, 10 to 18 mm broad, shiny brown with markings.

Distribution: Baja California (north-western Mexico).

Butia

The 8 species of this attractive, hardy South American feather palm genus occur in central and southern Brazil, Paraguay, Uruguay, and northern Argentina. They are solitary-stemmed, with or without an aboveground trunk. In species developing a proper trunk, its surface is clothed in old leaf stalk bases, or with age it becomes bare and grey, somewhat rough and ringed with scars. There is no crownshaft and the many long, pale-coloured, distinctly arching leaves are often strongly erect in their lower parts but may be drooping at the tips. Leaf stalks are stiff, with spines or spiny fibres along the margins, these becoming shorter in the upper part, or absent in some species; there is also greyish fibrous, shaggy material around the leaf stalk bases. The leaf blades have long-tapered, pointed leaflets, bluish-grey to green, sometimes divided at the apex and usually evenly arranged along the midrib though sometimes in groups, and with both ranks directed upwards forming a V in cross section.

Inflorescences arise among the leaf bases, each consisting of a strong main axis and numerous side branches; in bud the whole is enclosed in 2 large bracts. The outer bract is short and tubular, the inner large and woody, pointed at its apex and contracted at the base. It is finely veined or striated but not deeply grooved (as in *Arecastrum*, to which this genus is closely related), splitting down one side to release the flowers and remaining on the plant long after flowering. Flowers are yellow to reddish or purple, borne in groups of 3 (1 female and 2 males) on the lower parts of the side branches, but with male flowers only on the upper parts. The male flowers, which are shed soon after opening, have 3 sepals

and 3 larger petals with edges touching in bud, 6 stamens, and a 3-lobed sterile pistil. Female flowers have 3 sepals and 3 overlapping petals, and 6 sterile stamens. The ovary is 3-celled with single style and 3-branched stigma.

Fruits are spherical to egg-shaped with persistent petals and sepals attached to the base, yellow to reddish in colour, with a fleshy, finely fibrous outer mesocarp layer, and a thick, stony endocarp which has 3 pores near the base or in a more lateral position. The seed is non-ruminate.

HABITAT, USES, CULTIVATION   These palms grow in woodlands and grasslands in seasonally dry areas, in a variety of soils.

The fruits, produced in large quantities, are used for food. The sweet, juicy flesh may be strained to produce a jelly or fermented to make a wine.

B. capitata with its many forms and varieties has been widely cultivated in many parts of the world except the wet lowland tropics. It is moderately slow growing and with its greyish foliage and neatly overlapping leaf stalk bases makes an attractive specimen plant.

Butia species appear to hybridize readily with one another, also occasionally with the closely allied *Arecastrum* and *Syagrus*. A number of presumed hybrids have been recorded in cultivation.

These hardy palms will grow well under a wide range of conditions, from high-rainfall temperate to fairly dry subtropical. *B. capitata* survives moderately heavy frosts. Propagation is from seed, which is slow to germinate (often 6 months or more); subsequent growth of seedlings is also usually slow.

B. capitata Butia or Jelly Palm

A variable species, with many forms differing chiefly in trunk height and diameter, degree of arching of the leaves, and fruit shape, size, or colour. The trunk may be from 1 to 5 m or more in height and from 30 to 50 cm in diameter, covered in overlapping leaf bases, or with age becoming bare, ringed and somewhat rough. The crown is moderately dense, the erect, arched leaves 1.5 to 2.5 m long; the stout leaf stalks have spines on the margins and fibrous material between the bases. Leaf blades have numerous tapering bluish-grey leaflets, sometimes forked at the apex, each rank of leaflets directed upward, forming a V-shape.

Inflorescences are about 1 m long, the large, persistent woody bracts smooth and without hairs at maturity, variable in colour from cream to dull purplish; flowers are creamy-yellow to reddish. The fruits are spherical (sometimes with flattened ends) to egg-shaped or somewhat conical, yellow to orange, mostly around 25 mm long and 22 mm in diameter. Distribution: central-southern Brazil, Uruguay, northern Argentina.

Calamus

Climbing rainforest feather palms, *Calamus* species have prickly stems which are mostly very slender. The genus is large, containing about 370 species occurring in tropical Africa and Asia, the Malay Archipelago, New Guinea and north-eastern Australia, and out into the Pacific as far as Fiji.

Most species have multiple stems, generally climbing,

Butia capitata

68

but a few have stiff, erect stems. There is usually no distinct crown, the leaves being distributed along the stems below the apex at wide intervals. The leaves have short stalks and a greatly varying number of evenly spaced, usually lance-shaped, but in some species rhombic or wedge-shaped leaflets and a tubular sheathing base. Leaf bases, leaf stalks, midribs and frequently the leaflets are armed with numerous spines: the types of spines and their patterns of distribution over these organs are important distinguishing features for species. Arising from the top of the leaf sheath opposite the leaf stalk there is frequently a long flexible extension armed with hooked spines, which acts as a grappling organ for climbing: it is known as a flagellum (plural flagella) and is actually a modified, sterile inflorescence. This is shown by the fact that the true, flower-bearing inflorescences occupy the same position relative to higher leaves on the plant, and that there are often intermediate organs, with both hooked portions and flowering branchlets. In some species the climbing organ is not this modified inflorescence, but a slender extension of the main leaf stalk with hooked spines known as a cirrus. It is rare for both types of climbing organ to be present in the one species.

The inflorescences, male and female on separate plants, are long and slender, with a number of branches, each sub-tended by a tubular bract; each branch has a number of short branchlets with crowded flowers; bracts persist, though often in a withered state, when flowers open. Flowers are white to cream, the male flowers usually occurring singly and the female in pairs, one of the pair usually sterile; all are subtended by bracteoles. All flowers have 3 sepals, 3 petals, 6 stamens and a pistil, but in the males the latter is a non-functional pistillode, while in female flowers the sterile stamens are united into a ring. The ovary is 3-celled with 3 erect ovules, a short style and 3-lobed stigma; the outer surface of the ovary is covered with minute overlapping scales.

The fruits are globular and covered with overlapping scales. They have a thin, dry mesocarp. The seed has an endosperm which is ruminate or non-ruminate and an enveloping fleshy aril (outgrowth of the seed-stalk) which is edible in some species.

HABITAT, USES, CULTIVATION   *Calamus* species are inhabitants of rainforests in tropical and subtropical regions of high rainfall, from sea level to elevated mountain areas, reaching their greatest diversity in Indonesia, Malaysia and the Philippines.

It may not be generally realized that the well-known and widely used cane furniture is made from the strong flexible stems of *Calamus* and closely related genera. Collection, processing and export of cane is an important industry in Malaysia, Singapore, Indonesia and the Philippines. Even in the Western World the different types of cane have innumerable uses, for example in basketry and for handles of many kinds. In their native regions the leaves of these palms are used for thatching buildings; the stems are used for a great many purposes, from construction of buildings to suspension bridges. In northern Australia these plants have common names such as Lawyer Cane or Wait-a-while, the latter being most applicable as the long spiny tendrils are most effective in this regard.

Calamus caryotoides

Calamus muelleri

Calamus australis

Little attention has been given to the cultivation of *Calamus* species which, as well as making graceful scrambling plants in established moist shrub areas, are most attractive as potted plants for warm, shaded positions, although growth is often slow at first.

Propagation is from seed which may take 3 or 4 months to germinate and must be very fresh.

C. caryotoides Fishtail Lawyer Cane

A slender clustering palm with stems only about 7 to 10 mm in diameter, and leaf sheaths densely armed with short needle-like spines. Leaves are small, 20 to 30 cm long, with no stalk and only 8 to 10 shiny wedge-shaped leaflets with truncate or broadly V-shaped, finely toothed apexes, widely spaced along the midrib. The two terminal leaflets are often fused to form a fishtail shape. The spines on the leaf sheath extend on to the leaflet edges and very sparsely on to both leaf surfaces. The small cream flowers are borne on the outer or middle branchlets of the inflorescence. Fruits are almost spherical, yellowish, about 12 mm long and 10 mm in diameter.

This palm makes an elegant small pot plant in warmer areas. Its growth is quite fast and it has proved surprisingly cold hardy.

Distribution: Australia: north-eastern Queensland.

C. muelleri Wait-a-while

A slender-stemmed scrambling palm with multiple stems, about 8 to 12 mm in diameter, its leaf sheaths clothed densely in short, fairly weak greyish spines, and the stems smooth where sheaths have fallen. Leaves are 30 to 60 cm long with a very short stalk, leaflets not very numerous, lance-shaped and evenly spaced along the midrib. The flagella are slender, armed with numerous small sharp hooks. The leaflets have small spines on the edges and towards the base on the upper and lower surfaces. The cream flowers are borne on the upper side branches of the inflorescence. Fruits are globular, hard and yellowish when fully ripe. They grow to about 12 to 15 mm in diameter.

Distribution: east coast of Australia (north-eastern New South Wales, south-eastern Queensland).

C. australis Lawyer Cane

A robust, multistemmed, tall, scrambling palm, which has stems about 15 mm in diameter. The leaf sheaths of this Lawyer Cane Palm are densely armed with long, reddish-brown, needle-like spines, usually joined at their bases into groups. Leaves are about 1 m long with short, sparsely spiny stalks, the gently arched midrib bearing green leaflets tapering to the apex and evenly spaced along it, the leaflets without spines on either surface, but usually with small marginal spines. Flagella are long, armed with strong, hooked spines. Inflorescences have numerous small cream flowers arising on upper side branchlets. Fruits are globular, creamy coloured, about 12 mm in diameter.

Distribution: Australia: north-eastern Queensland.

Carpentaria

A tall, elegant feather palm, confined to the lowland region around Darwin in tropical northern Australia, is the only known species in this genus. It was given its name by the botanist Odoardo Beccari in the mistaken belief that it came from the Gulf of Carpentaria, which in fact is quite some distance away. Its smooth ringed trunk to about 20 m tall and 12 to 15 cm in diameter and its distinctive crownshaft give it a resemblance to some *Veitchia* or *Archontophoenix* species. The crown has strongly arching leaves, 3 to 4 m long with short leaf stalks and arching midribs, pendulous at the tips. The leaflets are broad, shiny deep green above and waxy bluish-green beneath. Each leaflet has one or more ribs and tapers to the apex which has one or two teeth on the lower edge. The uppermost and lowermost pairs of leaflets are markedly broader with several teeth and ribs.

The inflorescences, several present at the one time, appear large, branched and spreading. They grow to about 1.5 m long. Each is enclosed in bud by 2 long bracts which fall before the greenish-yellow flowers open. The flowers, separate male and female on the same inflorescence, are arranged in groups of 2 or 3 in the lower parts of the branchlets, with 1 female flower and 1 or 2 male; in the upper part all flowers are male. Male flowers are large with 3 overlapping sepals, 3 petals with edges touching in bud, numerous stamens, and a sterile pistil longer than the stamens; the female flowers have 3 sepals, 3 petals overlapping in bud, and minute sterile stamens. The 1-celled ovary has 1 ovule and a small, 3-lobed stigma. The fruits are almost spherical, about 20 mm long and 15 mm in diameter, bright scarlet, with a scar from the stigma at the apex; the outer layer of mesocarp is thick and juicy and the inner layer has crowded straight black fibres; the seed is ellipsoid, with non-ruminate endosperm.

HABITAT, USES, CULTIVATION   This tropical palm grows in patches of rainforest along the banks of streams, in low flat country, usually close to the heads of saltwater estuaries.

It has been frequently planted in Darwin as a street and park tree where it has proved fast growing and highly ornamental, but has as yet been little used elsewhere. It requires humid tropical or subtropical conditions with a plentiful supply of water for satisfactory results and will not withstand cold or dry conditions.

Propagation is from seed which germinates within about 1 to 3 months from sowing; fresh seed is necessary.

C. acuminata (syn. *Kentia acuminata*)
For description see above under genus.

Caryota

Highly ornamental palms with a unique foliage type, and adapting readily to cultivation, members of the *Caryota* genus are medium to tall, solitary or clump-forming. They occur in tropical areas of the Malay Archipelago, eastern Asia and Australia (Cape York Peninsula only). There are some 12 different species of this genus. Unlike other palms which have the leaves divided in a pinnate (feather) or palmate (fan) manner, those of *Caryota* are bipinnate, that is, each of the primary leaflets is further divided into leaflets. These are more or less triangular with the outer corners elongated and the apical side toothed, in a fishtail shape, hence the common name of Fishtail Palms. In common with the genera *Arenga* and *Wallichia*, in mature plants the first flowers appear

71

among the upper leaf bases, then each successive flowering occurs lower down the stem until ultimately that trunk dies. In single-stemmed species like *C. urens*, this means the death of the whole palm.

Inflorescences have a short stalk and numerous long, pendulous flower-bearing branchlets, sheathed in bud by several overlapping thin-textured bracts. They are usually male and female, alternating in successive leaf axils, or with flowers of both sexes on the one, in groups of 3 with 1 female between 2 males. Male flowers have 3 sepals, 3 long petals with edges touching in bud, and numerous stamens. Female flowers have 3 small sepals, 3 rounded petals overlapping in bud, and an ovary with 2 to 3 cells, each with an ovule, and a 3-lobed stigma. Fruits are 1 to 3-seeded, globose, with a tough skin and thick mesocarp which contains irritant crystals. The seeds are more or less hemispherical, or with 2 inner faces and rounded back, and have a thick, hard seed coat.

HABITAT, USES, CULTIVATION   These palms grow in a variety of habitats, though usually on hill slopes, ridges or rocky outcrops. Most are from high rainfall tropical areas, but a few occur in regions of strongly seasonal rainfall, or on high mountains, or subtropical hill regions of mainland Asia. The smaller-growing multiple-stemmed species are mostly forest undergrowth palms, while the tall solitary species emerge above the forest canopy, or occur in openings in the forest. Growth is often very rapid.

Sago and sugar are produced from the cut stems and inflorescences of these palms and alcoholic drinks are derived from the fermentation of these products. The leaf bases provide a fibre from which brooms and similar products are made.

All species of the genus appear hardy in subtropical and warm-temperate areas provided severe frosts are not experienced. They make very attractive pot or tub specimens for indoor use or outdoor areas such as courtyards and lawns, especially the multistemmed species.

C. maxima (syn. *C. rumphiana* in part)

A tall single-stemmed species, with grey, widely-ringed trunk to about 20 or possibly 30 m high, and 20 to 40 cm in diameter. The crown is very elongated with leaves persisting a considerable way below the apex of the trunk. The leaves are widely spaced with long stalks and are 4 to 6 m long, drooping at the apex. Leaflets (on adult plants) are pendulous, narrowly triangular to almost linear, with a long drawn-out point on one side, 20 to 45 cm long. Inflorescences grow to about 2 m long, fruits are pinkish-red, 2 to 3 cm in diameter, 1 or very rarely 2-seeded.
Distribution: Malay Peninsula, Sumatra, Java.

C. mitis

A multistemmed species with crowded trunks of greatly mixed height, forming a clump usually less than 1.5 m across at the base. The trunks grow to about 10 m (usually much less) and are 5 to 15 cm in diameter, with well-spaced rings. The crowns have few leaves but collectively appear dense. The ascending leaves have long midribs and are about 2 to 4 m long. The spreading leaflets are broadly to narrowly tri-

angular, very asymmetrical. Inflorescences are 25 to 45 cm long with crowded pale cream flowers; the fruits are yellowish-green turning orange or dark red, 7 to 15 mm in diameter, 1-seeded.

Distribution: widespread in South-East Asia and Malay Archipelago.

C. no (syn. C. rumphiana in part)

A very large solitary-trunked palm, the distantly ringed grey trunk thicker in the middle, up to 70 cm in diameter at this point. It grows to a height of up to 20 m or more. The crown is moderately elongated, rather open, with strongly ascending leaves 5 m or more long and about 4 m wide. The lateral stalks but not the midribs are often drooping; leaflets are semi-pendulous, narrowly triangular, 30 cm or more long. Inflorescences are 2 m or more long with cream flowers; fruits ripen to purplish-black, and are 2-seeded, about 30 mm in diameter.

Distribution: Borneo

Caryota no

C. urens Jaggery Palm

A robust but not very tall solitary-trunked species, the Jaggery Palm has a distantly ringed grey trunk to about 12 m high, 30 to 40 cm in diameter in the lower part, tapering somewhat toward the apex. The crown is usually elongated, fairly dense, with ascending, arching leaves about 4 m long. Leaflets are wedge-shaped, about 20 to 30 cm long, and pendulous. Inflorescences are very large, 1.5 to 3 m long with cream to green flowers, reddish fruits, which are 1 to 2-seeded, about 20 mm in diameter.
Distribution: India, Sri Lanka, Malay Peninsula.

Ceroxylon

This beautiful but rarely cultivated genus includes the tallest of all palms. Its 17 or so species occur in South America in the elevated parts of the Andes in Venezuela, Colombia, Ecuador, Peru and Bolivia. *Ceroxylon* species have a smooth distinctly ringed trunk which has a whitish waxy covering and may be slightly swollen toward the mid-point. The crown is open with a number of erect to arched and spreading long leaves, their sheathing bases not forming a proper crownshaft. The leaf stalks are short and without spines; the blades have numerous long leaflets contracted at the apex into a point, evenly spaced and crowded along the midrib and drooping to varying degrees.

The inflorescences, with a long stalk, and branched into numerous slender branchlets, arise among the leaf bases, with male or female inflorescences on separate plants. The stalk has about 5 to 7 large, overlapping bracts which enclose the inflorescence in bud. Flowers are borne singly on the branchlets; the male flowers have 3 united sepals, 3 petals joined at the base, 6 to 15 stamens, and a minute sterile pistil. Female flowers have sepals and petals similar to the male and small sterile stamens, and a 3-celled ovary with 3 spreading, recurved stigma-lobes. Fruit is globular, smooth to slightly rough, orange or red to purplish-black, with a thin fleshy mesocarp layer, and remains of the stigma low down on one side. Seeds have non-ruminate endosperm, with embryo in a lateral position near the base.

HABITAT, USES, CULTIVATION   Palms of this group grow in elevated areas from about 1500 m to 4000 m in valleys and sides of hills in moist forest, often wreathed in clouds.

The hard wax coating the trunks was at one time exploited commercially but since the process involved felling the tree, it is unlikely that this use still continues.

These attractive palms, reported to reach up to 60 m high, have very rarely been successfully cultivated except in cities and towns close to their native regions; however, there are two old specimens of *C. alpinum* growing in the large palm collection of the Royal Botanic Gardens, Sydney, Australia. Propagation is by seed, but little is known about the germination requirements.

C. alpinum (syn. *C. andicola*, *C. ferrugineum*) Andean Wax Palm

A tall feather palm with a ringed trunk to about 30 m high and 20 to 30 cm in diameter, pale grey, with a thin layer of hard wax. The crown of the Andean Wax Palm is moderately

dense, its spreading leaves with broad sheathing bases but not forming a true crownshaft; leaves are 2 to 3.5 m long, leaf stalks very short and, together with sheathing bases, covered thickly in white woolly scales. Numerous, crowded, leaflets are regularly arranged along the midrib. They are long and narrow, pointed at the apex, deep glossy green above, silvery-whitish beneath. Inflorescences arise among the leaf bases, a number present at the one time, 1.5 to 2 m long, arching and hanging below the crowns. The inflorescence stalk has about 7 large bracts; these and the midrib are covered densely with brown woolly scales. Flowers are pale yellow. Fruits are globose, 17 to 19 mm in diameter, orange-red with a finely warted surface and fleshy orange mesocarp.

Distribution: Colombia: slopes of the Andes to west of Bogota, between 1500 and 2000 m altitude. *C. alpinum* has been confused in the past with the taller (to 60 m) *C. quindiuense* which occurs in the same region but between 2000 and 3100 m.

Chamaedorea (syn. *Collinia, Neanthe, Eleutheropetalum*)

Over 130 species comprise this Central and South American feather palm genus, making it among the largest of all palm genera. The majority are natives of the Central American countries, from southern Mexico to Panama, but a substantial number occur in the north-western countries of South America.

These are all fast-growing, fine, ornamental palms, slender inhabitants of the forest understorey. A few are moderately tall, with solitary trunks rarely up to 10 cm diameter, but most have bamboo-like stems, smooth and green with prominent but well-spaced rings and around 2 cm diameter or less. Many of the species are clumping or colony-forming (stems branching off underground rhizomes), but there are also many which are both small and single-stemmed. A few are even climbers, either with long flexible stems simply resting on branches of trees and shrubs or, in the case of *C. elatior*, actually grappling on to them by sharply reflexed upper leaflets.

There is often no properly formed crownshaft in Chamaedoreas, the sheathing leaf bases generally being distributed back down the stem to well below its apex; however some species have reasonably distinct crownshafts. Leaf stalks and midribs are always very slender, green and smooth; leaf blades are divided into few to many thin-textured leaflets or, in a few species, undivided except for an apical cleft. Leaflets vary from straight and very narrow to fairly broad and gently curved into a slight S shape, with forward-pointing sharp apexes. They are mostly multi-veined, though usually with one central vein more prominent, and their attachment to the midrib is elongated, often as long as the leaflet's width, not constricted and strongly folded as in most feather palms. A peculiarity of many, but not all, species is the way the leaflets, as they die, fall from the midrib, often leaving several bare, wand-like, dead midribs persisting below the crown.

Male and female flowers are on separate plants. Inflorescences are mostly small, rather fleshy and brittle, with fairly few side branches or completely unbranched, though male inflorescences have more slender and numerous branches than the female. A characteristic feature is the sheathing of the inflorescence, in early bud stage only, by a series (3 or more) of overlapping, thin, papery, tubular bracts on the stalk. Male flowers are spirally and singly arranged, or clustered in longitudinal rows; they have 3 sepals forming a fleshy cup, joined together to varying degrees, 3 petals also basally fused to varying degrees, their upper parts with edges touching in bud, 6 stamens, and a fairly large sterile pistil. The solitary female flowers have similar sepals and petals, though with the latter often overlapping in bud, and up to 6 minute sterile stamens. The ovary has 3 cells, each with 1 ovule, usually only 1 cell develops into a fruit, but 1 or 2 underdeveloped cells may be attached to its base.

Fruits are round to elongated, small, red or black with thin, soft flesh, and a small seed which has non-ruminate endosperm and embryo in a lateral position. As the fruits enlarge the female inflorescence in most species turns a bright orange colour and becomes thicker and fleshier.

HABITAT, USES, CULTIVATION   All species come from high-rainfall tropical regions, though often at moderately high altitudes. Most are plants of the rainforest undergrowth, growing in fairly dense shade, with roots mainly in the humus layer of the forest floor, or on banks of fast-flowing streams. The native peoples of Central America eat the inflorescence buds of a number of species, using them as a green vegetable. Leaves of other species are used for thatching, as are the leaves of many palm genera.

Chamaedorea has many species already well established in cultivation, and many more with potential as attractive ornamental palms. Provided that their basic requirements of shade, mild temperatures and adequate moisture are met they are among the easiest of palms to grow successfully. A particularly rewarding characteristic is their speed of development, with flowers and fruits produced when only a very few years old; if seeds are required, though, it should be remembered that plants of both sexes must be grown together, and hand-pollination may be needed. A number of hybrids between different species have been raised in this way, but this should not be encouraged unless parentage is recorded and the hybrids have horticultural virtues not possessed by species. Chamaedoreas are especially useful in small gardens, it being possible to accommodate quite a selection of species in a small area. The smaller, more delicate species such as *C. elegans* should be reserved for the most protected, shady and humid positions; some of the larger-growing ones will tolerate full sun though usually at the cost of somewhat scorched or bleached foliage.

It is as a source of small, highly decorative pot plants that this group outdoes all other palm genera. The well known Parlour Palm, *C. elegans*, is already just about the most commonly sold palm in small pots, but all species are adaptable for use in this way. Those of bamboo-like growth-habit are effective in larger pots and tubs, in the same manner as *Rhapis*, though they should not be kept on patios or balconies in full sun. Unlike many other palms, Chamaedoreas may tolerate occasional drying out of their potting soil without apparent ill effect, though this is not recommended.

Propagation is mostly by seed, with time for germination anything from under 1 month to more than 6, depending on species and freshness of seed, or by division in the case of some of the multistemmed species. A further technique applies to a few species which produce rings of abortive aerial roots up the stem, namely air-layering. On such a plant, when it gets taller than desired, new roots can be regenerated on the stem by tying a ball of damp sphagnum moss around the chosen point and enclosing it in an air-tight wrapping of plastic; when sufficient roots are developed, the stem is cut below this point and the upper part replanted. Unfortunately the lower part is usually incapable of sprouting new leaves, though it may remain green for years, so this is only a means of rejuvenating, not multiplying a plant.

NOTES: 1. The juice of the fruits in most species is said to be irritant to the skin. 2. Being of Greek derivation, the genus name should be pronounced with a hard *ch*, i.e. ''Kammy-dory-a''. Only names derived from names of French persons or places, e.g. *Chambeyronia*, should have *ch* pronounced as ''sh''.

Chamaedorea costaricana

C. costaricana Bamboo Palm

This is one of the most densely clumping species, forming bamboo-like clumps to over 2 m wide at the base, the massed crowns being much broader. Stems of the Bamboo Palm grow to about 3 or 4 m tall, and are 1.5 to 2.5 cm in diameter, with very long smooth green internodes. The drooping leaves extend back down the stem and are 50 to 100 cm long with long leaf stalks and many (around 40) narrow-lanceolate pale green, very thin leaflets which fall from the midrib as they die.

Inflorescences emerge from the lower leaf sheaths, and are as long as the leaves, pendulous, the long stalk sheathed in several narrow bracts which are dry and pale by flowering. The yellow flowers give way to black fruits, spherical and 8 to 10 mm in diameter, on coral-red inflorescence branches.
Distribution: Costa Rica.

C. elatior

A clumping species with weak climbing stems to 4 m or more long, 1.5 to 2 cm in diameter, often largely covered in persistent leaf sheaths. Leaves very variable, with very short to long leaf stalks, blades from short, 2-lobed but otherwise undivided on younger stems, to sometimes 3 m long on taller stems. Leaflets widely spaced on these adult leaves, narrow-lanceolate, deep green, near base and apex modified into stiff, narrow, straight climbing hooks sharply reflexed downward with thickened base. Inflorescences break through the bases of leaf sheaths, with recurved, bracted stalks, branches to 30 cm long in female, shorter in male inflorescence. Fruits are black with a waxy bloom, 10 mm in diameter, on pale orange to pinkish or brownish branches.
Distribution: central and southern Mexico, Guatemala.

C. elegans (syn. *Collinia elegans, Neanthe bella*) Parlour Palm

Always solitary-stemmed, occasionally to 2 m tall but reaching maturity (i.e. flowering) when only 30 cm high with no visible stem. Stems of the Parlour Palm are 8 to 16 mm in diameter, green, with closely spaced rings, from which rings of thick, stubby, abortive aerial roots develop with age. The crown is compact with leaves all clustered near the stem apex; leaf stalks are 10 to 30 cm long, blades 20 to 40 cm long with regularly arranged lanceolate deep green leaflets. Inflorescences are usually longer than the leaves, many at once emerging from the leaf sheaths erect with long, straight, many-bracted stalks. The branches are short on a very short rhachis, turning red after flowering even without fruit. Fruits are black, globose, 6 mm in diameter. Depending on geographical origin, the dimensions of this palm are very variable.
Distribution: southern Mexico, Guatemala.

C. ernesti-augusti (syn. *Eleutheropetalum ernesti-augusti*)

Solitary-stemmed palms, to 2 or sometimes 3 m tall, stems 12 to 15 mm in diameter, fairly closely ringed and producing aerial roots with age like those of *C. elegans*. The crown is very small, and compact with the leaves all close to the stem apex; leaf sheaths are broad, loose, and the leaf stalks short, under 10 cm. Leaf blades are mostly 20 to 40 cm long, almost as broad, always undivided but 2-lobed with large apical cleft, multi-ribbed, upper margins shallowly toothed. Inflorescences are numerous, emerging from the tops of the

Chamaedorea elegans

78

leaf sheaths. They are erect, with straight, bracted stalks, male with a number of slender branchlets, female reduced to a single fleshy spike or with one or two side branches held close against the rhachis, colouring bright orange after flowering whether or not fruits are set. Fruits are ellipsoid, to 14 mm long, 8 mm in diameter, black when ripe.
Distribution: southern Mexico, Guatemala, Honduras.

C. glaucifolia

An attractive, solitary-stemmed, relatively sun-tolerant species sometimes reaching heights of 5 or 6 m. The stem is 2 to 3 cm in diameter, fairly closely and prominently ringed, often with small stilt roots at the base. The crown is moderately compact, with leaves distributed a little way below the stem apex; leaves are long and strongly ascending, 1.5 to 2 m or more in length with numerous long, very narrow, straight leaflets, waxy bluish-green on both sides, somewhat clustered into groups and carried in a number of planes, giving a plumose leaf.

Inflorescences arise from sheaths of old leaves below the crown, shorter than leaves, erect, with relatively long bract-covered stalks and short stiff branches near the apex. Fruits are black, globose, about 6 mm in diameter, on red branches.
Distribution: southern Mexico.

C. klotzschiana

A solitary-stemmed palm to about 2.5 m tall with a stem about 2 cm in diameter, green and fairly closely ringed. The crown is moderately compact with leaves crowded at the stem apex, their sheathing bases forming an apparent crownshaft. The leaves are about 1 m long, erect to spreading with a short leaf stalk and straight midrib; leaflets lanceolate, fine-pointed, quite broad, somewhat concave and crumpled, gathered in tight groups of 2, 3 or 4 on either side of the midrib, the groups being opposite one another and separated by long intervals of bare stalk. Inflorescences emerge below the crown, spreading, only half as long as the leaves, with few branches equalling the short, dry-bracted stalk in length. Flowers are greenish-yellow, fruits black, 8 to 10 mm in diameter, on orange branches.
Distribution: southern Mexico.

C. metallica (formerly misnamed *C. tenella*)

A beautiful small, slow-growing species with a solitary stem no more than 1 m tall, 8 to 12 mm thick, dark green, with close rings and aerial roots near the base. The crown is very compact, but the leaves are distributed down the stem to a little below the apex. Leaves are erect to somewhat spreading, with very short, slender stalks; leaf blades undivided except for a shallow apical notch, wedge-shaped, about 20 to 25 cm long, 10 to 15 cm wide, thick-textured, several-ribbed, shallowly-toothed an upper margins, slightly concave and contorted near the apex, deep grey-green with a marked metallic sheen at least on the upper side. Inflorescences are small, slender, erect, with cream flowers, the male with a short stalk and very short, weak side branches, the female unbranched with short fleshy flower-bearing spike carried vertically, at an angle to the stalk. Fruits are ovoid, black, about 12 mm long, 9 mm in diameter.
Distribution: southern Mexico.

Chamaedorea glaucifolia

C. microspadix

A clump-forming species with stems to about 3 m tall, usually much less, 9 to 12 mm in diameter, deep shiny green with moderately widely spaced prominent rings; new growths diverge at a wide angle from the bases of older stems before turning upward, so producing rather open clumps. Individual crowns are fairly open, with leaves distributed well below the stem apexes; leaves are deep dull green, 30 to 50 cm long, with short leaf stalks and relatively few broad, thin, fine-pointed, regularly-spaced leaflets. Inflorescences are carried below the crowns, markedly shorter than the leaves, spreading, with short stalks sheathed in dry bracts and with drooping branches and white flowers. Fruits are orange-red, spherical, to 12 mm in diameter, freely produced in cultivation, fruiting inflorescences not colouring much. A hardy species, moderately cold tolerant.

Distribution: eastern Mexico.

C. seifrizii

A fairly robust clump-forming species, occasionally reaching 3 m or taller but forming dense clumps while much lower; stems deep green with moderately widely spaced prominent rings, about 1.5 to 2 cm in diameter, all growing straight and erect. Crowns are fairly open with ascending, slightly arching and twisted leaves arising a little way back down the stem from the apex. Leaves are about 60 cm long, with short stalks and narrow, crowded, straight leaflets. Inflorescences emerge below the crowns, only about half as long as the leaves, with short stalks and spreading branches. Fruits are black, about 6

Chamaedorea klotzschiana

Chamaedorea metallica

Chamaedorea microspadix

mm in diameter, on orange branches. One of the more sun-tolerant species.

Distribution: eastern Mexico.

C. tepejilote

One of the largest solitary-stemmed species, highly variable in its native state with stems of some plants as little as 2 m tall and 1.8 cm in diameter; and others (representing different populations) up to 7 m or more tall and 10 cm in diameter, but always smooth and green with prominent rings which may be closely to widely spaced (though spacing is not more than twice stem-diameter). The crown is few-leaved, the sheathing leaf bases forming a narrow crownshaft, though in vigorously growing plants the leaves are distributed a good way down the stem below the apex. Leaves with stalks to 50 cm, usually much shorter, and straight, steeply ascending midrib to 2 m long from which arise at regular intervals a number of long, lanceolate, finely pointed leaflets up to 7 cm or more broad with several prominent ribs on the upper surface; the leaflets fall from the midrib with age.

Short inflorescences are borne below the crown; the males spreading, with short stalks, many slender branchlets and bright yellow flowers in rows; the females are longer, thick and fleshy, with reflexed stalks, pendulous midrib and fewer branchlets than the male. Fruits are ovoid to ellipsoid, blue-green ripening to black, 13 to 20 mm long, 7 to 8 mm in diameter, on thick orange branches. This fast-growing species is cultivated for its edible young inflorescences, with selected forms perpetuated.

Distribution: throughout Central America, from eastern Mexico to Colombia.

Chamaerops

This widely cultivated, low, clustering fan palm may be grown in many locations outside the tropics. It is a genus of 1 species extending from the Atlantic coasts of Portugal and Morocco eastward through the whole Mediterranean area except Egypt. It usually forms large clumps with a number of stems but in some forms the stem is solitary. Heights of plants vary in the wild, some even being stemless; in cultivation they are commonly from 2 to 3 m tall, but the solitary-trunked type may reach 6 m or more. The trunk surface is usually covered with leaf-base fibres from the old sheaths. In very old plants, or where leaves have been removed, the stem may be bare and ringed in the lower part.

The crown has a number of stiff spreading leaves on slender flattened leaf stalks, the margins of which are armed to varying degrees with forward-pointing sharp spines; the bases of the leaves have a short sheath which disintegrates into coarse woven fibres; the leaf blades are bluish to greyish-green, palmate and about three-quarters of a circle in outline, being divided deeply, sometimes almost to the apex of the leaf stalk, into tapered spreading segments each of which is again divided at the apex.

The short, stiff inflorescences which arise among the leaf bases are male or female on different plants, the male inflorescences being more densely flowered than the female. Occasional flowers may be bisexual or there may be separate

Chamaedorea tepejilote

Chamaerops humilis, inflorescence

male and female flowers on the same plant. The flower stalk is flattened and branches are fleshy with numerous small flowers. The whole is surrounded by a large bract, tubular in the lower part and expanded and flattened in the upper part, terminating in a pointed apex. This bract splits down one side, becomes gaping and allows floral branches to expand; within the large bract is a smaller less enclosing bract and small inconspicuous bracts at branches.

Flowers each have 3 spreading sepals and 3 petals. Male flowers are bright yellow and have stamens united at the base into a fleshy disc. The yellow-green female flowers are similar with the bases of the filaments cup-shaped and the anthers erect but usually sterile. The ovary has 3 separate globose cells joined at the base, each containing 1 ovule and tapering into a short style with minute stigma; only 1 ovule usually develops into a fruit. Fruits vary in shape and size from globular to oblong, and in colour from yellow to dull orange or brown. They have a tough skin and a slightly fleshy, fibrous mesocarp layer. The seed endosperm is shallowly ruminate and with a deep fold of the seed coat into the endosperm down one side.

HABITAT, USES, CULTIVATION   Plants grow naturally in poor, often rocky soils in various vegetation-types and in Spain cover large areas of waste land. They are often found on rocky and sandy seashores and on hot cliffs of mountain ranges up to at least 1000 m altitude, where they may be snow-covered in winter.

The leaves have been used for weaving into various articles such as baskets and hats, for cordage, for paper making and crushing into fibres for stuffing. Fibres from the leaf sheaths are used for weaving into carpets under the name of African hair. Fine fibres from the leaves have been used as a flax substitute.

This palm will grow most successfully in a sunny location with well drained soil in a temperate climate. There are many selected forms in cultivation which have frequently been given varietal names. A large clump makes a fine lawn or courtyard specimen; it may also be grown in a large tub for many years. Propagation is usually from seed which germinates in 2 to 3 months. Being a clustering palm it can doubtless be propagated by division of existing plants, though this is rarely attempted.

C. humilis Mediterranean Fan Palm
For description see above under genus.

Chambeyronia
Rare but highly ornamental solitary-trunked palms go to make up this, one of the 15 or so genera of palms endemic to New Caledonia. The genus consists of one somewhat variable species and a second recently discovered species. They are medium to tall feather palms with a well-defined crownshaft. The relatively few, large leaves have very short leaf stalks, stout midribs and broad leaflets of regular width and spacing. Near the apex of the leaf they become progressively shorter and slightly narrower. Each leaflet has a thick, prominent midvein and two prominent marginal veins, appearing as

greatly thickened edges to the leaflet; its apex is narrowed fairly abruptly into a fine point.

The inflorescences appear below the crownshaft, usually only one or two at a time, and fairly small, with short stalks and few, thick, contorted branches. In the bud stage they are enclosed in 2 thin-textured, flattened, short, broad bracts, of equal length, one inside the other, cast off together well before the flowers open. The quite large flowers are in groups of 2 male and 1 female at the bases of the branches, and pairs of male only on the upper parts of the branches. The males are asymmetric, 3-cornered, and green in bud, the non-overlapping petals opening to reveal numerous long white stamens. Female flowers have overlapping petals enclosing a fleshy 1-celled and 1-ovuled ovary terminated by a short 3-cornered stigma.

The fruits are quite large, ellipsoid, reddish with the remains of the stigma forming a broad scar right at the apex and enlarged petals and sepals adhering to the base. The fleshy mesocarp of the fruit is finely fibrous, and the large ovoid seed has a reticulate pattern of surface markings but plain white endosperm, with the embryo right at the base.

HABITAT, USES, CULTIVATION   *Chambeyronia* grows on densely forested mountain slopes to altitudes of about 1000 m in a region of very high year-round rainfall. It is doubtful that it has any significant uses other than as an ornamental. For this purpose it is of great value, if suitable growing conditions can be provided, its main (at least in *C. macrocarpa*) feature, being the colour of the expanding central leaf. For the first week or less after it begins to expand this leaf is translucent and anything from a russet colour through various shades of orange or red to a deep bronzy-purple. Only one or two new leaves may be produced each year, so enjoyment of this spectacle must be fleeting.

Despite its great beauty this palm seems to be rare in cultivation. The reason for this could be because of scarcity of seeds, or because the climate and soils of many palm-growing areas do not suit it. The fact that it has been grown successfully in Sydney and Rio de Janeiro may indicate its climatic preferences.

C. macrocarpa (syn. *C. hookeri, Kentiopsis macrocarpa*)
This species is said to reach 20 m or more in height in its native state, the smooth but slightly ringed brownish trunk having a diameter of 10 to 15 cm. The crownshaft is green with a purplish-brown scurfy coating, and the large leaves are strongly arched with the outer part pointing vertically downwards. The leaves are 2 to 2.5 m, long and leaflets may be over a metre long and up to 10 cm wide. The inflorescences are only about 30 cm long with white male and green female flowers, and the red fruits are 4 to 6 cm long and about 3 cm in diameter.
Distribution: New Caledonia.

Chrysalidocarpus

These slender feather palms with gracefully recurving leaves are much used in tropical landscaping. The genus of about 20 species occurs in Madagascar, the Comoro Islands and Pemba Island off Tanzania. They have multiple or solitary, smooth, ringed trunks. The crown has a few to a number of arching leaves usually in 3 vertical ranks; the leaf stalks are slender, without spines, and the encircling, sheathing leaf bases almost form a crownshaft in some species; the leaf blades have a number of long, narrow leaflets each with a single midrib, and tapered to the apex; leaflets are evenly spaced along the midrib and arise in the one plane, or sometimes in different planes, giving the leaf a plumose appearance.

The inflorescences, which are among the leaves at least in the bud stage, have a number of spreading branches and in bud are enclosed by 2 bracts, the lower outer one short and the inner one long and pointed; both are shed when the flowers open. Flowers are separate male and female, arranged in groups of 3 with 1 female between 2 males on the lower part of the branchlet but with paired or solitary male flowers only on the upper part. Male flowers have 3 overlapping sepals, 3 petals with edges touching in bud, 6 stamens and a distinct sterile pistil. Female flowers have 3 sepals, 3 petals overlapping in bud and tiny sterile stamens. The ovary has 3 cells, but only 1 of these contains an ovule. Fruits are ovoid with a fleshy mesocarp and a scar from the stigma at the base; the seed has a non-ruminate endosperm.

HABITAT, USES, CULTIVATION   These tropical palms grow in forest areas of high rainfall, mostly in richer soils.

Of the 20 or so species, only a few are generally known in cultivation and one species, *C. lutescens*, is widely grown in tropical and subtropical areas for various landscaping uses and as a potted decorative plant for indoor and outdoor use. It adapts well also to cooler regions where buildings are heated and there is adequate light available. Propagation is usually by seed which germinates satisfactorily, some species taking longer than others to germinate. Clump-forming types such as *C. lutescens*, which make numerous suckers, can be propagated by division of existing plants or possibly by detachment of single suckers which mostly have aerial roots.

C. cabadae

A cluster palm with smooth, green stems to about 9 m tall and 12 cm in diameter, distinctly ringed with greyish leaf scars. The sheathing leaf bases are long and glaucous, with the long leaves arching; the leaf stalks are short; the leaf blades have many light green leaflets, evenly spaced along the midrib, their 2 ranks directed upwards and becoming arched. The inflorescences are erect and horn-like in bud, the open flowers being creamy-yellow; fruits are ellipsoid, about 10 mm long, bright red.
Distribution: named from a cultivated specimen; precise native origin unknown.

C. lucubensis (syn. *C. madagascariensis* var. *lucubensis*)

A solitary-trunked palm to about 10 m high and about 20 cm in diameter, greenish with prominent rings and tapering to the apex. Leaves 2 to 3 m long, clearly arranged in 3 vertical rows, each with a short, sheathing base with a white mealy coating towards the top; leaf stalks are about 30 to 50 cm long; leaf blades with numerous leaflets arising from the mid-

rib in different planes, giving the leaves a plumose appearance. The inflorescences are broadly branched with many fine branchlets. Fruits are ellipsoid.
Distribution: Nossi Be Island, off north-western Madagascar.

C. lutescens (syn. *Areca lutescens*) Yellow Palm, Golden Cane Palm, Butterfly Palm
A slender, multi-trunked palm, developing with age numerous crowded stems, the tallest to about 9 m high and 6 to 10 cm in diameter. The stems increase by suckering, usually at or slightly above ground level, or sometimes from the trunk 1 m or more above the ground. Sheathing leaf bases are long and narrow, with a whitish, mealy appearance, becoming yellowish. The few leaves are in 3 rows, to about 2 m or more in length with a yellowish arching midrib and yellow leaflet midveins; the leaf stalks are about 60 cm long; leaflets upward-pointing, evenly spaced along the stalk, narrow and gracefully arching. The inflorescences are few-branched, with a downward-curving stalk; flowers are yellow. The fruits are pale yellow to violet-black, narrowly ovoid, about 18 mm long.
Distribution: Madagascar.

C. madagascariensis (syn. *Areca madagascariensis*)
A multi-stemmed palm, growing to about 10 m high, the stems to about 15 cm in diameter, greyish, closely ringed; leaf bases are short and broad and the leaves 2 to 3 m long on short stalks. Numerous leaflets arise in different planes along the midrib, giving the leaves a plumose appearance. Inflorescences are broadly branched with numerous small branchlets. The flowers are yellow. Fruits are ellipsoid, yellowish.
Distribution: Madagascar.

Cocos

This is the Coconut Palm, highly valued by man and cultivated throughout the wet tropics. The genus, now regarded as having only 1 species (*C. nucifera*), was formerly interpreted as including a number of other species which are now placed in separate genera, although some nurserymen still use the old name of *"Cocos plumosa"* for the widely cultivated palm *Arecastrum romanzoffianum*. The geographical origin of *Cocos* is not known though various theories have been put forward in this regard and it is generally thought to be from the west Pacific or Indian Ocean islands. It is widely distributed throughout tropical coastal parts of the world between latitudes 26° north and south.

This palm has a number of different forms or varieties cultivated in different parts of the world, varying in stature from dwarf types to the typical tall-growing, slender Coconut Palm, and representing a wide range of fruit colour, shape and size.

The grey trunk grows to 30 m high and about 20 to 30 cm in diameter, usually with an enlarged base. It has distinct crescent-shaped leaf scars and vertical cracks and is commonly curved to varying degrees. Although usually solitary, the trunk may occasionally sucker in young plants. The crown of large pinnate leaves (6 m or more in length) has no crownshaft and the bases of the stout yellowish-green leaf stalks and adjoining trunk are clothed in strong light brown woven fibres; the leaf stalks are about 1 m long, and the leaf blades have numerous long, tapered, yellowish-green, single-veined

Chrysalidocarpus madagascariensis

leaflets, evenly spaced along the midrib. This midrib is gently twisted, so that the upper leaflets are in a vertical plane.

The inflorescences arise among the leaf bases; they are once-branched only from a thick central axis or rarely reduced to a spike, and grow to about 1.8 m. In the bud stage they are enclosed in a tough woody tubular bract which splits down one side and persists when flowers open. Male and female flowers are carried on the same plant, with one or two triads of both sexes at the base of each side branch, and male only along the remainder of its length. The small male flowers have 3 short sepals, 3 petals with edges touching in bud, 6 stamens and sterile pistil minute or absent. The fairly large female flowers have 3 sepals and 3 petals, all overlapping in bud, and 6 sterile stamens united into a ring. The ovary is 3-celled with 3 ovules, only one of which develops into a fruit; the stigma is short. The large fruits are usually ovoid and vary in colour from green to ochre-yellow or orange-red, turning brown and dry before falling off. The outer mesocarp layer is a thick, dry and very fibrous husk and covers a hard woody endocarp with 3 openings or pores at the base. A very thin seed coat covers the endosperm which is non-ruminate and is divided into a narrow peripheral zone of fairly hard, white, oily flesh and a central part which is in liquid form, being a mixture of a sweet watery fluid and oil.

HABITAT, USES, CULTIVATION   The Coconut Palm commonly grows among various forms of vegetation on tropical seashores and on alluvial plains extending inland where conditions are suitable, such as the presence of a high ground-water table, but it avoids waterlogged areas.

The Coconut Palm is a most important plant with innumerable uses in addition to being a source of food and attractive too. It is of the greatest economic importance in many of the less industrialized parts of the world. Millions of tonnes of copra (the dried endosperm of the fruit which is cut open and allowed to dry) are produced annually. Copra yields coconut oil, used in margarine, soap, candles, and the like, and the endosperm is also grated to make the well known shredded coconut so widely used in cooking and confectionery. The fresh white endosperm is a source of food and cooking oil in many countries; the leaves are used for thatching and weaving into mats, baskets etc. and the trunk is also used as a source of timber. The fibres of the mesocarp, or husk, comprise the familiar coir of doormats, etc. In some areas, for example the Philippines, the stalk of the inflorescence is tapped to obtain a sugary sap which is fermented into an alcoholic beverage. The watery fluid of the green fruit makes a delicious drink, being cool even in hot tropical areas.

As well as being planted for commercial purposes and to provide food and drink, Coconut Palms are most attractive palms for single and group planting. The Pacific Islands would lose much of their charm without the numerous swaying Coconut Palms helping to provide island magic.

These palms require warm tropical conditions with a high rainfall and high ground-water level, but will not grow successfully in waterlogged soil and will not tolerate cold. Although they will grow in elevated areas to about 1000 m in equatorial regions they are not as vigorous in growth and may not flower.

C. nucifera Coconut Palm
For description see above under genus.

Cocos nucifera, fruit

Coccothrinax

These graceful, slender, thin-leaved fan palms belong to a genus of 20 species occurring in the West Indies and southern Florida, with one species extending to northern South America. They are closely related to *Thrinax* and were formerly included under that genus. They have a solitary trunk which is often slender and smooth with a pale surface or covered with dead leaf bases and matted brown fibres. The crown consists of smallish, thin-textured leaves with flexible, slender petioles, their bases surrounded by matted brown fibres from the leaf sheaths; the leaf blades are palmate, glossy green above and lighter green to silvery-grey beneath, usually almost circular in outline and divided into radiating segments which may be stiff or flexible and drooping, and either pointed or 2-lobed at the apex.

Inflorescences are mostly shorter than the leaf stalks, with slender arching midribs sheathed in narrow, tubular bracts, which subtend a number of pendulous side branches; these branch at least once again into numerous fine branchlets with crowded, white or yellow, stalked flowers, borne singly along them. Flowers are bisexual, with petals and sepals fused together into a single small, 6-pointed, star-like disc, half hidden below the much larger stamens, which are 9 to 12 in number and also have their broad-based filaments united into a disc at the base; above them is the spherical or somewhat flattened ovary, with 1 cell and 1 ovule, and short style terminating in an obliquely cup-shaped stigma.

Fruits are small, round, brown or purple to black, with thin, pulpy mesocarp. The spherical seeds are irregularly grooved from apex part-way to the base, some with 5 deep furrows, others with shallow, less regular, branching grooves giving the seed a brain-like appearance. Grooves of this type correspond to deep penetrations of seed endosperm by the seed coat and therefore these seeds are ruminate.

HABITAT, USES, CULTIVATION   Like the genus *Thrinax*, palms of this group grow in forests, frequently in soil derived from limestone in tropical coastal areas, and sometimes in poorly drained ground.

Coccothrinax species have similar uses to those of *Thrinax*. The gracefully radiating leaf segments and the symmetrical arrangement of the leaves add to the attractiveness of these palms and their slow growth rate makes them satisfactory for potted specimens in warm areas.

Propagation is from seed, fresh seed taking from 2 to 3 months to germinate. Growth is fairly slow, especially in the earlier stages.

C. alta

A tall slender palm with a smooth, slightly ringed, pale grey-brown trunk, 8 to 10 m tall and about 15 cm in diameter near the base, the upper part often covered with loosely woven matting of old leaf bases. There are about 15 leaves in the crown; the leaf stalks are about 1 m long; leaf blades are nearly circular, about 1 m across, bright green above, silvery beneath, divided to about half to two-thirds their depth into rather broad segments, tapering to 2-lobed apexes. Inflorescences are 30 to 50 cm long with white flowers. The globose fruits are shiny brown to black, 8 to 10 mm in diameter. Distribution: Puerto Rico.

C. crinita

A palm with trunk 4 to 9 m high and 15 to 20 cm in diameter, densely covered with a shaggy, hair-like mass of light brown fibres with projecting leaf bases. The 15 to 25 leaves in the crown are about 2 m long with slender leaf stalks about 1 m in length and circular blades 60 to 70 cm broad, shiny green above and greyish beneath, divided into tapered segments almost to the base. Flowers are yellow, on inflorescences about as long as or longer than the leaves. Fruits are purplish-black.
Distribution: Cuba.

C. miraguama

A slender, somewhat variable palm with a trunk either smooth and grey or covered with leaf bases and brown raised fibres, from 4 to 5 m high and 10 to 15 cm in diameter. The 30 or so leaves in the crown are 1.5 to 2 m long with slender leaf stalks about 1 m in length; the leaf blades are 60 to 100 cm across and carried at an angle to the leaf stalks, shiny green above and greyish beneath, divided to half or more of their depth into stiff, pointed segments. Flowers are yellow on much-branched inflorescences among the leaf bases. Fruits are globular, deep red to black, about 10 mm in diameter.
Distribution: Cuba.

Coccothrinax crinita

Coccothrinax miraguama

Copernicia

Known as Wax Palms, these make attractive specimen plants and are particularly striking when young. They occur in the West Indies (Cuba and Hispaniola only) and South America. The genus of 25 species consists of fan palms with short or tall, usually solitary trunks, or in a few species forming a clump of several stems. The trunk, depending chiefly upon its age, is covered to a varying extent by leaf bases, or is smooth and marked with distinct leaf scars. Usually it is of even diameter throughout, but may be somewhat spindle-shaped.

The leaves, which may be very large, form a dense crown, without crownshaft, often with the leaves closely crowded and the old leaves creating a dense skirt-like thatch around the trunk. The leaf stalks may be long, short or virtually absent; their margins are armed with spines while the surfaces may be smooth, hairy or waxy and the bases sometimes spiny. The leaf blades are palmate to very shortly costapalmate, fan-shaped to circular or wedge-shaped, and divided to about half to one-third of their depth into tapered segments; the leaf surface may or may not have a coating of wax.

Inflorescences arise among the leaf bases and are much branched with enclosing tubular bracts which persist after the flowers open. Flowers are very small, bisexual, yellowish to brownish, solitary or in groups of 2 to 4. Each flower or cluster is subtended by a small bracteole. The sepals and petals are both fused for about half their length into a tube, the petals being longer; the 6 stamens have the lower part of the filaments united into a tube. The ovary consists of 3 1-celled segments, fused at the apex into a single style; only one usually develops into a fruit. Fruits are egg-shaped to spherical with endosperm deeply ruminate.

HABITAT, USES, CULTIVATION   This group of tropical fan palms grows in various locations in savannahs and forests where they occur as individuals, or in stands mixed with other vegetation in relatively dry areas often subject to flooding, such as along the banks of streams and the edges of lakes, usually near sea level or sometimes extending to the side of low hills.

In their natural habitat *Copernicia* species are used for various purposes, the trunk being used for fencing and building, and the leaves for thatching and weaving into various articles such as mats, baskets and hats. Wax may be obtained from the leaves of various species, but *Copernicia prunifera* is grown extensively in Brazil for the commercial production of carnauba wax. This wax is widely used in various types of high quality polishes and has other potential uses.

These palms grow well in warm areas although growth is slow. Propagation is by seed which takes about 2 to 3 months to germinate.

C. alba Caranday Palm

A tall slender fan palm with a solitary trunk 8 to 30 m high and 17 to 22 cm in diameter, grey and smooth in older plants. The leaf bases of the Caranday Palm remain attached in younger specimens. The crown is dense; leaf stalks are slender, 70 to 80 cm long, with coarse teeth on the lower part of the margins; leaf blades are light green, flat to cupped upwards, with a dense waxy coating on the surface. They are

Copernicia baileyana

89

Copernicia ekmanii

divided to about half or more of their depth into tapered segments, sometimes drooping.

Inflorescences are slender, about 1.8 m long, extending beyond the leaves, with yellowish flowers. Fruits are ovoid, 20 mm long, 17 mm in diameter.

An attractive fan palm for warm areas with a plentiful supply of moisture, and useful for production of wax.
Distribution: Paraguay, northern Argentina, Bolivia and adjacent region of western Brazil.

C. baileyana Bailey Copernicia
A large palm with a solitary trunk, spindle-shaped or of even width, 10 to 15 m high, up to about 60 cm in diameter. It is smooth with inconspicuous leaf scars, or with leaf bases remaining attached. The dense crown carries erect, broad leaf stalks to about 1.3 m long and armed with coarse spines. The leaves have a waxy surface and are divided to about one-third of their depth into stiff tapered segments.

Inflorescences are about 3 m long, much-branched, extending beyond the leaves, with numerous yellowish flowers. The dark brown fruits are ovoid, 18 to 20 mm long, 18 mm broad.
Distribution: Cuba.

C. ekmanii
A small palm with a solitary trunk 3 to 4 m high, with old leaf bases on the lower part. The short leaf stalks are stiff and spiny, about 30 cm long, white in colour, and waxy. The light green leaf blades have a whitish coating of wax and are distinctly undulate, about 1 m broad, divided to one-third or more of their depth into tapered, stiff segments. Inflorescences are short, about 80 cm long, and have many branches. Fruits are ovoid, about 20 mm long, 17 mm broad.
Distribution: Haiti.

C. glabrescens Guano Palm
This slender palm has a rough trunk 4 to 6 m high, 12 to 15 cm in diameter, sometimes suckering from the base. It has a fairly open crown. The slender leaf stalks are about 1 m long with toothed margins. Leaf blades are circular in outline, light green, with a light coating of wax and divided to about half their depth into tapered segments. Inflorescences are slender, 2 m long, extending beyond the leaves. The globular fruits are 17 mm in diameter.
Distribution: Cuba.

C. macroglossa Cuban Petticoat Palm
A palm with a solitary trunk 4 to 5 m high, 16 cm in diameter, being covered with a dense skirt of dead leaves, the lower part being bare and smooth in older plants. The dense crown has leaves closely arranged. Leaf stalks are very short to 30 cm long; blades are shortly costapalmate, wedge-shaped and light green with a waxy coating, divided to about one-third of their depth into tapered segments which are at first erect, later drooping. Inflorescences are slender, about 2 m long, extending well beyond leaves, and bear brownish flowers. Fruits are ovoid, 16 mm long, 15 mm in diameter.
Distribution: Cuba.

C. prunifera (syn. C. cerifera) Carnauba Wax Palm
The Carnauba Wax Palm is fairly slender with a solitary trunk 10 to 15 m high and 15 to 25 cm in diameter, with distinct leaf scars on the upper part of the trunk in older plants and the

lower 3 m or so covered with distinct persistent leaf bases. Younger plants have leaf bases to about two-thirds the length of the trunk.

Inflorescences are 1.5 to 2.7 m long, extending beyond the leaves. Flowering branchlets have no tubular bracts. The ovoid fruits are about 27 mm long and 22 mm in diameter. Distribution: north-eastern Brazil (confined to the region east of the mouth of the Amazon).

C. rigida Jata Palm
A tall palm with a solitary trunk to 15 m high and 25 cm in diameter, often with a skirt of dead leaves below the dense, globose crown. There are no leaf stalks, the blade having a wide costa which looks like a leaf stalk. The light green blades are about 1 m long, narrowly wedge-shaped, with a waxy coating on the surface, and shallowly divided into broad segments which are at first erect, later drooping. Inflorescences are slender, about 2 m long, extending beyond the leaves, with brownish flowers in clusters of 2 to 4. Fruit are ovoid, 18 mm long, 17 mm in diameter.
Distribution: Cuba.

Copernicia macroglossa

Copernicia rigida

Corypha

The most massive of all fan palms, these need tropical
conditions and ample space. They occur in India and eastward
through tropical Asia, the Malay Archipelago and northern
Australia. The genus is represented by about 8 species. They
differ from most other palms in that flowering only occurs
once, usually at 20 to 50 years, when the apex of the plant
becomes a huge inflorescence, and after flowering and fruiting, the palm dies. The tall, robust, solitary, close-ringed
trunks are usually covered in leaf bases in younger plants.
Leaves are very large with long stiff thick leaf stalks which in
some species have spiny margins, each stalk being split at the
base where it joins the trunk. The large, stiff, erect blades are
strongly costapalmate and distinctly undulate, being divided
from about a third to half their depth into broad, stiff
segments.

The enormous inflorescence which develops from the
whole apex of the palm has a thick central axis which is a
continuation of the trunk. At the base of this are a series of
leaves grading from the normal foliage leaves formed prior to
the inflorescence developing, to much shorter leaves with
very small blades, and finally to sheaths without blades, which
are the inflorescence bracts (this palm is thus a perfect illus-
tration of the way bracts are derived from leaves). Higher up,
each bract subtends a major lateral branch, of which there are
quite a number; these also are sheathed in large tubular
bracts, subtending much shorter side branches, which are in
turn branched again, and finally again into the small flower-
bearing branchlets. There are therefore 4 orders of branching
from the central axis, and the resulting branchlets number
many thousands, with flowers in the millions.

Flowers are bisexual, grouped in small clusters on the
branchlets, small, white to cream, usually with an unpleasant
odour; each has 3 sepals, 3 petals, 6 stamens and a 3-celled
ovary, each cell with a single ovule, only one of which usually
develops into a seed; the apex of the ovary narrows into a
short style with a shortly 3-lobed stigma.

Fruits are spherical, usually with small protuberances
at the base, representing the two undeveloped cells of the
ovary and a tough skin enclosing a firm, succulent mesocarp.
The spherical seed has a non-ruminate endosperm, without
any lateral or basal intrusion of the seed coat of the sort found
in related Coryphoid fan palms (e.g. *Livistona*). It sometimes
has a central cavity.

HABITAT, USES, CULTIVATION   *Corypha* species grow in
tropical monsoonal areas in woodlands and forests, chiefly in
flat, low-lying land.

In areas where Corypha species occur naturally, use is
made of the leaves for various purposes, such as covering
walls and roofs of buildings, for weaving into baskets and
similar objects and, in the Philippines, for weaving into high
quality hats. Sugar is obtained from the cut inflorescence and
is fermented into an alcoholic beverage.

These palms require warm tropical conditions and may
be grown as large ornamental specimens where ample space is
available. Growth may be very slow in the early stages,
particularly where the temperatures are lower. The disadvantage of the relatively short life of these palms is more than
offset by the wonderment aroused by their spectacular mode
of flowering and fruiting.

Germination from seed takes about 2 to 3 months and fresh seed should be used where possible.

C. elata Gebang Palm

The Gebang Palm is tall, with a solitary, closely ringed trunk 15 to 20 m high and 50 to 70 cm in diameter. The large, erect leaves are 4 to 6 m long, and have thick, stiff, greyish or yellowish leaf stalks, 2 to 4 m long, with closely spaced blackish spines on the margins, gradually broadening into the sheathing base. The blades are shorter than the leaf stalks, light green, almost round in outline, but cut off almost squarely at the base, undulate, curved downward along the midrib and divided to about half their depth into broad segments, each tapering to a shortly 2-pronged apex.

The huge, much-branched terminal inflorescence is 3 to 4 m high, fairly dense and almost circular in outline, the main branches straight and ascending in flower, with branchlets pendulous, but becoming more horizontal and gently arching with the weight of the developing fruit. Flowers are white to cream in enormous numbers; fruits are round, 20 to 25 mm diameter, olive-green to brownish.

Distribution: southern India, Sri Lanka, Malay Peninsula, Malay Archipelago, northern Australia.

C. umbraculifera Talipot Palm

A very large palm with closely ringed trunk to 25 m high and 60 to 90 cm in diameter. The leaves are very large, 5 to 6 m long, in a tall dense crown; leaf stalks are equal to or shorter than the leaf blades, green and massive with smooth margins, abruptly demarcated from the sheathing base by a projection or auricle on either side. The sheathing base is edged with spinous fibres. Blades are light green, up to 3 m long and 5 m broad, divided to about one-third their depth into broad stiff segments, each terminating in a short 2-lobed apex.

Inflorescences are very large, about 6 m tall, roughly circular in outline, with the main branches arching below horizontal. The drooping branchlets give the branches a feathery appearance at flowering. The flowers are cream and the brownish fruit round, 3 to 5 cm in diameter.

Distribution: southern India and Sri Lanka, but only associated with human habitation; exact wild origin unknown.

Cyrtostachys

Colourful, slender, clump-forming palms comprise this genus of 8 species occurring from Malaysia to the Solomon Islands. The stems are smooth, green to brown and distinctly ringed. The crowns are small with arched leaves and smooth crownshafts which may be a striking reddish colour; leaf stalks are short and slender and the blades have a number of long leaflets tapered to a pointed apex and evenly spaced along the midrib.

The inflorescences are below the crownshafts and are slender and branched into slender spikes, the whole enclosed in bud by tubular bracts with the upper one pointed, becoming deciduous when flowers open. The flowers are separate male and female, spirally arranged in groups of 3 in pits, with a female between two males. Male flowers have 3 overlapping sepals and 3 petals touching in bud; stamens are 9 to 15 with the filaments joined at the base and the small sterile pistil is 2 to 3-branched. Female flowers have 3 sepals and 3 petals with edges touching in bud; the sterile stamens are united into a

Corypha elata, fruiting specimen on left

Corypha umbraculifera

small 6-toothed ring. The ovary is incompletely 3-celled with 3 stigmas. Fruits are egg-shaped to nearly spherical with the old style attached. The seed is egg-shaped with non-ruminate endosperm.

HABITAT, USES, CULTIVATION   This group of palms grows in moist forests, frequently in swampy areas.

Two of the species of these clump-forming palms are frequently cultivated in warm tropical areas with plentiful moisture. They will not tolerate cold or dry conditions. They make very attractive specimens with the bright red crownshaft presenting a striking appearance. Plants from seed often take some time to form a coloured crownshaft and propagation is commonly carried out by dividing suckers from existing plants and growing them on under nursery conditions. Seeds germinate within 2 to 3 months but require heat for satisfactory results.

Cyrtostachys renda

C. renda (syn. *C. lakka*) Sealing Wax Palm, Lipstick Palm
An attractive clump-forming palm for moist tropical areas,
this species has a number of slender, smooth, green to brownish, distinctly ringed stems 5 to 10 m high and 4 to 7 cm in
diameter. The small crowns have several arched leaves about
1 to 1.5 m long. Crownshafts are about 60 cm long and a
striking shade of red. Leaf stalks are short, 15 to 30 cm,
slender and red in colour; blades have a number of leaflets
tapered to the apex and evenly spaced along the midrib with
both ranks directed forward and inwards in a V-shape.

Inflorescences arise below the crownshaft, their slender
and branched stalks becoming red; flowers are greenish. The
obovoid fruits are tapered to the apex, black with a red base.
Distribution: Malay Peninsula, Borneo.

Dictyosperma

An attractive feather palm, widely cultivated but almost
extinct in its natural habitat. This is a genus consisting of 1
species only, though formerly treated as 2 or more, with
several varieties. It occurs only in the Mascarene Islands
(Mauritius, Réunion and Round Islands). The slender, solitary
trunk is grey to blackish, closely ringed and expanded at the
very base. It grows to 20 m in height and 10 cm or more in
diameter. The trunk is surmounted by a distinct crownshaft,
from whitish to green or reddish in colour, often softly
woolly, formed from the bases of the long graceful pinnate
leaves which are erect or spreading and up to 3 m long. The
leaf stalks are short (15 to 30 cm long), coloured greenish,
whitish or reddish, with sharp edges. The leaf blades have
numerous long leaflets, tapering to a pointed apex and often
divided into 2 thin points; the midvein is distinct on both
surfaces and lateral veins are distinct, particularly in younger
plants where they are of contrasting colour; leaflets are evenly
but closely spaced along the midrib and are spreading to
drooping. The midrib is usually slightly twisted so that the
upper ranks of leaflets are in a near-vertical plane.

Inflorescences arise below the crownshaft and are short
and much branched, 40 to 100 cm long, with short stiff stalks;
in bud stage they are enclosed in two large papery bracts, one
inside the other, which are flattened and tapered to a pointed
apex, falling when the flowers open. The flowers are
numerous, creamy-yellow to dark reddish, near the bases of
the branches arranged in groups of 3 with 1 female between
2 male, but nearer the ends of the branches they bear
solitary or paired male flowers only. All flowers have 3 sepals
and 3 larger petals. The edges of the petals touch in male
flowers and overlap in female. Male flowers have 6 stamens
with large anthers and an almost equally long 3-toothed sterile
pistil. Female flowers have 3 small sterile stamens grouped on
one side of the 1-celled ovary which is obscurely divided into 3
stigmas at its apex. The fruits are narrowly egg-shaped or
somewhat bullet-shaped, and coloured purplish-black, often
with a waxy bloom. They are 16 to 18 mm long and 8 to 10
mm in diameter, with stigma persisting. The seed endosperm
is ruminate, with embryo at the base.

HABITAT, USES, CULTIVATION   This palm is a forest
dweller in its native islands, where it is now almost extinct.

Dictyosperma album, with its previously recognized
varieties, *rubrum*, *aureum* and *furfuraceum*, is widely cultivated in tropical and warmer temperate areas as an attractive

Dictyosperma album

95

specimen feather palm, when adult closely resembling *Archontophoenix* with which it may easily be confused. In cultivation a plentiful supply of water is required and a protected warm position, as leaves burn readily in drying winds. In young plants the veins are dark red to yellow, which adds to the attractiveness of the palm. Propagation is from seed which germinates in 2 to 4 months from sowing.

D. album (syn. *D. rubrum, D. album* var. *rubrum, D. album* var. *furfuraceum*) Princess Palm
For description see above under genus.

Drymophloeus

Small to medium-sized slender feather palms form this genus of 15 species which occur in the Moluccas, New Guinea, and the Solomons and nearby islands. They have smooth, ringed, solitary trunks and slender crownshaft. The crown has arched leaves, with a short leaf stalk; the blades are divided into a relatively few broad, wedge-shaped leaflets with a distinct midvein, raggedly toothed at the apex, being often 3-pointed; there are usually a pair of broad leaflets at the apex of the leaves.

The inflorescences are below the crownshaft, fairly short and few-branched and enclosed in bud by 2 bracts; the outer lower one or prophyll is shorter and the inner upper one longer and persistent. The flowers are separate male and female on the same inflorescence and are spirally arranged on the rather fleshy branchlets, with 1 female flower between 2 male, often on the upper part of the branchlets reduced to pairs of 1 male and 1 female or solitary males. The male flowers have 3 overlapping sepals and 3 petals with the edges touching in bud; there are numerous stamens with thread-like filaments; the sterile pistil is large, swollen and hollow at the base. The female flowers are nearly spherical with 3 broad, short sepals and 3 petals broadly overlapping in bud; the sterile stamens are minute and sometimes fused to form a ring. The ovary is on a short stalk with 1 cell and 1 ovule and a sessile stigma with 3 lobes.

The fruits are egg-shaped to ellipsoid, red in colour with the remains of the stigma attached at the apex; the mesocarp is pulpy with stinging crystals and coarse fibres and the endocarp is thin; the seed endosperm is ruminate or non-ruminate with the embryo at the base.

HABITAT, USES, CULTIVATION   This group of slender palms grows in the moist shaded undergrowth of rainforest in high rainfall tropical regions. The black wood from the trunk is used locally for making spears, arrow heads and the like.

Under cultivation, these palms require moist tropical conditions. They require to be grown in a shaded, protected position and will not tolerate cold.

Propagation is by seed which should be fresh and requires from 1 to 2 months to germinate.

D. pachycladus (syn. *Rehderophoenix pachyclada*)
A slender palm with a slightly tapered, smooth, distinctly ringed trunk about 10 to 18 m high and 5 to 10 cm in diameter. Crownshaft is smooth, green, and the crown is small with arching leaves to about 3 m long; the blades have broad, light green leaflets. The spreading inflorescences are about 1 m long with stalks about 50 cm long. The red oblong fruits

Drymophloeus pachycladus

are up to about 25 mm in length.
Distribution: Solomon Islands: San Cristobal.

Elaeis

Tropical palms which are important commercially, and are also cultivated as ornamentals. The genus of 2 species is allied to the Coconut Palm and occurs in tropical Central Africa, Central America and northern South America. It consists of feather palms with a solitary trunk, erect or creeping, with roots emerging from the creeping part. The surface of the trunk has old leaf bases persisting or scars in older palms. The crown is dense with a large number of erect, spreading to drooping, long leaves; leaf stalks are short with a broad base and have spiny, fibrous projections along the margin from the leaf sheath, wearing away on older leaves to jagged spines. The leaf blades have numerous long leaflets with prominent midribs and are tapered to a point. They are arranged singly or in groups along the midrib, arising sometimes in different planes.

Inflorescences are male and female on the one plant or sometimes both male and female flowers are present on the one inflorescence. They arise among the leaf bases in large, very dense clusters, with innumerable small flowers, enclosed in bud stage in 2 large fibrous bracts which finally become deciduous. Male or female flowers are usually on separate inflorescences on the same plant or sometimes both on the one inflorescence. Male flowers are single or in pairs in recesses on the branchlets, each with 3 sepals, 3 petals with edges touching in bud, 6 stamens and a small sterile pistil. Female flowers are subtended by 2 to 3 small bracts and have 3 sepals, 3 petals overlapping in bud, a ring of small sterile stamens and a 3-celled ovary with 3 spreading stigmas.

Fruits are egg-shaped to oblong, sometimes irregular in shape, and deep orange to reddish-black in colour, in dense clusters. The outer mesocarp layer is fleshy and oily. There is usually only 1 seed, enclosed in a woody endocarp which has 3 pores in the upper part; the seed endosperm is not ruminate.

HABITAT, USES, CULTIVATION   This group of palms grows in more or less open forest in moist, sandy soils, often poorly drained. The African Oil Palm, *E. guineensis*, is taking over from the Coconut as the world's most valuable oil-producing palm and is widely cultivated in tropical areas for this purpose. It yields two distinct types of oil, "palm oil" from the mesocarp, and "palm kernel oil" from the seed endosperm. Both have a wide range of uses in the manufacture of margarines, icecream, soaps, shampoos, detergents, cosmetics, lubricating oil additives and fluxes. Under good conditions, plants bear fruit after 3 years and plantations may yield 5 tonnes of oil per hectare per year at maturity. This palm is also commonly planted as an ornamental subject and makes an imposing specimen in tropical areas. The South American species with a creeping trunk is not as well known in cultivation, even though oil can be produced from the fruits. These palms require tropical conditions and a plentiful supply of moisture for satisfactory results.

Propagation is from seed which takes about 2 to 5 months to germinate under hot conditions; deep containers should be used for potting on.

Elaeis oleifera

E. guineensis African Oil Palm

This is a large palm to about 20 m high or more commonly 10 m, with trunk usually about 30 to 60 cm in diameter; leaves are 4 to 5 m long and leaf stalks about 1 m with spiny fibrous margins. The blades have numerous long, narrow, pointed leaflets, in clusters and arising in different planes, giving the leaves a plumose appearance; lower leaflets are short and spinous. Inflorescences are very short and dense, arising among the leaf bases. Fruit are reddish-black, ovoid, 3 to 4 cm long, in large clusters with numerous projecting, pointed bracts.

Distribution: Tropical West and Central Africa; widely cultivated in other tropical areas.

E. oleifera (syn. Corozo oleifera) American Oil Palm

A smaller palm than *E. guineensis*, the trunk creeping and rooting underground, becoming erect with age and 2 to 4 m tall. The leaves are about 4 m long; the leaf stalks are about 1.5 m long with hooked spines on the margins. The blades have numerous long narrow leaflets, all in the one plane. Inflorescences are similar to those of *E. guineensis* but lack the numerous bracts between the fruits. Fruits are egg-shaped to oblong, 2 to 3 cm long, 1.5 to 2 cm in diameter, orange-red at maturity.

Distribution: Central America and northern South America, from about Costa Rica to the lower Amazon.

Eugeissona

These are interesting, clump-forming feather palms. The genus of about 7 species occurs in Borneo and the Malay Peninsula. They have an underground or short to tall trunk, covered with spiny leaf bases, or rough with leaf scars; aerial roots are frequently formed from the trunk. The crown lacks a crownshaft and has long, arching leaves; leaf stalks are stiff and spiny with a clasping prickly base. The blades have numerous long narrow leaflets, each tapering to a point, often with bristles on the midvein.

Inflorescences are terminal, with a stiff, erect main axis from which arise many short side branches, which in turn branch into numerous short branchlets each terminating in a pair of large flowers, one male and soon falling, the other bisexual. The inflorescence stalk, rhachis, branches and branchlets are all clothed in numerous overlapping bracts. Flowers are large and unusual: the sepals are joined into a bell-shaped tube with 3-lobed apex, and covered by overlapping bracts; the 3 petals are up to 10 cm long, narrow, woody and stiffly pointed with edges touching in bud; there are from 24 to 70 stamens which develop before the ovary, then fall off. The ovary is incompletely divided into 3 cells with 3 ovules, only 1 of which develops into a seed; the style is hard with a 3-lobed apex.

Fruits are ovoid, large and covered with innumerable very small scales; the mesocarp layer is fleshy and corky with numerous longitudinal fibres; it encloses a woody endocarp which has an aperture at the base and 6 to 12 internal ribs intruding into the seed, 3 almost to the centre. Apart from these intrusions the seed endosperm is non-ruminate.

HABITAT, USES, CULTIVATION   These tropical palms occur in rainforests in coastal lowlands to lower mountain areas, both adjoining swamps, rivers and on hillsides, and in some forests are regarded as weeds following timber felling.

The leaves are used for thatching walls and roofs of dwellings, and sago is obtained from the trunks of larger species. The immature seeds are sometimes eaten, and the abundant pollen of *E. utilis* is reported to be eaten by the Bornean forest people.

These palms are suitable for cultivation only in the tropics in areas of high rainfall. They have as yet been little planted for ornament.

Propagation is from seed which takes several months to germinate.

E. utilis

A clump-forming palm 12 to 15 m high, the trunks 25 to 30 cm in diameter, covered with spiny leaf bases or surface bare with rough leaf scars and numerous short roots forming a mound at the base. Leaves are up to 9 m long, erect and becoming arched; the leaf stalks are long with the lower broadened part covered in short sharp spines. The blades have numerous narrow leaflets tapered to the apex, crowded along midrib, distinctly drooping. Inflorescences are very large, arising vertically from the centre of the crown with densely crowded main branches, each with many branchlets bearing a single, large, purplish-black flower about 8 to 9 cm long. Fruits are ovoid, brownish, 8 to 10 cm long and 5 to 6 cm in diameter, covered with numerous small overlapping scales and with a persistent style.

Distribution: Borneo.

Euterpe

Gently arching leaves are a feature of these medium to tall feather palms which are all South American except one which extends up the Central American isthmus as far north as Belize (formerly British Honduras). The genus has 18 species. The palms are unarmed, and solitary or with clustered trunks. All have long, narrow, green crownshafts and the leaves have numerous, regularly spaced, pendulous, narrow leaflets, each drawn out into a fine point. The very symmetrical rows of pendulous leaflets give the leaves of some species an appearance like those of the well known "Kentia", *Howea forsterana*.

Inflorescences are typically Arecoid, enclosed in bud by two large tubular bracts, one inside the other and cast off together before flowering. Many slender flowering branchlets, pendulous in some species, stiffly spreading in others, arise from a short, thick inflorescence stalk. Flowers are in groups of 3, 1 female flanked by 2 earlier-opening males. The male flowers are slightly asymmetric and have 6 stamens; the female flowers are reduced to a large fleshy ovary terminated by 3 fleshy stigma lobes and enclosed by tightly-sheathing petals and sepals. As the fruit develops the remains of the stigma shift around to a lateral position on its surface.

The more or less spherical fruits are purple to blackish with a thin, pulpy mesocarp and an inner fibrous endocarp covering the seed. The hard white endosperm of the seed may or may not be ruminate, depending on species.

HABITAT, USES, CULTIVATION   Mainly forest-dwelling palms of high-rainfall regions, some *Euterpe* species occur in

Euterpe oleracea

extensive riverine swamps, others in dense river-bank forest, and yet others on steep mountain slopes, sometimes on limestone. Some species are economically important in their native countries. The best known product derived from them is palm hearts (palmito), consisting of the innermost unexpanded leaves from the centre of the crownshaft, usually cut out as a neat cylinder of crunchy, sweetish white tissue. In Brazil there is quite a large industry based on the collection, canning, and to a limited extent, export, of this product which is derived mainly from *E. edulis*. Its harvesting kills the palms and there has been concern expressed about their continued survival, but their numbers are so large and their growth sufficiently fast that with sensible management of stands production can probably be sustained indefinitely. The fruits of a number of species are eaten. Wallace, in his classic *Palm Trees of the Amazon* (1853), describes how in Para the ripe fruits of *E. oleracea* were used to prepare a favourite drink, "assai", which was "a thick creamy liquid, of a fine plum colour", and with a nutty flavour. This drink is still popular in the Amazon towns.

Cultivation of *Euterpe* species presents few problems in a suitably warm and humid climate. The seeds germinate rapidly and growth of young plants is also fast. As with most forest-dwelling Arecoids, a sheltered position is appreciated, with plentiful supply of moisture, though mature plants should be able to tolerate full sun.

E. oleracea Assai

The Assai Palm is a moderately robust species with trunks up to 25 m tall and up to 18 cm in diameter, forming clusters of up to about 12. Often it will reach its mature height while still remaining solitary except for a few suppressed suckers at the base. There are only 8 to 14 leaves in each crown, up to 3.5 m long, but mostly shorter. The drooping narrow leaflets are about a metre long. Several smallish, spreading inflorescences are carried at the one time below the crownshaft. Fruits are purplish-black, up to 1.5 cm in diameter. This species occurs mainly in swampy ground, often on sandy soils. Distribution: widespread in tropical Brazil and extending to the north coast of South America in the Guyanas, Venezuela and Trinidad, but not to any of the west coast countries.

Gaussia

Slender feather palms with solitary ringed trunks, usually swollen at the base and tapering to the apex, comprise this genus of 2 species occurring in Cuba and Puerto Rico.

The crowns are light and open with a limited number of erect to arched leaves with erect, long, sheathing bases, forming an indistinct crownshaft. Leaf stalks are short and the leaf blades have a number of broad leaflets, each tapered to a point and crowded along the midrib usually dropping from it before the whole leaf falls.

The inflorescences arise among the leaf bases and remain on the trunk after the subtending leaves have fallen. Each has a long stalk, 6 to 8 tubular bracts sheathing the inflorescence in bud, and slender branchlets. Separate male and female flowers are arranged in rows of 4 to 5 with the lowest flower in each row being female and the remainder male. Flowers of both sexes have 3 sepals and 3 petals which in bud overlap near the base but have edges touching in the upper part. Male flowers have 6 stamens and a small sterile pistil, female flowers have 6 tiny sterile stamens and a 3-celled ovary with 3 ovules and a 3-lobed stigma; usually only 1 ovule develops into a seed. Fruits are small and obovoid with a thin fleshy mesocarp layer; the seed has a non-ruminate endosperm.

HABITAT, USES, CULTIVATION   These tropical palms occur in forests in shallow rocky soils, commonly on limestone cliffs and ridges in hilly areas.

The two species of *Gaussia* are not often cultivated, being found chiefly in botanical gardens in warmer areas. They require protection and shade during their early development stage.

Propagation is from seed which takes from 1 to 3 months to germinate.

G. attenuata

A tall slender feather palm with a solitary, smooth, ringed trunk, swollen at the base with a mound of dense prop-roots and tapering towards the apex to about 15 m high and 8 to 10 cm diameter at the narrower part. The crown has about 6 to 8 erect to arched leaves 1 to 1.5 m long plus some old leaves without leaflets; leaf bases are broad, erect and sheathing, forming an indistinct crownshaft. Leaf stalks are about 30 to 50 cm long; leaf blades have numerous light green leaflets tapered to a point and crowded along the midrib, arising in slightly different planes and giving the leaves a somewhat plume-like appearance.

Inflorescences are long and slender, arising among the leaf bases and remaining after subtending leaves have fallen; the tiny flowers are greenish-yellow. Fruits are small and egg-shaped, tapered towards the stalk, about 15 mm long, yellow to orange-red.

Distribution: Puerto Rico (West Indies).

Gronophyllum

Tall feather palms found in tropical forests and woodlands, this genus of about 14 species occurs in the Celebes, Moluccas, New Guinea and northern Australia. The solitary, ringed trunks sometimes have vertical markings and may be swollen around the mid-point. The crown consists of a number of arched leaves and a long, prominent crownshaft. The leaf stalks are short and without spines; the leaf blades have a number of long leaflets, each tapered to a toothed or 2-cleft apex or pointed, crowded and evenly spaced along the midrib.

The inflorescences appear below the crownshaft, each with a thick, short stalk and branched into slender branchlets, enclosed in bud stage by 2 large, thin bracts which are shed before the flowers open. Separate male and female flowers are usually arranged in 2 rows on the branchlets in groups of 3, each group with 1 female flower between 2 males. Male flowers have 3 pointed sepals, 3 petals tapering to the apex with edges touching in bud, and 6 to 12 stamens, and a minute 3-lobed sterile pistil; female flowers have 3 rounded sepals, 3 petals overlapping at base with the upper part extended and the edges touching in bud; the sterile stamens are very small or absent, and the ovary is 1-celled with 1 ovule and a simple stigma. Fruits are ovoid with the old stigma attached and have a thin fleshy mesocarp. The seed endosperm is ruminate or non-ruminate.

Gronophyllum ramsayi (photograph: Doreen Hand)

HABITAT, USES, CULTIVATION   These tropical forest-dwelling palms grow in regions of monsoonal rain, often in areas subject to flooding.

Gronophyllum has received limited attention in cultivation and is not well known; the Australian species is occasionally cultivated in Darwin, northern Australia.

Propagation is from seed which requires heat for satisfactory results.

G. ramsayi (syn. *Kentia ramsayi*)

A medium to tall robust palm with grey to greenish ringed trunk 10 to 15 m high and 20 to 30 cm in diameter, frequently enlarged around the mid-point and tapering to the apex. The crown is compact with a number of distinctly arched leaves and a very prominent, glaucous crownshaft to about 1 m long. Leaf stalks are short and the blades have numerous, long, light green leaflets, tapering to a toothed apex and crowded along the midrib, forward-pointing with both ranks of leaflets directed inwards in a V shape.

Inflorescences arise below the crownshaft, each with a short thick stalk, and forked twice into a broom-like panicle, the branches drooping as they grow longer. Flowers are cream; fruits are oblong to egg-shaped, yellow to brown, about 12 mm long.

Distribution: northern Australia, in Arnhem Land.

Hedyscepe

A genus of a single species confined to Lord Howe Island in the south-west Pacific. This compact feather palm has a smooth, closely ringed, greenish to greyish, solitary trunk, 6 m or higher and 9 to 12 cm in diameter. It is surmounted by a distinct, pale bluish-grey, glaucous crownshaft formed from the bases of the spreading, strongly arched leaves, which grow to about 1.5 m long. The leaf stalks are short and stiff and the blades have many closely and evenly spaced leaflets, each tapered to a pointed apex, both ranks directed upwards.

Inflorescences are borne below the crownshaft, and are about 40 cm long. They have a short stalk and fleshy branchlets, are pendulous in fruit, and are enclosed in bud stage by 2 flattened bracts, tapering to the apex, which are shed before the flowers open. Flowers are small, separate male and female on the one inflorescence, yellow to orange-yellow, all with 3 narrow sepals and 3 angled petals, their edges touching in bud in male flowers and overlapping in female. The male flowers have 9 to 12 stamens, female flowers have 3 sterile stamens. Fruits are egg-shaped, about 50 mm long and 40 mm broad and a dull, deep red. The remnants of the stigma are attached at the apex; the seed has a non-ruminate endosperm and the embryo is at the base.

HABITAT, USES, CULTIVATION   These palms grow in elevated areas from 450 m to about 900 m altitude in moist forests and on cliffs above the sea, much of the time in mist and drizzle from moisture-laden clouds.

This feather palm has similar requirements in some respects to those of the genus *Howea* but is generally slower in growth and its leaves tend to burn more readily when exposed to hot winds. As an ornamental it has not been used to any great extent. Like *Howea* it is quite unsuitable for tropical or near-tropical climates, but at the same time will only endure the mildest frosts, and only succeeds in humid

Hedyscepe canterburyana

coastal conditions. Propagation is from seed, behaving similarly to that of *Howea*.

H. canterburyana (syn. **Kentia canterburyana** Umbrella Palm

For description see above under genus.

Howea (*Kentia*, in part)

Graceful adaptable feather palms make up this genus of 2 species which occur only on Lord Howe Island in the south-west Pacific. When specimens were first collected in 1870 the Victorian botanist von Mueller mistakenly placed them in the genus *Kentia*, by which name they were known for many years: the name "Kentia Palm" is still widely used by nurserymen. *Howea* was named as a distinct genus in 1877 by Odoardo Beccari, a leading palm authority of that era, the name referring of course to Lord Howe Island. The genus consists of feather palms with smooth, distinctly ringed, solitary trunks. The graceful crown has a number of leaves with long, slender, smooth petioles and broad, fibrous-margined, sheathing bases which do not form a crownshaft. The blades have numerous leaflets, tapering to a pointed apex and very evenly spaced along the midrib.

The inflorescences arise among the leaf bases, each consisting of an unbranched spike or 3 to 5 spikes joined at the base by a very short, flattened stalk, surrounded by a common short bract. Each spike is enclosed in a long, papery, cylindrical bract which is shed before the flowers open. Flowers are male or female, arranged with a female flower between 2 male, in recesses on the thick spike. Male flowers are creamy brown and have 3 overlapping sepals, 3 much larger, woody petals with edges touching in bud, numerous short stamens and a small sterile pistil; female flowers are green and have 3 sepals, 3 petals which are all overlapping and a 1-celled ovary with 3-lobed stigma. Fruits are ellipsoid, with thin, dry, very fibrous mesocarp and papery endocarp. Seeds have a non-ruminate endosperm and the embryo is towards the base on one side.

HABITAT, USES, CULTIVATION   These palms are generally found in coral sands or basaltic soils near the sea or sometimes up to about 450 m elevation, often forming pure stands, or, in the case of *H. belmoreana*, as a forest understorey on steep slopes.

Howea species have been widely cultivated in Europe and the U.S.A., also in New South Wales. As well as being used for outdoor planting, these palms are extensively used as indoor potted specimens, both for domestic and commercial premises. They are tolerant of low light, lower temperatures and dry atmosphere which most palms will not tolerate, and even poor cultivation methods. Plants may also be kept in the same container for many years.

For outdoor use *Howea* species require temperate, moist, coastal conditions and will not withstand any but the lightest frosts or a hot or dry climate. They have rarely been grown successfully in the tropics. Plants prefer at least partial shade in their young stages of growth but adult specimens tolerate full sun and exposure to wind, *H. forsteriana* being the hardiest in this respect. They will grow successfully in various types of well drained soils of medium to high fertility. Plants in pots and tubs should preferably have a well drained potting mixture with a reasonable quantity of humus material.

Propagation is from seed which should be ripe, i.e. coloured, and used while fresh for best results; germination occurs within 2 to 12 months and may be assisted by the use of artificial heating. Seed is always in great demand and since the supply is limited, it is usually expensive.

H. belmoreana (syn. *Kentia belmoreana*) Belmore Sentry Palm, Curly Palm

The Belmore Sentry Palm has a trunk to about 6 m high, 8 to 15 cm in diameter. The leaves are 2.5 to 3 m long and distinctly arched towards the apex. The leaf stalks are about 1 m or more in length and the many leaflets long, dull green on both surfaces, closely spaced along the midrib with both ranks of leaflets directed upward in a V-shape.

Inflorescences are single spikes about 2 m long. The fruits are almost spherical to ellipsoid with a slightly extended

Howea belmoreana

apex, to about 4 cm long and 2 to 3 cm in diameter, shiny green, becoming greyish-brown or, rarely, reddish when ripe.
Distribution: Lord Howe Island.

H. forsteriana (syn. *Kentia forsteriana*). Forster Sentry Palm, Kentia Palm, Thatch Palm

A tall palm with trunk to about 15 m high and 12 to 15 cm in diameter. The leaves are 3 to 4 m long, at first erect with leaf stalks later bending and becoming slightly drooping; the leaf stalks are 1 to 2 m long; the leaflets are very evenly spaced along the midrib and droop downwards in a very regular curve.

Inflorescences are about 1 m long with 3, 5 or rarely 7 spikes, fused at the base into a short, flattened stalk. Fruits are ellipsoid, evenly tapered to both ends, about 3 to 4.5 cm long, 2 cm in diameter, ripening through dull orange to deep dull red.
Distribution: Lord Howe Island.

Hydriastele

These delicate feather palms are not widely cultivated. There are about 8 species in the genus, occurring in New Guinea, and northern and north-eastern Australia. They have slender ringed trunks and may be solitary or multiple-stemmed. The stem is surmounted by a slender crownshaft. The leaf stalks are short; the leaf blades have numerous leaflets of unequal width, not tapering to the apex which often has a cut-off, ragged appearance.

Inflorescences appear below the crownshaft and consist of a very short stalk from which arise many slender, wiry, flower-bearing branches in a broom-like group; in the bud stage the inflorescence is enclosed by two thin bracts which are shed when the flowers open. Flowers are small, the separate male and female in groups of 3 with 1 female between 2 larger males. These groups are arranged in rows on the branchlets. Male flowers have 3 sepals, 3 petals and 6 stamens, but no sterile pistil; female flowers have overlapping kidney-shaped sepals which enlarge after the flower is fertilized. The petals are joined for about half their length with the upper edges touching in bud. There are no sterile stamens. The 1-celled ovary has a small 3-lobed stigma. Fruits are small, red, egg-shaped to spherical, with the remains of the stigma at apex, and a thin fibrous mesocarp. The seed has a basal embryo and a ruminate or non-ruminate endosperm.

HABITAT, USES, CULTIVATION   *Hydriastele* species occur in swampy areas or at edges of streams in tropical rainforests, mostly in richer soils.

These palms have received limited attention under cultivation as they are very tender and are easily damaged by drying winds; they require a moist tropical protected location for satisfactory results.

Propagation is from seed which should be fresh. Germination may take up to a year and requires ample warmth.

H. wendlandiana (syn. *H. douglasiana*)

A slender feather palm usually with a clump of 8 or fewer smooth ringed trunks and light crowns of spreading leaves 1 to 2 m long. The crownshafts are slender; leaf stalks 30 to 40 cm long. The blades have broad unequal leaflets, usually grouped on the midrib, their apexes truncate and toothed. The inflorescences are slender-branched, below the crown-

Hydriastele wendlandiana

shaft, about 30 to 35 cm long with short stalks, and bear cream flowers. Fruits are egg-shaped, about 8 mm broad, and red.

Distribution: Australia: northern Queensland, Northern Territory.

Hyophorbe (syn. *Mascarena*)

An interesting genus of 5 species of feather palms confined to the Mascarene Islands. All have solitary ringed trunks, variously swollen in some species or of fairly uniform thickness in others. The trunk is surmounted by a smooth, prominent crownshaft which is swollen at its base. The number of leaves in the crown is fairly few, between 5 and 10 in an adult plant. Above the short thick stalk of each leaf, the leaflets are crowded along the rather arched leaf midrib with the two ranks of leaflets pointing upwards to form a V shape, at least in the earlier part of the life of that leaf.

A group of inflorescences, at various stages of expansion, encircles the top of the trunk below the crownshaft. Most of the growth of the inflorescences takes place only after the enclosing leaf bases have been shed. Each bud is upward-curving, and tightly sheathed by 4 to 9 overlapping green tubular bracts, giving it the appearance of a sharp-pointed green horn. As the inflorescences mature the lower bracts are successively cast off, leaving the uppermost 1 or few enclosing all the flower-bearing branches, until those, too, finally shed. This arrangement of bracts is not known in any other genus of feather palms with stout trunks and well-developed crownshafts.

The many wiry inflorescence branches each bear numerous short rows of orange to white flowers. On each row the lowest flower is female and above it there are 3 to 7 male flowers. The ovary of the female flower has 3 compartments, but only 1 ovule usually develops into a seed. The fruits, produced in large numbers on pendulous stalks, are ellipsoid to spherical or pear-shaped, red, brown to black in colour, with the perianth remaining attached; the fleshy mesocarp layer is thin.

HABITAT, USES, CULTIVATION   In their natural habitat on the Mascarene Islands all species of *Hyophorbe* are threatened with extinction. None has been recorded as occurring on more than one island of the group; they grow in forests (or formerly-forested places) from low coastal areas to about 700 metres altitude on volcanic soils, or limestone.

Two species of *Hyophorbe* are frequently cultivated in tropical and subtropical regions. They make curious but attractive specimen plants due to their swollen trunks and arched leaves. They grow best in tropical lowland areas near the sea. They would make interesting potted specimens where temperatures are warm enough, or in heated glasshouses.

Plants are propagated from seed which germinates within approximately 3 months.

H. lagenicaulis (syn. *Mascarena lagenicaulis*) Bottle palm
A feather palm with a solitary, grey, smooth, closely ringed trunk usually vertically fissured, to about 6 m in height. It is enlarged at the base sometimes to 70 cm in diameter and tapers at the apex to 10 to 30 cm in diameter. The crown of 4 to 8 leaves has a basal smooth green waxy crownshaft, markedly broader at the base. Leaves are 1 to 2 m long with a short leafstalk 10 to 15 cm in length, the leaf stalk being

Hyophorbe lagenicaulis

distinctly arched; leaflets are greyish-green tapered to the apex and crowded and evenly arranged along the leaf midrib with both ranks of leaflets directed upwards.

The inflorescences arise below the crownshaft and are arched upwards in bud stage, becoming spreading and much branched when open. They are carried on a thick, stiff stalk. Flowers are small, cream and numerous. Fruits are ellipsoid to spherical, about 20 mm long and 10 to 12 mm in diameter, smooth and orange to black when ripe, and produced in large numbers.

Distribution: Mascarene Islands: known only from the tiny Round Island off Mauritius, with only about 15 wild plants surviving; widely planted in the tropics.

H. verschaffeltii (syn. *Mascarena verschaffeltii*)

A small feather palm with a grey, solitary, distinctly ringed stout trunk to about 5 m high. It is of fairly uniform thickness, to about 25 cm in diameter, and becomes swollen to varying degrees in older plants. The small crown of 5 to 10 leaves has a smooth, green, waxy crownshaft which is distinctly swollen at the base. The leaves are 1 to 1.5 m long with smooth short leaf stalks 6 to 9 cm long. Their tapered leaflets, bright green above and greyish beneath, are arranged along the arched leaf midrib in different planes, often presenting a somewhat untidy appearance.

The inflorescences arise below the crownshaft and are erect in bud stage, becoming spreading and much branched when open, and carried on stiff stalks. Fruits are elongated, somewhat ellipsoid, 2 to 3 cm long and 1.5 to 2 cm broad, and beaked at the end to one side. They are very numerous, bright orange to red, and hang in large clusters.

Distribution: Mascarene Islands: island of Rodriguez.

Hyphaene

This genus of about 4 species occurs in Africa, Madagascar, Arabia, Palestine, India and Sri Lanka, and consists of fan palms with solitary or multiple trunks, stemless or, rarely, prostrate.

In some species the trunk branches dichotomously (dividing regularly and repeatedly in a forked manner); the old leaf bases may remain attached or the trunk may be distinctly marked with leaf scars. The crown has a number of erect to spreading leaves and there is no crownshaft. The long leaf stalks have strong, forward-pointing teeth along the margins and are split at the base into a Y shape where they join the trunk. The old leaf sheaths are without distinct marginal fibres; the blades are costapalmate, almost circular in outline, distinctly arched downwards along the costa and folded inwards and divided for about half to two-thirds their depth into stiff, tapered, pointed segments.

The inflorescences which arise among the leaf bases are short and branched, with tubular persistent bracts on the stalks, and a tubular bract subtending each branch. The flowers are small with male or female on separate plants. Male flowers are arranged in small pits in groups of 3 on the floral branchlets; there are 3 sepals which are joined at the base, and 3 broad, ovate petals joined at the base with the tips overlapping in bud; there are 6 or 7 stamens with the filaments united into a ring and there is no sterile pistil. The female flowers, slightly larger than the male, have 3 overlapping sepals and 3 smaller, broadly ovate, overlapping petals. The 6

Hyphaene compressa (photograph: Barbara Briggs)

sterile stamens are united into a membranous ring. The ovary has 3 cells with 2 cells being non-functional; the stigma is minute and 3-lobed.

The fruits may be spherical, oblong, egg-shaped or pear-shaped, usually brown or dull orange in colour. Sometimes they are obviously lobed or constricted in the middle and often they are depressed at the apex and base; frequently there are knobs at the base representing the undeveloped ovary cells. The mesocarp is dry and fibrous and the outer coat is shiny and dotted. The seed is enclosed in a hard endocarp and the endosperm is non-ruminate with a central cavity.

HABITAT, USES, CULTIVATION   *Hyphaene* species commonly occur in hot dry areas in poor or exhausted soils with impeded drainage. Some species occur near the sea coast while others are found in inland regions.

In their native habitats, the leaves are used for thatching and for weaving into articles such as baskets and mats. The fibrous, sugary mesocarp makes a poor source of food and the sap, obtained by tapping the crown of the palm, is fermented into a poor quality alcoholic beverage. The seed was formerly used as a source of vegetable ivory.

H. compressa East African Doum Palm

The East African Doum Palm is about 15 m tall, its trunk forking repeatedly high above the ground, with sometimes up to four generations of branching evident. Individual crowns are small, the total leaf length often under 1 m, the slender leaf stalks longer than the glossy green blades which are divided to more than half their depth into stiff, tapering seg-

Hyphaene coriacea

ments. Inflorescences are short. Fruits are about 7 to 8 cm long, top-shaped to pear-shaped or ovoid, often somewhat asymmetrical, obscurely 3-angled.

Distribution: tropical East Africa. Further north-west in Africa this species is replaced by the similar Doum Palm *H. thebaica*, which apparently extends from Egypt to sub-Saharan West Africa, west to Senegal. However these large palms have been poorly studied and their exact distributions are not clear.

H. coriacea (syn. *H. crinita*, *H. natalensis*) Doum Palm

A palm with a single trunk or several stems, inclined outwards or sometimes branching dichotomously. The crown of this Doum Palm has greyish-green leaves about 2 m long; leaf stalks are 1 to 1.5 m long with strong, blackish teeth on the margins; blades are greyish-green, divided to about two-thirds their depth into stiff, pointed segments. Inflorescences are short and thick, with a few branches. The fruits are globular to pear-shaped, 5 to 6 cm long, about 5 cm in diameter and depressed at the apex.

Distribution: south-eastern Africa.

Jubaea

A tall, solitary feather palm with a straight leaden-grey trunk of massive thickness, *Jubaea* grows to 25 m tall and 0.8 to 1.3 m in diameter near the base. It is sometimes slightly thicker near the mid-point. With age the trunk contracts to a smaller diameter near the top, and is patterned shallowly with wide, diamond-shaped leaf scars. The genus consists of a single species only, occurring over a restricted area of central coastal Chile and now very rare in the wild state. There is no crown-shaft and the huge, dense crown consists of a large number of long, straight leaves 4 to 5 m long, arranged in distinct near-vertical rows. The leaves are a dull, deep green above, paler beneath. In some plants all leaves are steeply ascending but in others they become spreading and finally drooping. The broadened shovel-like leaf bases do not encircle the trunk at any visible stage and are edged with sparse fibres which are sometimes all shed, leaving smooth margins. Leaf stalks are short in relation to total leaf length and are smooth-margined. The very numerous leaflets are straight, forward-pointing, in 2 regular rows, each shortly 2-lobed at the apex.

Inflorescences are many, arising among the leaf bases, fairly short (about 1.5 m) and dense. Each consists of a thick stalk, bearing at its base a short tubular bract and a much larger club-shaped, pointed, semi-woody, smooth-surfaced bract which encloses the whole inflorescence in bud, and a slightly shorter central stem from which arise many thick, undulate flower-bearing branchlets. Many old hanging bracts persist among the lower leaf bases. Inflorescences and bracts are erect in flower but pendulous in fruit.

The purplish flowers are separate male and female on the 1 inflorescence, in groups of 2 male and 1 female between them at the bases of the branchlets, but solitary or paired males towards the ends. Male flowers have 3 narrow, angled sepals, joined at the base, 3 much longer, thick, pointed petals, their edges touching in bud, about 30 stamens, and a minute sterile pistil. Female flowers have 3 broad sepals, 3 petals overlapping and curling around one another in bud

and sterile stamens united into a membranous cup. The ovary has 3 cells, only 1 of which develops a seed.

Fruits are pale yellow, 4 to 5 cm long, almost spherical, with bases flattened and apexes slightly pointed with remains of the stigma attached. The thick mesocarp is fleshy and finely fibrous and separates freely from the thick bony endocarp which is pointed at both ends. Three equally spaced lines run the whole length of the endocarp, and alternating with them are 3 black pores slightly below the median position. The seed has a thin coat and a non-ruminate endosperm with a fairly large central cavity.

HABITAT, USES, CULTIVATION   *Jubaea* occurs in pure stands, now greatly reduced, in a few valleys not far from the coast, where the climate is temperate and moist but without extremes of cold.

Until quite recently this palm was exploited by the Chileans for its abundant sugary sap. Unfortunately the tree had to be felled to obtain it. The sap is said to have been allowed to exude from the felled trunk for a period of up to 2 years, up to 160 litres being yielded by each tree. The sap was used for making a wine, or by prolonged boiling thickened into "palm honey". The species is now protected by law in Chile. The seed endosperm is also edible, tasting just like coconut, hence the name *coquito* or "little coconut".

Cultivation presents few problems in a suitable temperate climate, but growth of these massive palms is slow and it is generally later generations who get the benefit from their planting. A deep, open-textured soil, well-drained but with ample subsoil moisture is preferred, and full sun suits this palm best. It tolerates moderately severe frosts, but on the other hand makes very poor growth in tropical or near-tropical climates. The thick-shelled seeds may take 6 months or more to germinate and must be fresh when planted.

J. chilensis (syn. *J. spectabilis*) Coquito Palm,
Chilean Wine Palm
For description see above under genus.

Jubaeopsis

A palm for a well-watered environment, the single species in this genus occurs in the far north-east of South Africa. It is a feather palm growing to about 6 m, whose trunk bears old leaf bases or is marked with leaf scars. The crown has a number of long arched leaves (4 m or longer) and does not have a crownshaft; the leaf stalks are about 1 m long, without teeth on the margins and the blades have numerous long, narrow, light green leaflets, tapered to their apexes, which are unequally 2-toothed or shortly divided. The midveins are prominent and the leaflets are evenly spaced along the midrib in the one plane.

The inflorescences arise among the leaf bases, with a stalk about 1 m long and numerous simple, long floral branches; in the bud stage, the inflorescences are enclosed by 2 bracts, the outer, lower one short and fibrous and the upper, inner one large, smooth, woody and spindle- or club-shaped with a pointed apex; this bract splits down one side to release the cream flowers, and then remains hanging on the plant. The stalkless flowers, separate male or female on the same inflorescence, are arranged along the floral branchlets, chiefly in groups of 3 with 1 female between 2 male. The male flowers may also occur singly, particularly on the upper part of the branchlets, and more rarely there may be solitary female flowers. The male flowers have 3 sepals overlapping at the base and 3 long, angled petals with edges touching in bud; there are from 8 to 16 stamens and the sterile pistil is small, with 3 lobes. The female flowers are ovoid with broad, overlapping sepals and 3 longer petals, overlapping except for the tips which touch in bud; the sterile stamens are united into a shallow lobed cup. The ovary has 3 cells, only 1 developing a seed. The fruits are almost round, and yellow when ripe. They are beaked at the apex with old stigmas attached. The mesocarp is thin and fibrous; the seed is enclosed in a hard, bony endocarp with 3 pores at the sides; the endosperm is non-ruminate with an internal cavity.

HABITAT, USES, CULTIVATION   This palm occurs near the coast on the banks of rivers in alluvial soils close to the water. *Jubaeopsis* has received limited attention for cultivation and for successful results requires a warm-temperate type climate with a plentiful supply of water, particularly subsoil water. Propagation is from seed and, as with other Cocosoid palms, germination may be slow or irregular.

J. caffra Pondoland Palm
For description see above under genus.

Jubaeopsis caffra

Korthalsia

An interesting group of tropical climbing palms, this genus of 26 species occurs through most of the Malay Archipelago, from the Andaman and Nicobar Islands in the west to the Philippines and New Guinea in the east and also in the Malay Peninsula. They are spiny, scrambling palms with slender, strong, flexible stems clothed with spiny leaf sheaths or are smooth and shiny with widely spaced leaf scars where the sheaths have fallen.

The leaves are distributed along the stems and do not form a crown. The long sheathing leaf bases are armed to varying degrees with spines and gradually taper into long, slender leaf stalks usually armed with hooked spines directed downwards. An unusual feature of the leaf sheaths is an apical extension beyond the leaf stalk, known as an ocrea, which in some species is swollen and hollow, forming a specialized organ which harbours ants; its shape varies between species.

Unlike most species of the allied genus *Calamus*, the leaf sheaths never bear spiny flagella, but instead the midrib in the upper leaves is extended into a long, whip-like, spiny end which becomes attached to adjoining plants and serves as a climbing organ. This is known as a cirrus. The leaflets are rhomboid, trapezoidal, or wedge-shaped or rarely elongate, with each leaflet attached to the spiny midrib by a short distinct stalk, which is a most unusual feature in palms. The upper parts of the leaflets are toothed or notched, giving them a ragged appearance.

The inflorescences are terminal and have a varying number of branches, each again branched into several dense spikes of small flowers. The stalks and branches are sheathed in persistent, tubular pointed bracts; the flowers are subtended by small membranous bracts. Unlike in the genus *Calamus*, the axis of the inflorescence is not extended into a spiny flagellum. The small flowers are bisexual with a bell- to cup-shaped calyx with 3 small lobes. The 3 longer petals are united in the lower part; there are 6 short stamens and the ovary is covered with tiny overlapping scales. The fruits are ovoid to oblong with a small, pointed apex and are covered with scales, arranged with their edges overlapping. The fruits have no fleshy layer but the seed within has an outer layer, or aril, which is fleshy. The seed endosperm may or may not be ruminate.

HABITAT, USES, CULTIVATION   This group of climbing palms are strictly inhabitants of tropical rainforest in areas of high rainfall. They occur in lowland and elevated areas, commonly along the banks of streams and sides of moist mountain valleys.

The common name of Rotang is applied to these climbing palms, a name shared with the genus *Calamus* and other climbing palm genera of this region. The long, strong, flexible stems of *Korthalsia* are widely used in undeveloped areas for various purposes such as a tying material. They are not sought after as a major commercial source of cane, for example for cane furniture, as the surface is not shiny.

Cultivation of these interesting climbing palms for ornamental purposes has received limited attention. They would be a useful addition in established large gardens in moist tropical areas or as unusual potted specimens.

Propagation is from seed which needs to be fresh for satisfactory germination.

K. laciniosa (syn. *K. teysmannii*)

A robust, high-climbing palm with long, flexible stems, 2 to 3 cm in diameter. Adult leaves are 130 to 150 cm in length, ending in a long, strong, spiny cirrus; leaf stalks are 10 to 12 cm long and the midribs have strong hooked spines. The leaf sheaths have short spines and an ocrea 8 to 10 cm long fraying to a ragged apex. The blades have 8 to 9 leaflets on either side of the midrib; leaflets are rhomboid with a wedge-shaped base, 25 to 35 cm long and 8 to 10 cm broad with 11 to 15 main veins. The upper end of each leaflet is irregularly toothed and notched and the apex is drawn out into a short narrow point.

The large inflorescences grow to 1.5 m and have a number of branches. Fruits are 20 to 24 mm long, 17 to 18 mm broad, somewhat top-shaped with a flattened top and pointed apex. The surface is covered with straw-coloured scales. This is one of the largest-growing species.

Distribution: South-East Asia, Sumatra, Java and Philippines.

K. rostrata (syn. *K. scaphigera*)

A slender, climbing palm with long, very thin stems, 5 to 17 mm in diameter. Adult leaves are 40 to 45 cm long. The sheathing bases have short spines, with an ocrea of the ant-harbouring type which is distinct, elliptical, and bears short spines. The leaf stalks are slender and of variable length, armed with spines; leaflets are few in number, wedge-shaped, 12 to 23 cm long and 4 to 7 cm wide, each with 7 main veins. The upper part is irregularly, raggedly toothed and notched with the apex drawn out.

Inflorescences are about 60 cm long, with slender branches. Fruits are ovoid, 15 to 16 mm long and 10 to 11 mm broad with a small pointed apex; they are covered in light brown or reddish scales.

Distribution: South-East Asia, Sumatra, Borneo.

Laccospadix

A small, elegant, shade-loving feather palm which is native to the mountains of north-eastern Queensland. The 1-species genus is allied to *Howea*. It consists of slender feather palms, with multiple trunks about 3 m high and 5 cm in diameter. It sometimes occurs with a solitary, stouter trunk to about 6 m. It is covered with old leaf bases or closely ringed in older plants. The crown has a few arching leaves, 1.5 to 2 m long; the leaf stalks are long (about 1 m), slender and flexible, with the spreading bases carried close against the trunk, but not forming a crownshaft; the blades have a number of narrow leaflets, tapered to a point and evenly spaced along the midrib. The leaflets are a dull deep green.

The inflorescences, which arise among the leaf bases, are unbranched spikes about 1 m or more long, at first erect, with long stalks and enclosed in bud by 2 thin bracts, the lower one very short, both becoming deciduous. The flowers are separate male and female and are arranged in groups of 3 in recesses on the branchlets with 1 female between 2 male, the male flowers opening and falling before the female ones open. The yellow male flowers are larger and have 3 overlapping sepals and 3 petals with edges touching in bud; there are from 6 to 12 stamens and a small sterile pistil. Female flowers are green with 3 sepals and 3 petals all overlapping in bud. The ovary is 1-celled with 1 ovule. The 15 mm long fruits are ellipsoid with a fleshy, finely fibrous mesocarp; the seed endosperm is ruminate. The fruits ripen through yellow to bright red.

Korthalsia rostrata

HABITAT, USES, CULTIVATION   This palm grows in mountain areas of high rainfall at elevations of 500 to 1500 m where temperatures become cool at night; they grow beneath the rainforest canopy, usually in full shade.

Until recently this palm has received limited attention for cultivation but is an attractive small palm for moist warm to temperate and subtropical areas. Although from mountainous tropical areas, this palm is not very successful when grown in the lowland tropics. Propagation is from seed which with bottom heat will germinate within 2 to 3 months but may take 12 months or more under cooler conditions. Growth of seedlings may be slow in the early stages.

L. australasica (syn. *Calyptrocalyx australasicus*)
For description see above under genus.

Latania

These erect fan palms with their large, spreading, green to bluish leaves present a striking appearance. The 3 species of the genus occur in the Mascarene Islands. The plants have a solitary ringed trunk, sometimes with bulges at each of the old leaf scars, usually smoother towards the lower part and swollen at the base. The crown is dense with large stiff leaves; the long leaf stalks have sharp edges and are sometimes armed with shallow teeth towards the lower part and the expanded bases are split where they join the trunk. The large blades are costapalmate and are divided into broad, stiff segments which taper to a point. The terminal outgrowths (hastulas) on the leaf stalks, on the upper sides of the leaves, vary in shape in the 3 species. The leaf stalks and leaf blades are strongly tinged with blue, red or yellow in the different species and in mature leaves the undersides of the leaf stalks and blades have a whitish-grey, waxy or woolly coating.

The inflorescences, which are among the leaf bases, are shorter than the leaves, being either male or female on separate plants, each having a different appearance. The long stalks in each sex are covered with several tubular bracts. In the male inflorescences the numerous branches arise from within a tubular bract and each branch has a number of spikes or branchlets radiating out in a hand-like manner. These branchlets are covered with small overlapping bracts and the flowers occur singly in the recesses formed between the bracts. The male flowers have 3 sepals and 3 petals, divided to the base or almost so there are from 15 to 30 stamens in a bunch and the sterile pistil is column-shaped. The female inflorescences have a number of single branches with small sheathing bracts, with 3 sepals and 3 petals overlapping in the lower part, and sterile stamens united into a cup. The ovary is 3-celled with 3 ovules. There are 3 stigmas. Fruits are large, oblong to obovoid, green to yellowish-green, with 1 to 3 seeds. The mesocarp is fleshy; each seed is covered with a separate envelope of woody endocarp and the endosperm is not ruminate.

HABITAT, USES, CULTIVATION   Species of *Latania* grow in tropical island conditions with distinct seasonal rainfalls, a hot wet summer and comparatively dry winter and are often found close to the sea in exposed positions. As well as the bold appearance given to the plants by the unusual shape and colour of the leaves, the leafstalks, costa, and main leaf veins, and sometimes the trunk in younger plants, have colours of bluish-red to yellow, and provide a striking contrast against the foliage of other plants.

These hardy palms have been widely grown in tropical areas and are able to withstand conditions of exposure and seasonable dry and wet periods. The rate of growth varies according to conditions and may be slow or reasonably fast. For best results under cultivation an open, sunny position is required. Propagation is from seed, which requires to be fresh and takes usually 1 to 2 months to germinate. As plants are deep rooted, they should be potted on in their early stages and for pot cultivation a deep container with well drained soil gives the best results.

L. lontaroides (syn. *L borbonica, L. commersonii*)· Red Latan

The Red Latan Palm has a trunk 10 to 16 m high and 20 cm or more in diameter, greyish with bulges at upper leaf scars. The leaves are 2 to 3 m long, greyish-green to lightly glaucous; the leaf stalks are about 1 m in length, sometimes with a few teeth, reddish to violet and scurfy. The hastula is very broad and rounded. Leaf blades are 1.5 to 2 m broad, undulate, curved downwards, with segments 6 to 8 cm broad. Inflorescences emerge from among the leaf bases, the male ones drooping; flowers are brownish. The fruits are pear-shaped, 3.5 to 4.5 cm long and 2.5 cm broad, greenish-brown in colour.

Distribution: Réunion Island (Mascarene Islands).

L. verschaffeltii Yellow Latan

A tall palm with a rough, greyish trunk, 12 to 16 m high and 20 cm or more in diameter. The light green leaves of the yellow Latan Palm are about 2 to 3 m long, with leaf stalks, costa and ribs yellow. Leaf stalks are about 1 m, often with teeth on the margins in the lower part and scurfy beneath; the hastula is small and only slightly projecting. Leaf blades are about 2 m broad, undulate, rounded in outline, divided into segments 5 to 6 cm broad and tapering to a slender apex.

Inflorescences are among the leaf bases, the male ones 2 to 3 m long and drooping, with brownish flowers; fruits are egg-shaped, greenish-brown, 4 to 5 cm long.

Distribution: Rodriguez Island (Mascarene Islands).

Latania verschaffeltii

Licuala

The unusual leaf shape found in these small to medium-sized tropical fan palms makes the genus instantly recognisable. It consists of about 100 species, native in tropical Asia from north-east India to southern China and throughout the Malay Archipelago to New Guinea and the Solomon Islands, with a single species in north-eastern Australia. These palms have solitary or multiple trunks, often partially covered with leaf bases and brown fibres, and sometimes below ground level. The small to moderately large crown, without a crownshaft, consists of leaves with slender leaf stalks, toothed on the margins, at least towards the base; the blades are palmate or slightly costapalmate, mostly circular in outline, sometimes undivided but more usually divided right to the leaf stalk into wedge-shaped multi-ribbed segments, which are squarely truncate at the apex with regular notches between the ends of the leaf ribs.

The long slender inflorescences arise among the leaf bases, each with few to numerous branches which are further divided into flower-bearing branchlets. The rhachis is sheathed in overlapping tubular bracts and each branch has a separate bract which remains on the plant when the flowers open. Flowers are cream to yellow, bisexual, with sepals joined into a tube which is 3-lobed or 3-toothed at the apex; petals are also joined, forming a longer 3-lobed tube. There are 6 stamens with filaments united at the base. The ovary has 3 cells with separate 1-celled segments joined at the top forming a single style with a 3-lobed or small unlobed stigma, usually only 1 ovule developing into a seed.

Fruits are spherical to egg-shaped, usually red, with a thin fleshy mesocarp. The seed is intruded from the basal side by the seed coat with the intrusion variable in shape and form; endosperm is not ruminate or may appear ruminate due to branching of the intrusion.

HABITAT, USES, CULTIVATION   These palms grow in tropical rainforests, along the banks of streams and in swampy and low-lying areas which are often subject to flooding, in alluvial soils, or on hillsides and moist gullies, sometimes at moderately high altitudes.

One of the few local uses recorded for this genus is that the large, thin leaves of some species are used for wrapping food in lieu of paper, for sale in village markets.

Most species of *Licuala* are suitable subjects for cultivation in warm climates in partly shaded areas where there is a constant supply of moisture. If planted in more exposed positions, the leaves may burn. They make attractive and unusual potted specimens for use in sheltered positions in the tropics or for artificially heated environments in temperate climates, and will grow successfully in conditions of low light. Propagation is from seed which takes from 3 to 6 months to germinate and requires heat in cooler areas for successful results.

L. gracilis

A small clump-forming palm with stems 1 to 1.2 m high and 2 to 3 cm in diameter with leaf bases and fibres attached. The crown has small leaves, the leaf stalks slender and flattened, almost 2-edged, 50 to 70 cm long, with short spines on the lower parts of the margins; the blades are palmate, deeply divided into broad wedge-shaped, truncated segments, the middle segments longer, about 30 cm long, toothed along the apexes. Inflorescences are shorter than the leaves with a few branches only, the stalk being short with flattened bracts. Fruits are small and spherical.
Distribution: Java.

L. grandis

An attractive slender palm with a solitary trunk, about 2 to 3 m high and 5 to 6 cm in diameter, with old leaves remaining on the plant a little below the crown. The dense crown has shiny dark green leaves closely arranged; the leaf stalks are slender, 50 to 100 cm long, toothed on the lower parts of the margins. Blades are usually undivided but sometimes divided into 3 or more broad segments, almost circular in outline, undulating closely, 60 to 90 cm broad. Inflorescences arise from among the leaf bases. They are longer than the leaves and openly branched, pendulous, with flowers loosely arranged on

Licuala gracilis

116

the branchlets. The crimson, shiny fruits are about 12 mm in diameter, spherical in shape.
Distribution: New Hebrides.

L. lauterbachii

A robust palm with a solitary stem to 6 m in height and 5 to 6 cm in diameter. The leaves are large, on long slender leaf stalks (about 1.3 m long) with short marginal spines on the lower part. The leaf blades are more or less circular, divided into long, wedge-shaped segments. The flowers are borne on branched inflorescences, 1 m or more in length. Fruits are spherical, about 12 mm in diameter.
Distribution: eastern New Guinea and Bougainville Island, in lowland forests to about 400 m altitude.

Licuala grandis

117

Licuala paludosa

L. paludosa

One of the larger species of the genus and of variable growth, solitary or possibly clump-forming, with stems 4 to 6 m high and 6 to 9 cm in diameter with the old leaf bases and fibres attached in the upper part. The dense crown has moderately large leaves. The leaf stalks are robust, 1 to 1.5 m long with strong downward-directed spines on the margins; the blades are palmate, circular, 1 to 1.3 m broad with leaf stalks joining from beneath, divided to the leaf stalk into a variable number of wedge-shaped segments with truncated, toothed apexes. The inflorescences arise among the leaf bases, about 1 m or more long with a number of spreading branches; flowers are cream. The small spherical fruits, 8 mm in diameter, are shiny red.

Distribution: Malay Archipelago, Malay Peninsula, Thailand and Indo-China.

L. ramsayi (syn. *L. muelleri*)

The only species occurring in Australia and probably the largest-growing of the whole genus. The solitary trunk grows to 5 to 12 m high and 7 to 10 cm in diameter, often with leaf bases and fibres remaining attached on the upper part. The dense crown has long leaves whose stalks are 1 to 1.5 m long with spines on the lower parts of their margins. The blades are almost circular in outline, 1 m or more broad, mid-green, divided into wedge-shaped segments of varying width; the segments are sometimes joined at the apex or the leaf may be completely undivided when young. Inflorescences are stout, much-branched, as long as or longer than the leaves. The flowers are cream and the fruits orange-red, and spherical, 9 to 10 mm in diameter, sometimes longer than broad.

Distribution: north-eastern Queensland, New Guinea.

L. rumphii

A densely clump-forming palm growing to about 3 to 4 m high with leaf bases and fibres remaining attached to the stems. The crowns are dense, the leaf stalks about 1 m long with spines on the lower parts of the margins. Leaf blades are shaped like three-quarters of a circle, and may be up to 1 m broad; they are divided to the leaf stalk into a number of wedge-shaped segments which are shallowly toothed at their truncate apexes. The inflorescences are stout and elongate, equal to or longer than the leaves, with branches densely covered with cream flowers; fruits are ellipsoid.

Distribution: Celebes, Moluccas (eastern Indonesia).

L. spinosa

A tall cluster-palm, more sun-tolerant than other species, with stems 3 to 5 m high and 4 to 8 cm in diameter, with leaf bases and fibres attached on the upper parts. Crowns are of medium density, the leaves having stalks 1 to 1.5 m long, angled beneath, flat above and armed along the margins with robust, curved spines. Leaf blades are circular in outline, about 1 m broad, divided into many wedge-shaped segments which are shallowly to fairly deeply toothed on their truncate apexes. Inflorescences are 1 to 2.5 m long, the spreading branches bearing numerous cream flowers. Fruits are spherical to slightly egg-shaped, 9 to 10 mm long and 8 mm wide and red in colour.

Distribution: western Indonesia, Philippines, Malay Peninsula, Thailand.

Licuala spinosa

Linospadix (syn. *Bacularia*)

These miniature feather palms are at their most attractive when carrying their slender, necklace-like spikes of brilliant red or pink fruits. The genus consists of about 7 species with 5 occurring in Australia and the remainder in New Guinea. They have slender ringed stems about 1 to 3 cm in diameter and usually not more than 3 m tall, solitary or forming several stems. The crown is small and consists of small leaves, usually under 1 m in length; the leaf stalks are short and slender with the sheathing bases not forming a proper crownshaft. The leaf blades have a varying number of leaflets, often having both narrow and wide leaflets on the same leaf. The wide leaflets are toothed or notched at the apex and the narrow ones taper to a point; some species have leaflets of fairly equal width and spacing.

The inflorescences occur among the leaf bases and consist of unbranched spikes covered in the bud stage by two thin papery bracts, the lower one short and hidden among the leaf bases, the upper one attached much higher on the stalk, becoming deciduous when the flowers open. The many flowers are spirally arranged in groups of 3, with 1 female flower between 2 male. Male flowers are larger and creamy-yellow with 3 roundish, overlapping sepals and 3 large egg-shaped to oblong petals with edges touching when in bud. There are 6 to 15 stamens; the sterile pistil is absent or minute. The male flowers open and fall off before the female flowers open. The female flowers are smaller than the male and green, with 3 overlapping sepals and 3 overlapping petals;

Linospadix palmeriana

the sterile stamens are reduced to minute teeth; the ovary is 1-celled; there are 3 tiny stigmas. The small fruits are nearly spherical, spherical, or narrow-cylindrical, with a fleshy and juicy mesocarp; the seed has a non-ruminate endosperm.

HABITAT, USES, CULTIVATION *Linospadix* species grow in shaded rainforests and along small streams in various types of acid soils; the roots are confined chiefly to the upper humus layers of the soil.

Except perhaps for *L. monostachya*, these palms are not often cultivated and for satisfactory results require a heavily shaded, protected position with an ample supply of moisture. A dry atmosphere and strong sunlight usually result in damage to the leaves. The growing medium should be well drained and rich in humus; watering must not be neglected. When plants are used for indoor decoration, they should be periodically removed to a moist shadehouse or glasshouse. Propagation is from seed and germination may be slow, sometimes taking up to 12 months.

L. monostachya Walking-stick Palm
A slender palm, with a solitary trunk to about 3 m high and 2 to 3 cm in diameter. The leaves are about 1 m long with slender leaf stalks and the blades usually have leaflets of variable width.

Inflorescences are about 1 m long, at first erect, but becoming pendulous. Fruits are globular to narrow-obovate, 1 cm long, ripening to bright red.
Distribution: Australia: north-eastern New South Wales and south-eastern Queensland.

L. palmeriana
A very slender palm with several ringed stems, only slightly thicker than a pencil and up to 1.5 m high. Leaves of young plants are 20 to 30 cm long, often with only 2 pairs of broad, slightly S-shaped, curved leaflets; adult leaves have more numerous leaflets, varying in width and less curved.

Inflorescences are small and slender with cream flowers. Fruits are small, red.
Distribution: Australia: north-eastern Queensland.

Livistona
Mostly medium-sized to tall fan palms with masses of creamy to yellow flowers followed by densely clustered, attractively coloured fruits, *Livistona* species make striking, robust landscape specimens. This genus has about 30 species of which more than half are native to Australia, the remainder occurring in various parts of the Malay Archipelago and South-East Asia. They may be small or large and, with one exception, are solitary-trunked. Most species when mature cast their leaves off cleanly, leaving a grey or brown trunk which may have fine vertical fissures. A few, however, have trunks clothed in old leaf bases, though only on the lower part. The crown is usually moderately dense, consisting of numerous leaves which often hang beneath it for some time after dying. Their sheathing bases consist of mats of fibre wrapped around the stem apex and terminating on the side opposite the leaf stalk in a long parchment-like tongue; the group of these pale-coloured tongues projecting above the trunk apex is a distinctive feature of the genus: although found in other fan palms they are more conspicuous and less

ragged in *Livistona*. The leaf stalks are generally fairly long and often armed with sharp teeth on the margins, though these teeth frequently disappear as the plant reaches maturity. The blades are slightly to strongly costapalmate, usually strongly undulate, divided to at least half their depth into many segments which are generally narrow and 2-lobed but in a few species may be broader and several-lobed.

Inflorescences arise among the leaf bases, varying from about half the length of the leaves to considerably longer than them, and erect to spreading and arching. They consist usually of a short to moderately long stalk and mostly an elongated midrib from which arise a number of more or less pendulous side branches, which sometimes branch once again before the flower-bearing branchlets. The inflorescences are sheathed in bud by a series of similar overlapping tubular bracts, usually 2-lobed at the apex.

The flowers are borne singly or in small clusters on the branchlets, and are shortly stalked or stalkless. They are all bisexual, or in some species apparently bisexual on some plants and functionally male only on others. Each flower has 3 small sepals, 3 larger ovate or triangular petals with edges touching in bud and usually hooded near the apex, 6 stamens with separate flattened filaments, and an ovary divided into 3 distinct lobes, each 1-celled with 1 ovule and tapering into a short style and minute stigma. Only 1 ovule develops into a seed.

Fruits are spherical to egg-shaped, brown to red, blue, or black, generally with a thin, oily mesocarp layer, often with grit-cells but not fibres, and a thin papery endocarp. The endosperm is pierced from one side by a corky intrusion of the seed coat. Often this has a mushroom-like shape though sometimes irregular lobes run through the endosperm; the embryo is in a position opposite the intrusion.

HABITAT, USES, CULTIVATION   Livistonas extend from warm-temperate to tropical regions where they occur in areas of regular high rainfall to monsoonal zones with a long dry season. In their natural habitat most species are restricted to situations where the soil is permanently moist, such as stream banks, swamps, soaks, or seepage zones on cliffs. Some species are associated with brackish water at the heads of estuaries. Most are light-loving plants with deep-rooted, tough-leaved seedlings adapted to full sun, though some are found in the fringes of rainforests, and have shade-tolerant seedlings.

The leaves of various *Livistona* species have been used for making such items as hats, fans and temporary roofing; whole leaves are often used for shelter. The oily fruits of a few of the species, as well as the edible apical buds, have been an item of diet of some forest peoples. The trunks have sometimes been used for constructional purposes or hollowed out and used as pipes.

The majority of *Livistona* species are hardy enough to be grown in warmer temperate and subtropical climates, with a few (*L. australis, L. decipiens, L. chinensis, L. saribus*) enduring winter temperatures of a few degrees below freezing without damage, as evidenced by their successful growth in central Florida and the Italian Riviera.

Planted outdoors these palms make splendid landscape specimens, the effect of the pendulous segment tips of most species being particularly graceful. The numerous flowers and

Livistona alfredii

Livistona australis

densely clustered fruits, carried for quite long periods, add to their appeal. Growth is generally rather slow; in a temperate climate *L. chinensis* may take 100 years to grow a trunk of 5 m. But in very warm, sheltered conditions with very moist soil, growth can be greatly speeded up. A deep sandy soil is usually favoured. Livistonas may also be used to good effect as pot or tub plants, though their slow early growth and the "messiness" of their fibrous leaf bases frequently make them less favoured for this purpose than feather palms. They require sufficiently deep containers for their strong root systems, and reasonably good light.

Propagation is from seed, which can be stored in a dry state longer than that of many other palms (though fresh seed is always preferable) and takes usually between 6 weeks and 3 months to germinate. Seedlings should be planted into deep containers at an early stage as they resent root disturbance.

L. alfredii Millstream Palm
A robust palm of very hot, dry tropical habitats where it grows in calcareous soils on permanent springs, the Millstream Palm is slow-growing, with a grey, ringed trunk with old leaf stalk stubs near the base. It grows to about 12 m high and 30 to 50 cm in diameter. The crown is dense. The leaf stalks are relatively short, unarmed, broad and whitish; leaf blades are large and very thick-textured, pale blue-grey on both sides with a waxy surface, divided to about two-thirds their depth into segments, each divided again into 2 long, finely pointed, slightly drooping lobes.

Inflorescences are shorter than the leaves, stiff, with pale pinkish-brown bracts and deep orange flowers, on some plants functionally male only. Fruits are large and spherical, 3.5 to 4 cm in diameter, with dark brown skin dotted with small paler spots; the flesh is thick and juicy. The seed endosperm is pierced by an irregularly branched plug of seed coat.

Distribution: Australia: lower Fortescue River region, Western Australia, just north of the Tropic of Capricorn. Of strictly limited occurrence and potentially an endangered species.

L. australis (syn. *Corypha australis*) Cabbage-tree Palm
The Australian Cabbage-tree Palm is a tall, robust species with a grey or brownish trunk, ringed, closely fissured, rough and somewhat spiny-fibrous. The trunk is free of old leaf bases at maturity, swollen only at the very base, if at all, and growing to 25 m high and 25 to 30 cm in diameter. The crown is dense; leaf stalks are long and slender, strongly spiny-margined on vigorous younger plants but unarmed on tall, old specimens. Leaf blades are thin-textured and deep glossy green on both sides or tinged brownish. They are very strongly undulate and circular in outline often with overlapping lower edges, divided to about two-thirds of their depth into segments which are in turn divided into 2 very long, fine-pointed pendulous lobes. The inflorescences are slightly shorter than the leaves, with thick straight rhachis sheathed in chestnut-brown bracts; flowers are bright creamy-yellow, functionally male only on some trees. Fruits are black, often slightly reddish-brown on one side, dull with thin waxy bloom, spherical and about 20 mm in diameter.

Distribution: temperate east-coastal Australia, from about Fraser Island in Queensland to far eastern Victoria.

L. chinensis (syn. *L. oliviformis, Latania borbonica*)
Chinese Fan Palm

The Chinese Fan Palm is a robust, slow-growing palm with rough, pale greyish-brown trunk, bare and closely ringed below the crown, lower down becoming corky with outer layers disintegrating in irregular plates, to about 12 m tall and 20 to 30 cm in diameter, slightly and gradually swollen at the base. The crown is dense; leaf stalks are shorter than leaf blades, broad, pale green, the margins unarmed or with small spines toward the base only; leaf blades are large, dull, slightly brownish-green on both sides, divided to about two-thirds their depth into segments which are again divided almost to their bases into very long, very finely pointed pendulous lobes.

Inflorescences are about as long as the leaf stalks, sheathed in bracts which are green at flowering, smooth and grey-brown by fruiting; the flowering branchlets are pendulous, bright creamy-yellow. Fruits are irregularly ovoid to spherical, to 25 mm long and 25 mm in diameter, glossy deep greyish-blue to pinkish-grey.

Distribution: southernmost parts of Japan, Ryukyu and Bonin Islands, and islands off southern Taiwan. (The usually-cultivated form with ovoid blue fruit is not known in the wild state; the round-fruited wild form is often distinguished from it under the name var. *subglobosa*).

L. decipiens

A very attractive species, similar in growth-habit, trunk characteristics and colouring to *L. australis* but not growing quite as tall. Its most remarkable feature is the very deep division of the leaves: blades are strongly costapalmate with long, thick costa from which a large proportion of the segment ribs arise; they are very large, over 2 m in length, and divided to within 5 cm or less of the leaf stalk apex or costa, the segments distinctly spaced out along the latter; each segment is divided for more than half its length into 2 very fine-pointed lobes, all of which hang quite vertically from about the point of forking, producing a curtain-like effect. The undersides of the leaf stalks, costa and ribs bear dense circular flat grey scales.

Inflorescences are similar to those of *L. australis* except that the flowers are in small clusters on stalks a few millimetres long arising from branchlets, these stalks lengthening in fruit to almost 1 cm, each appearing as the stalk of a single fruit. Fruits are slightly smaller than in *L. australis*, glossy black, without waxy bloom.

Distribution: Australia: central east coast of Queensland, from a little south of the Tropic of Capricorn north to Townsville.

Livistona decipiens

L. mariae Central Australian Fan Palm

A species of hot, very arid country, restricted to one valley in central Australia where it only occurs around permanent waterholes and soaks. It is a tall, robust palm, to 20 m or more tall, the pale grey ringed trunk about 30 cm in diameter except at the base where it is swollen for a little way above ground, with scattered old leaf stalk remains on the swollen part. The crown is fairly dense, with erect to spreading and drooping leaves on long straight leaf stalks, often over 2 m long, spiny-margined only at the base. The leaf blades are large, about 2 m long, very thick-textured and strongly ribbed, glossy green or brownish-green above, pale green with

Livistona rotundifolia

a thick, flaky layer of wax beneath, divided to more than half their depth into segments which are again divided into finely pointed, irregularly drooping lobes.

Inflorescences are long, erect, stout, and have tight bracts which are green at flowering, and bear white scales. Flowers are dense and creamy-yellow; and the fruits glossy jet-black, spherical, 15 to 20 mm in diameter. Seedlings and juvenile leaves are coloured bronzy-purple, intensified in strong sun; their segments are prickly-margined in the early stages.

Distribution: Australia: MacDonnell Ranges, near Alice Springs.

L. robinsoniana

A tall palm, with prominently ringed stems to 25 m high and about 20 cm in diameter. The crown is fairly dense with long, slender leaf stalks and somewhat drooping, deep glossy green, thin-textured leaf blades, divided to over half their depth into drooping segments which are shortly and bluntly 2-lobed at the apex. Inflorescences are shorter than the leaves with straw-coloured bracts and yellowish flowers. Fruits are orange, 15 mm in diameter.

Distribution: Philippines.

L. rotundifolia

Similar to the preceding species in habit and stature, *L. rotundifolia* has a fairly smooth, pale grey trunk. The leaves are erect to pendulous, with slender leaf stalks, spiny-margined only at the base; blades are shorter than the leaf stalks, glossy, deep green, divided to half or less their depth into straight segments, their blunt apexes shortly divided again, hardly drooping. Inflorescences are about the same length as the leaf stalks, branching near the base into 3 more or less equal, long slender branches, each with repeated clusters of short branchlets, and sheathed in reddish-brown bracts. The spherical fruits, about 20 mm in diameter, are black when ripe but pass through a very ornamental bright scarlet intermediate stage. Juvenile leaves are large and circular and very shallowly lobed.

Distribution: Indonesia, Philippines.

L. saribus (syn. L. cochinchinensis)

A robust palm, with solitary, pale grey ringed trunk to 15 or 20 m tall, about 30 cm in diameter. Crown is large and fairly dense, the leaves with straight leaf stalks, about 2 m long, their margins armed on the lower half with many strong, straight, spiny teeth, often 2 cm or more long, longer and more numerous in semi-juvenile plants. The blades are shorter than the leaf stalks, strongly contorted, dark green, divided to about half their depth into segments which are deeply forked into 2 finely pointed slightly drooping lobes. Inflorescences are longer than the leaf stalks, and rather open. Fruits are spherical, about 20 mm in diameter, glossy blue-grey when ripe with small white spots.

Distribution: South-East Asia, from northern Malay Peninsula to southern China; Philippines, Borneo. Very abundant in Indo-China.

Metroxylon

These interesting, large and fast growing feather palms grow best in moist tropical areas and require ample space. The genus of about 6 species occurs in eastern Indonesia, the Caroline Islands, New Guinea, the Solomon Islands, New Hebrides, Fiji and Samoa. They have solitary or multiple trunks, rough and ringed, or with leaf bases remaining attached, each trunk dying after fruiting. The crown is dense with numerous large leaves, without a crownshaft; leaf bases are broad and stem-clasping; leaf stalks are stout, smooth or armed with spines; the blades have numerous long, broad leaflets, tapered to the apex and crowded along the midrib, their midveins distinct and sometimes with spines on the upper surface and margins.

Inflorescences are huge, terminal, arising from the middle of the crown or rarely among the leaf bases. They have many branches with numerous flower-bearing branchlets; the stalks, branches and branchlets are sheathed or subtended by tubular, overlapping bracts, which are open in the upper part. The flowers are numerous, arranged in pairs and subtended by small bracts. Male and female flowers are similar in appearance with 1 male and 1 female together or the latter possibly bisexual. The 3 sepals are united at the base into a bell shape and the 3 petals have edges touching in bud. There are 6 stamens in both sexes. The ovary is 3-celled, with 3 ovules; the style is stiff with small 3-lobed stigmas, its surface being covered with small scales. In male flowers the size of the sterile pistil is greatly reduced. Male flowers open before the female flowers and then fall off.

Fruits are large, round to pear-shaped, and sometimes flattened or hollowed at the base or apex. The outer surface is covered with hard, shiny, overlapping scales; the inner layer is corky and fibrous. The seed is penetrated by the fleshy case and becomes hollow on one side, being horseshoe-shaped in cross section; the endosperm is not ruminate.

HABITAT, USES, CULTIVATION   Some species belonging to this group of tropical palms grow in lowland forest areas in swamps and other wet places, others occur in forests on the sides of hills.

The Sago Palms are widely cultivated in the Malay Archipelago, New Guinea and some Pacific islands as a source of food. The sago is obtained from the inner fibres of the trunk which is cut down and the starch washed from the fibres after preparation. These palms were formerly the commercial source of sago but in the Malaysian region the tubers of the cassava plant, *Manihot esculenta*, are now commonly used for sago. It has been calculated that the labour requirement for each kilogram of edible starch obtained from these palms is far less than for any other starch-producing plant. The hard outside of the trunk is used for building purposes and the leaves are widely used for thatching. The common Sago Palm, *M. sagu*, is cultivated for sago and thatching.

These palms make interesting large plants where there is ample space in moist tropical areas with a plentiful supply of water. Propagation may be from seed which takes some months to germinate, or with species such as *M. sagu*, suckers are commonly obtained from existing plants.

M. sagu Sago Palm

A large clump-forming palm with a trunk 8 to 10 m high and 30 to 60 cm in diameter, the Sago Palm is covered with leaf bases or roughly ringed. Leaves are large, erect, arching, 5 to

Metroxylon sagu

7 m long; the leaf stalks are long and robust, expanding into a spreading, clasping base; surfaces of both are smooth. The leaf blades have numerous broad, long, light green leaflets, tapered to a pointed apex; midribs are distinct, sometimes with prickles on the upper end and on the margins of leaflets; both ranks of leaflets are directed inwards forming a V shape.

The huge inflorescences arise from the top of the crown and are 5 to 7 m long with numerous branches and branchlets; fruits are globular, 2.5 to 4 cm in diameter with a pointed apex and covered with yellowish-brown scales.
Distribution: Moluccas, western New Guinea; widely cultivated in the Malay Archipelago, Peninsular Malaysia and the Solomon Islands.

M. vitiense

A large palm with a trunk 10 to 15 m high and up to 1 m in diameter, enlarging at the base, rough and ringed with short roots growing from the rings. The whole plant dies after fruiting.

The large, erect leaves are 4 to 5 m long; leaf stalks are very robust with a broad spreading base, armed with rows of spines. The leaf blades have numerous long, broad leaflets, tapered to the apex and becoming ragged with age. The leaflets are crowded along the spiny midrib, with spines on the upper side of the midveins and leaflet margins.

Inflorescences are huge, 2 to 4 m long, arising from the top of the crown, with numerous branches and branchlets. Fruits are large, spherical to somewhat ovoid, 6.5 cm long, covered with straw-coloured, hard, shiny scales.
Distribution: Fiji.

Microcoelum* (syn. *Syagrus*, *Cocos* in part)

Slender feather palms for moist, warm areas, *Microcoelum* species are ideal far shady corners, and containers. There are 2 species in this genus which occurs in Brazil. They have a solitary, ringed trunk and the crown has several small leaves, without a crownshaft. The leaf stalks are slender and without teeth on the margins; the blades have a number of narrow leaflets, tapered to the apexes which are narrowly 2-toothed or 2-lobed; leaflets are evenly arranged along the midrib.

The slender inflorescences arise among the leaf bases and are branched once only into many slender, short branchlets. They are covered in bud with 2 bracts, the lower short and the upper one long and tough, with longitudinal grooves and splitting down one side. The small yellow flowers are separate male and female, spirally arranged on branchlets in groups of 3 on the lower part, with 1 female between 2 male, but with paired or solitary male flowers only toward the branchlet ends. The male flowers have 3 sepals and 3 petals with the edges touching in bud; there are 6 stamens and the sterile pistil is minute. The female flowers with 3 sepals and 3 petals which overlap except at the tips of the petals, have tiny sterile stamens united into a ring. The ovary is 3-celled with 3 ovules, only 1 of which forms a seed. The fruits are egg-shaped with a spongy, fibrous mesocarp which, with the outer skin, splits into 3 parts, exposing the papery endocarp which has 3 pores at the base. The endosperm is not ruminate and is hollow.

HABITAT, USES, CULTIVATION   These palms are inhabitants of forests with high rainfall, where they chiefly grow under the forest canopy.

Microcoelum weddellianum

*See Appendix IV (p. 189)

They grow best in tropical and subtropical areas with a moist atmosphere and a plentiful supply of water. As they naturally grow in low light and the rate of growth is slow, they make particularly good potted specimens in warm indoor conditions with an ample supply of moisture. Potted specimens have been known to have the trunk reach less than 1 m in 20 years. When grown outside, moist warm conditions in a shaded protected position are required. Seeds germinate readily within 2 to 3 months with warm conditions.

M. weddellianum (syn. *Cocos weddelliana, Syagrus weddelliana*)
A slender, small palm with a greyish trunk to about 3 m high and 5 cm in diameter. The leaves are about 1 m long, strongly arched; leaf stalks are slender with reddish-black scales on margins, also on midrib. The leaflets are glossy green above, whitish beneath, drooping with age.

Inflorescences are about 1 m long, with yellow flowers. Fruits are ovoid, about 2 cm long, straw-coloured or dull orange, splitting to reveal the brownish endocarp.
Distribution: southern Brazil.

Nephrosperma

This is an elegant, single-trunked feather palm of medium size, which has been grown as an ornamental for over a century in the tropics and European hothouses. The genus of a single species occurs as a native in the Seychelles, an isolated group of small islands in the Indian Ocean. It is interesting to note that there are six genera of palms native on the Seychelles, all endemic and each having only one species. Among them is the famous ''Double Coconut'', *Lodoicea*.

Nephrosperma has a fairly smooth, grey trunk which grows to about 10 m tall and up to 15 cm in diameter, although usually more slender. The longish, slender leaf stalks are flared at their bases into the broad sheaths which do not form a proper crownshaft. They are armed with bristly spines on younger plants. The leaves are up to 2 m long and have closely spaced, narrow, pendulous leaflets, sometimes up to a metre long. These vary in width on the one leaf, the broadest about 5 cm wide, and each is forked shortly at its apex. Inflorescences arise from among the leaf bases and are very conspicuous because they are much longer than the leaves.

In bud the arching inflorescences are semi-erect and spear-like, enclosed in a very narrow pointed bract. The branched part of the inflorescence is short in relation to the slender, arching stalk. The inflorescences may total 3 to 4 m in length with the branches up to 75 cm. The thin, lax green branches bear very small flowers in rather widely spaced groups of mostly 2 male and 1 female. Male flowers have small overlapping sepals, oblong petals which do not overlap one another in bud, and about 40 stamens. The smaller female flowers are more globular with overlapping sepals and petals. Staminodes are fused into a cup-like organ around the base of the fleshy, 1-celled ovary. The red fruits are nearly spherical, up to 15 mm in diameter, but can be laterally compressed and more broad than long. The remains of the stigma are present as an off-centre, small, but prominent point.

The fruits ripen through yellow to cherry-red and have a thin, dry flesh covering a thin fibrous layer. The seed fills most of the fruit and its endocarp is strongly ruminate.

Nephrosperma vanhoutteanum

HABITAT, USES, CULTIVATION   *Nephrosperma* occurs widely through the lowlands of all the larger Seychelles islands, up to an altitude of about 600 m, most commonly rooting in small pockets of soil between rock slabs, either on stream banks or in ravines or clefts in exposed cliffs. Less commonly it is found as an understorey tree on forested hill slopes. The Seychelles are granite islands, with mainly reddish, lateritic soils. It is doubtful that this palm has any traditional uses except occasionally for thatching. Although valued as an ornamental, it has never been a common palm in cultivation. If climate is suitable it appears to have no special requirements apart from reasonable shelter from strong winds, a well drained soil and plentiful moisture. Its seeds should germinate freely and relatively quickly.

N. vanhoutteanum
For description see above under genus.

Normanbya

This is a very beautiful feather palm, the single species of the genus, commonly known as the Queensland Black Palm. It was named after the Marquis of Normanby in the late 19th century and it occurs in a small area of north-eastern Queensland. The slender, solitary, smooth trunk grows to about 20 m high and 10 to 15 cm in diameter, tapering to about 10 cm just below the crownshaft. It is distinctly ringed, with fine vertical corrugations and the base is bulbous. The crownshaft is a distinctive, pale, ashy grey with brown on the upper part. The crown has about 9 to 12 arched leaves, about 2 to 2.5 m long. The leaf stalks are short, 30 to 60 cm; the blades have numerous broad, wedge-shaped leaflets, toothed or notched at the apex. The leaflets are dull dark green above and glaucous bluish-white beneath. In young plants the leaflets arise along the midrib in the one plane but in mature plants they are divided to their bases, each into a number of segments which are in different planes, giving the whole leaf a distinctly plume-like appearance.

Inflorescences arise below the crownshaft and are much branched, about 50 cm long, and enclosed in bud by 2 tubular bracts which are shed when flowers open. The whitish flowers are separate male or female, arranged with 1 female flower between 2 male on the lower part of the branchlets and only paired or solitary males appear on the upper part. The male flowers have 3 overlapping sepals and 3 petals with edges touching; stamens are numerous and the sterile pistil is as long as the stamens; female flowers have 3 sepals and 3 petals which are overlapping and there are 3 small sterile stamens. The ovary is 1-celled with 1 ovule. The fruits are ovoid, pointed and large (4 to 5 cm long, 3 cm in diameter), and the mesocarp is fleshy with crowded, straight fibres; the seed endosperm is ruminate. The colour of the fruits varies from dull salmon-pink to purplish-brown.

HABITAT, USES, CULTIVATION   Restricted to a limited area in north-eastern Queensland, this palm grows in lowland rainforests of high rainfall, close to rivers and streams, often in slightly swampy areas and chiefly in gravelly alluvial soils.

In its natural habitat *Normanbya* is a very handsome palm. The wood of the trunk is hard and dark and was used by the Aborigines of the area for making spears. To date only limited use has been made of this attractive palm in cultiva-

Normanbya normanbyi

tion, although it has been known in tropical botanical gardens for about a century. A warm, moist, protected, partly shaded position, particularly in the early stages, is required for successful results under cultivation.

An interesting feature of this palm is the manner in which, in young plants, the very broad, wedge-shaped leaflets with a toothed, jagged apex and a number of veins arise in the one plane, whereas in mature plants, the leaflets split into several narrow segments which lie in different planes, presenting a plume-like appearance.

When grown as a potted specimen a deep container with well drained soil, rich in humus material, should be used and the plants kept in a position protected from direct sunlight, with a plentiful supply of water.

Propagation is from seeds which germinate within about 3 months, sometimes almost immediately they are sown. Seeds deteriorate quickly and are often difficult to obtain.

N. normanbyi (syn. *Ptychosperma normanbyi*) Queensland Black Palm
For description see above under genus.

Nypa

The remarkable clump-forming Nipah Palm is the only species in its genus, the botanical characters of which are so different from those of all other palms that it has sometimes been regarded as comprising a separate family. Its main area of occurrence is the Malay Archipelago (Indonesia, Philippines, Papua New Guinea) but it also extends along the mainland Asian coast as far west as the Bay of Bengal in eastern India, also in some of the westernmost Pacific Island groups, with a few scattered occurrences in tropical Australia. Always found growing on tidal creek-banks, its thick horizontal stems are buried deep in soft mud, and are branched dichotomously to form large colonies; upward-pointing aerial roots also protrude from the mud. From each buried stem apex the massive pinnate leaves rise vertically to a height of 5 to 7 m, with thick straight leaf stalks almost circular in cross section, and stiff, regularly spaced leaflets about 1 m long.

Close to the leaves the inflorescences also rise from the mud, to a height mostly under 1 m above the surface. The stout, bracted inflorescence stalks are terminated by globular heads of dull purplish female flowers, below which are several lateral branches bearing short dense spikes of yellow male flowers. After shedding their pollen these male flowers and their branches quickly shrivel up leaving only the terminal cluster of fruits developing from the female flowers. A number of features of the fruits, including their arrangement in heads, are more like those found in *Pandanus* than in most other palms, but current opinion is that *Nypa* is a perfectly natural, if somewhat exceptional, member of the palm family.

A remarkable point about this genus is its antiquity; fossil fruits and pollen identical with the present-day species have been found in various parts of the Northern Hemisphere in strata up to 100 million years old, which puts the genus back close to the time when flowering plants are believed to have first appeared.

HABITAT, USES, CULTIVATION   The Nipah Palm is very

Nypa fruticans, inflorescence

abundant over most areas of swampy coastal lowland in some parts of its range. It requires brackish water which must be subject to tidal rise and fall, so as to cover its leaf stalk bases daily. Deep mud is necessary for its establishment. Often it forms very narrow fringes along the steeply shelving banks of the many small tidal creeks which penetrate the lowlands, but broader stands also occur.

It is a plant highly valued by the peoples of the regions where it grows: the leaves provide one of the best thatching materials and are also woven into walls; even the strong leaf stalks have many structural uses. The cut inflorescence stalks produce large quantities of sugary sap, used mainly as a source of alcohol, and the immature fruits are prized for the delicious flavour and creamy texture of their seed endosperm.

Cultivation is only possible in the tropics under conditions resembling the plants' wild habitat. It seems that tidal conditions are not absolutely essential, as evidenced by its successful growth in Bogor Botanic Gardens, Indonesia, where a large stand has been established in a swampy depression close to a fast-flowing river in this hill region. Perhaps the tidal requirement only operates in relation to seed germination or seedling establishment. We do not know anything about techniques or length of time for germination, but within its native area germinating seeds are often washed up on beaches, sometimes in large numbers.

N. fruticans Nipah Palm
For description see above under genus.

Oncosperma

Five tall, spiny feather palm species comprise this genus, widely distributed through South-East Asia and the Malay Archipelago, from Sri Lanka to Indo-China and the Philippines. The densely clustered trunks are smooth and ringed, though on older trunk bases the rings usually disappear. Between the ring scars on the upper trunk are numerous downward-pointing, very sharp black spines which, however, are soon shed leaving most of the trunk unarmed. There is a distinct but rather short crownshaft which, together with the short leaf stalks and midribs of the leaves, is also strongly spiny. Leaflets are numerous, closely and evenly spaced, or in one species clustered in groups, those of each rank in the one plane, each leaflet long and narrow and with its apex tapering to a fine point.

Inflorescences arise below the crownshaft, each consisting of a short stalk, once or twice branched into many pendulous flower-bearing branchlets. The stalk bears 2 large, semi-woody bracts of almost equal length, the inner closely enfolded by the outer which is flattened with a broad keel running right around it. Both bracts may be armed with spines; they enclose the whole inflorescence in bud and are shed together just before flowers open.

Flowers are separate male and female on the one inflorescence, in groups of 2 male and 1 female near the bases of branchlets, and paired or solitary males only on higher parts. Male flowers have 3 small, pointed sepals, 3 larger, angled petals with pointed apexes and edges touching in bud, 6 to 12 stamens, and a prominent cylindrical sterile pistil. Female flowers are much smaller than male, with 3 short sepals and 3 slightly larger circular petals, their edges overlapping in bud except at the pointed apexes and 6 minute sterile stamens. The egg-shaped ovary has 1 to 3 cells and a minute stigma in an off-centre position.

Fruits are round, 1-seeded, purple to black, with the remains of the stigma markedly off-centre; they have a fleshy and mealy or slightly fibrous mesocarp, and thin endocarp. The round seed has a strongly ruminate endosperm.

HABITAT, USES, CULTIVATION   *Oncosperma* species occur in a variety of habitats. *O. tigillarium* is found only in brackish-water coastal swamps or creek banks, or on sandy or rocky seashores, often in great abundance. *O. horridum* and some other species occur further inland, in valleys or on hill slopes at altitudes of up to 1500 m, with crowns sometimes up among the canopy trees of the rainforest.

The inhabitants of regions where these palms occur put them to many uses. The trunks yield a "wood" stronger and more durable than that of most other palms. It is used extensively for house construction, especially for the foundation piles of raised houses and, split into planks, for floors. It also finds many uses in boat-building and fishing. The apical bud or "cabbage", especially of *O. horridum*, is edible and one of the most prized among palms of this region. The fruits are sometimes eaten also.

Cultivation of *Oncosperma* has been little attempted outside the regions where it occurs naturally, and even there only in a few city parks and botanical gardens. As park specimens, planted in low-lying areas or at water's edge, they look magnificent. It is doubtful that they can be cultivated successfully outside the humid tropics, except in hothouses.

Seeds of this genus germinate readily in under 2 months, if very fresh and if sufficient warmth is provided.

O. horridum

A large clump-forming palm, with usually only 6 to 12 mature stems per clump; these stems are closely crowded, pale grey, and smooth towards the base. They grow to 20 m or more and are about 25 cm in diameter. Crowns are fairly dense, with fairly stiff, erect to spreading leaves 4 to 5 m long; leaflets are closely and evenly spaced, both ranks held in a near-vertical plane though becoming somewhat drooping with maturity. Inflorescences are about 60 cm long, densely branched with yellow flowers. Fruits are purplish-black with a waxy bloom, about 18 mm in diameter, with finely granular surface.
Distribution: Malay Peninsula, Sumatra, Borneo, Philippines.

O. tigillarium (syn. *O. filamentosum*)

A densely clumping palm, with sometimes hundreds of trunks in old specimens, though in wild stands 15 to 30 would be more usual. Trunks grow to 25 m, possibly more, 15 to 20 cm diameter, and are smooth and grey near the base when old, usually slightly sinuous and spreading apart from one another with increasing height. Crowns are fairly open, the leaves 3 to 3.5 m long, regularly arching with all leaflets pendulous in two regular, curtain-like rows. Inflorescences are about 30 to 50 cm long, bright golden-yellow in flower. Fruits are purplish-black, about 10 mm in diameter.
Distribution: Malay Peninsula, western Indonesia, Philippines, Indo-China, always on or close to coasts.

Oncosperma tigillarium

Opsiandra maya

Opsiandra*

A tall slender feather palm is the single species of this genus, occurring wild in Guatemala and Belize (formerly British Honduras). It has a solitary, brownish-grey, distinctly ringed trunk, usually with a number of inflorescences projecting from the upper part at one time. The trunk grows to 20 m high and 15 cm in diameter and is slightly swollen at the base where it has a number of conspicuous thick roots. The crown is compact with erect, slightly arching leaves 2 to 3 m long, each with an ascending encircling base but not forming a definite crownshaft; the thick leaf stalks are grooved above and unarmed, about 60 cm long; the blades have a number of long narrow leaflets tapered to the apex, on the lower side with a distinct raised vein on either side of the midvein towards the edge. These leaflets are evenly spaced along the midrib, but on each side they are directed alternately upward and downward, resulting in rows of leaflets in several slightly different planes.

The inflorescences develop below the crownshaft, being represented at different stages of development at a number of points down the trunk. The inflorescences branch once with slender branchlets and are covered in bud by 4 tubular bracts on the stalk. The greenish flowers are separate male and female and are arranged in longitudinal rows of 2 to 3, the lower being the female, and with male flowers often occurring singly towards the apex of each branchlet. All flowers have 3 sepals and 3 petals which overlap in bud. Male flowers have 6 stamens and a small sterile pistil; female flowers have a 3-celled ovary and a 3-branched stigma. Fruits are almost spherical to slightly kidney-shaped, 10 to 15 mm in diameter with a thin, juicy mesocarp containing irritant crystals. They ripen through yellow to bright red. The seed is flattened to somewhat kidney-shaped; its endosperm is non-ruminate.

HABITAT, USES, CULTIVATION   This palm occurs over a somewhat limited area in forests at about 150 m or lower altitudes, with high rainfall and humidity.

Opsiandra has been cultivated in the far south of the United States and other subtropical areas where there is adequate moisture. A most interesting feature of this palm is the manner in which the first inflorescences are produced and remain in bud stage for some years while the trunk keeps growing above them, producing further inflorescences, until finally all begin to flower and fruit, progressing in the normal sequence from the lowest, oldest ones to the higher and younger, a whole range of stages being present at the one time.

These palms require a protected position, warmth, and a plentiful supply of water as their leaves burn readily. Fruits have stinging crystals in the pulpy outer layer and should not be eaten. Propagation is from seed which should be fresh; warmth is required for satisfactory results.

O. maya Maya Palm
For description see above under genus.

Orania

These are small to large feather palms with solitary, robust, smooth, ringed trunks. The genus with about 16 species occurs in the Malay Archipelago and north-eastern Australia.

*See Appendix IV (p. 189)

The crown of long leaves is light to moderately dense, without a crownshaft and with brown fibres from leaf bases covering the bases of the stiff leaf stalks. The blades have numerous slightly tapered leaflets, each with a single midvein; leaflets are evenly spaced along the midrib and the apexes are oblique and toothed, presenting a slightly ragged appearance.

The inflorescences which arise among the leaf bases vary according to species from erect to somewhat drooping; from short and densely branched to elongated and open, and from once to three times branched. They are enclosed in the bud stage in two large bracts, the lower one short and tubular and the upper, larger one club-shaped with a pointed apex and splitting down one side to release the flowers, finally being shed. Flowers are cream to yellow, either male or female on the one inflorescence, and arranged on the branchlets in groups of 3 towards the base, with 1 female flower between 2 male; towards the upper part of the branchlet, male flowers only occur singly or in pairs. All flowers have 3 tiny sepals and 3 petals; male flowers have 3 to 14 (6 in most species) stamens and a minute or absent sterile pistil; female flowers are larger with sepals and petals meeting at the edges in bud. They have 3 to 6 sterile stamens. The 3-celled ovary has 3 ovules and 3 spreading stigmas. Usually only 1 or 2 ovules develops into a seed, but there are usually some 2 or 3-seed fruits also present. Fruits are spherical, often quite large, green to yellow, with the persistent stigma attached to one side, and 1 or 2 small appendages near the base, representing undeveloped cells of ovary. The mesocarp is fleshy and fibrous in all species except *O. appendiculata*, and the endocarp is woody but thin. The spherical seed has the embryo to one side and endosperm non-ruminate, not intruded by the case. Seeds are said to be very poisonous.

HABITAT, USES, CULTIVATION   These feather palms grow in tropical rainforests in lowlands and on hillsides in mountain areas where some species grow in large stands.

The poisonous seeds are said to be used by native peoples in areas where they grow as a basis for a poison for arrow tips. The apical buds, edible in most other palm genera, are also poisonous.

These attractive palms are useful for specimen planting in tropical areas with higher rainfall. Although they are sometimes planted for ornament in their native countries, there has been very limited use of them in other parts of the world. Possibly the poisonous seeds and foliage may tend to act as a deterrent to their use. Propagation is by seed which is slow to germinate, producing a long extension of the cotyledon which requires a deep container, so it may be wise to plant them into their permanent position when the cotyledon appears.

O. appendiculata *

A robust feather palm with brownish-grey ringed trunk 6 m or more high and 30 cm in diameter. The crown is of light to medium density and carries leaves 3 to 4 m long; the blades have a number of long leaflets, dark green above, greyish beneath, apexes tapering to a narrow, obliquely toothed end, well spaced along the midrib and crowded towards end of leaf in a fan-like manner.

Inflorescences are among the leaf bases, pendulous, about 75 cm long and covered with woolly brown hair. The

*See Appendix IV (p. 189)

Orania palindan

flowers are white to cream. The orange-yellow fruits are spherical, about 25-30 mm in diameter, sometimes 2-lobed, with a large seed in each lobe.

Distribution: Australia: north-eastern Queensland.

O. aruensis

A robust feather palm with ringed trunk, 15 m or more high and 30 cm in diameter. The crown has large, erect to spreading leaves 4 to 5 m long; leaf stalks are at least 1 m long, and the blades have a number of long leaflets, well spaced along the midribs with oblique and toothed apexes.

Inflorescences emerge among the leaf bases to a length of about 1 m, and the branches are crowded. They bear yellow flowers of which the males have 3 stamens. Fruits are spherical, about 50 cm in diameter, dull yellowish-orange in colour.

Distribution: Aru Islands (far eastern Indonesia); may prove to be identical with *O. regalis* of Irian Jaya (West New Guinea), and if so, the latter name has priority.

O. palindan

A robust feather palm with a distinctly ringed, brownish-grey, solitary trunk, 5 to 7 m high and 20 to 30 cm in diameter. The light crown bears erect leaves, 2 to 4 m long; the stiff leaf stalks are 30 to 45 cm long, and the blades have a number of parallel, light green leaflets, crowded along the midrib with ragged apexes, more crowded at the end of the leaf. Drooping inflorescences arise among the leaf bases. Flowers are cream and the males have 6 stamens; fruits spherical, orange.

Distribution: Philippines: islands of Luzon and Sibuyan.

Orbignya

Large, commanding feather palms make up this genus of about 24 species. It is sometimes included in the closely allied genus *Attalea* and occurs from southern Mexico to subtropical South American regions. These palms, which may be low or quite tall, have a solitary trunk irregularly scarred to ringed, or with leaf bases persisting, particularly on the upper part. The dense crowns are without a crownshaft; the leaves are very long and erect, with broad bases ascending against the trunk and fibres on the margins extending to the broad leaf stalks. The blades have numerous long tapered mid-green leaflets crowded along the midrib, alternately arranged.

Inflorescences are long, arising among the leaf bases with a thick main branch and numerous side branchlets, surrounded in bud by 2 bracts, the lower, outer one tubular and the inner, upper one large, woody and spindle-shaped. They split down one side to release the flowers and remain hanging on the plant. Flowers are separate male or female, with branchlets of male and female flowers, rarely on separate plants. Male flowers are small with 3 tiny sepals and 3 larger ovate, lance-shaped petals joined at the base with the edges touching in bud; there are 12 to 14 stamens with elongate anthers, spirally twisted. Female flowers have 3 thick, leathery, ovate or lance-shaped sepals which are overlapping in bud; the petals are similar but overlap in a rolled manner. The egg-shaped 2 to 7-celled ovary has erect ovules at the base. The style is short with 2 to 7 large erect stigmas. Fruits are large, round to egg-shaped, beaked, with 2 to 6 seeds, and a fibrous mesocarp. The seeds have a hard bony endocarp with outside fibres, 3 to 6-pored near the base; the endosperm is uniform, with the embryo opposite one of the pores.

HABITAT, USES, CULTIVATION   These palms grow naturally in forest areas, extending to open country in tropical regions of higher rainfall, in various sites from coastal lowlands to valleys, foothills and elevated areas.

In their natural habitat, the leaves are used for thatching and in buildings and the leaflets for weaving numerous articles including mats, rain capes, baskets and the like. Young leaflets are used for making hats and the trunks are used for general construction purposes. The endosperm is rich in oil which has been used in commercial soap manufacture in Brazil. It has, however, proved inferior to the African Oil Palm (*Elaeis guineensis*) for oil production.

Apart from oil production, these large palms have received limited attention in cultivation as their slow growth and large size impose restrictions on their use. Propagation is by seed which germinates within about 3 to 4 months.

O. cohune Cohune Palm

A very robust tall feather palm with a greyish scarred trunk, or with leaf bases remaining attached in younger plants, 10 to 15 m high and 30 to 40 cm in diameter. The dense crown consists of many erect leaves curved outwards, about 10 m long and up to 2 m broad; the leaf stalks have very broad bases. The blades carry numerous broad, long leaflets, crowded along the midrib and carried in various planes, giving the leaf a plume-like appearance.

Inflorescences among the leaf bases are 1 to 1.5 m high with crowded side branches and numerous flowers. Fruits are large and ovoid, about 6 cm long, resembling small coconuts, and are produced in large quantities.

Distribution: southern Mexico, Guatemala, Honduras to Costa Rica.

Parajubaea

Handsome, cold-hardy feather palms with a smooth, solitary trunk, obscurely ringed. There are 2 species in the genus occurring in Colombia, Ecuador and Bolivia. The crown is spreading with drooping leaves and there is no crownshaft. The sheathing bases are densely covered with a mass of brown fibres; leaf stalks are short and unarmed, and the blade has numerous narrow leaflets, each tapering to a fine point. They are closely and evenly spaced along the midrib which is frequently twisted, bringing the leaflets into a more or less vertical plane, as in the Coconut Palm.

Inflorescences arise among the leaf bases and are short and very erect, with the stiff floral branchlets also erect. There are usually a number of inflorescences in various stages of development at the one time. In the bud stage each inflorescence is enclosed in a slightly woody, narrow, cylindrical bract which splits and remains hanging on the plant when the flowers open. The flowers are separate male or female on the same inflorescence, with the female flowers grouped singly near the bases of the branchlets and the male flowers on the mid and upper part. The male flowers have 3 small sepals and 3 larger petals with the edges touching in bud; there are about 15 stamens and the sterile pistil is 3-lobed. The female flowers have 3 sepals and 3 overlapping petals, the sterile stamens

being united in a ring at the base. The ovary is 3-celled, each cell with 1 ovule. Three separate stigmas arise from the ovary apex. The fruits are large and egg-shaped with a pointed apex, and the mesocarp is dry and densely fibrous; the endocarp is very thick and bony with 3 pores at the base. The 1 seed has a non-ruminate endosperm which has a small central cavity.

HABITAT, USES, CULTIVATION   Little has been recorded of the native habitat of this genus which was described in 1930 from the eastern side of the Andes in Ecuador. It is known, however, that *P. cocoides* is a species of high altitudes (3000 m or more), where it must frequently withstand temperatures well below 0°C. These palms appear to grow well in warm-temperate areas but have been little tried as yet in cooler climates, where they might be expected to make a useful addition to the small number of cold-hardy palms available. Two specimens in the Sydney Botanic Gardens have been in cultivation for many years, flowering and fruiting regularly. It has been suggested that cracking the hard endocarp assists in germination, although very fresh seed is known to have germinated readily without treatment.

P. cocoides

A tall palm with trunk about 15 m tall and 20 to 25 cm in diameter and slightly swollen at the base. The graceful leaves are about 3 to 5 m long and the leaflets are shiny dark green above and greyish-white beneath.

The stiff, erect inflorescences bear flowers which are purplish in bud and yellowish when open. Fruits are 4 to 5 cm in diameter, dark green, turning brown after falling.
Distribution: Ecuador, Colombia.

Pelagodoxa

There is only 1 species in this rare genus which occurred in limited areas of the Marquesas Islands but is now virtually extinct in the wild state. It consists of a slender feather palm with a solitary ringed trunk 6 m or higher and about 15 cm in diameter. The crown of large undivided or irregularly divided leaves 1.5 to 3.5 m long does not have a crownshaft. The leaf stalks are about 70 cm long and covered with scaly, felt-like hairs and are unarmed on the margins; the large broad blades (2 m or longer, up to 1.2 m wide) are pinnately veined and undivided when young, with a V-notched apex and the upper margins jaggedly toothed. They become torn to varying degrees by the wind, forming segments of irregular width. The upper surface is dark green and the lower surface greenish-white due to a covering of scale-like, white hairs.

The branched inflorescences, which are among the leaf bases, are 50 to 60 cm long and in bud are sheathed by a woolly, boat-shaped, pointed bract which is shorter than the inflorescence. The branches are subtended by bracts which are large in the lower part. Separate yellow male and female flowers are carried on the one inflorescence and are arranged in groups of 3 in pits, with 1 female flower between 2 males, or the flowers on the outer parts of the branchlets are all male. The male flowers open and fall before the female flowers open. The male flowers have 3 overlapping sepals, 3 petals with edges touching in bud, 6 stamens and a very small, sterile pistil. Female flowers are enclosed by 2 bracts, and have 3 overlapping sepals, 3 petals overlapping in bud, very small sterile stamens, and an ovary with 1 cell and 1 ovule. The brownish fruits are very large, 10 to 15 cm in diameter, and covered with a thick, corky, fibrous outer skin with pyramid-shaped projections; the endocarp is tough but thin and the seed endosperm is non-ruminate with a small central cavity.

HABITAT, USES, CULTIVATION   This rare species in its wild state occurs in narrow ravines in conditions of shade and high humidity. It is close to extinction in its natural habitat but has been successfully established in a number of the Pacific Islands. Due to the rareness of this palm and its strict require-ments for growth coupled with the limited number of fruit produced, its cultivation has been chiefly restricted to tropical botanic gardens or to the ardent collector who has conditions available for satisfactory growth. It is important that where this palm is to be grown it must be in a moist, warm, shaded position and free from wind. Propagation is from seed which, as well as being hard to obtain, may be difficult to germinate.

P. henryana
For description see above under genus.

Phoenicophorium
This most attractive feather palm with only a single species in the genus is confined to the Seychelles Islands. Over the years it has been known as both *Stevensonia* and *Phoenico-phorium*. It has a tall, slender, solitary, distinctly ringed trunk, 10 to 16 m high and 8 to 10 cm in diameter, spiny when young, becoming smooth in older palms. The close crown of broad, arched leaves 1 to 2 m long does not have a crownshaft. The leaf stalks are short, spiny, and expanded at the base in young plants, but in older plants are smooth and the sheathing bases have weak, appressed spines. The broad-oblong leaf blades, about 1 m wide, are undivided except for the margins, which are lobed to varying depths. In older palms they may be dissected to about one-third of their depth into narrow lobes, the apex of each being notched; the apexes of the blades have a small V-notch.

The erect inflorescences arise among the lower leaf bases and by the time the fruits ripen the lower leaves have fallen, bringing the metre-long inflorescence below the lowest leaf; the long stalks and slender branches are pendulous and sheathed in bud by 2 tubular bracts, the inner one being large, woody, spindle-shaped, finely ribbed and pointed at the apex. The small flowers, which are separate male and female, are arranged on the branchlets with 1 female between 2 male, often with males only on the upper part. The male flowers have 3 small sepals and 3 longer petals with the edges touching in bud; there are 15 or more stamens and a narrow sterile pistil. Female flowers have 3 small sepals and 3 broad petals overlapping in bud; the ovary is 1-celled with 1 ovule. The fruits are oblong-ovoid, 8 to 10 mm long and greenish-yellow becoming reddish when ripe with a thin mesocarp; the seed endosperm is ruminate.

HABITAT, USES, CULTIVATION   This tropical palm occurs from sea level to elevations of about 500 m in its native islands, where it grows in valleys, or on hillsides or ridges, and may occur in pure stands; it is believed that such stands are secondary and followed early clearing of rainforest. The leaves are said to have been used for thatching.

Phoenicophorium, with its broad, undivided leaves has been cultivated in moist tropical areas as an outdoor

Phoenicophorium borsigianum

specimen, or as a potted specimen in heated glasshouses in various parts of the world, although to a much more limited extent than one would expect, considering its striking appearance. Plants grown in the open require moist, tropical conditions with high rainfall and protection from winds; under dry or cold conditions, the edges of leaves burn readily.

Propagation is by seed which requires warmth and moist conditions for germination.

P. borsigianum (syn. *Stevensonia borsigiana*)
For description see above under genus.

Phoenix

These are hardy, ornamental feather palms belonging to a widely distributed genus which occurs throughout southern Asia, eastwards to south China, southwards to the Philippines and throughout most of Africa, with outlying species in the Canary Islands and Crete. The genus consists of some 17 to 18 species, a number of which are widely cultivated; one, the Date Palm, *P. dactylifera*, has been grown from ancient times for its sugary fruit. The trunks of *Phoenix* species may be single or multiple with the surface generally rough due to the leaf bases remaining attached or breaking away leaving rough, diamond-shaped scars. The crown is generally dense with the number of leaves varying, reaching a maximum in the massive crown of the Canary Island Date Palm, *P. canariensis*. The leaf stalks are short with the lowest leaflets being reduced to long, strong, stiff, sharp spines; the blades have numerous narrow, stiff leaflets, deeply folded at the base into a distinct upward-facing V. Other feather palms have the V facing downwards, so this character provides a simple means of identification for this genus. The leaflets are tapered to a sharp, pointed apex and are evenly spaced along the midrib.

The much-branched, erect, broom-like inflorescences arise among the leaf bases and have a flattened stalk with one bract at the base which encloses the inflorescence in bud, later falling. The flowers are separate male or female occurring on separate plants and are arranged singly on the inflorescence branchlets; the male flowers have the sepals united into a small cup and the 3 petals have edges touching; there are usually 6 stamens. The female flowers have the sepals united into a 3-lobed cup and the 3 petals overlapping; there are usually 6 sterile stamens, which are united or scale-like. The ovary has 3 distinct cells and 3 ovules. Fruits are oblong to egg-shaped, with a fleshy or pasty mesocarp. Seeds are elongate, cylindrical to slightly flattened with a distinct longitudinal groove; the endosperm is not ruminate. The thick fleshy fruit in the cultivated edible date, *P. dactylifera*, is the result of human selection over thousands of years.

HABITAT, USES, CULTIVATION   Species of *Phoenix* are found in a range of climates and habitats from warm-temperate to tropical and from semi-arid to wet conditions; however the majority come from tropical monsoonal regions with a well marked dry season alternating with a season of heavy rain. Nearly all are sun-loving palms, growing in open forests, savannah woodlands or low scrub thickets. Most grow naturally in alluvial soil on the moist banks of streams where their roots have permanent access to ground water, although sometimes deep down. There are also cliff and swamp-dwelling species: one inhabits brackish-water swamps in South-East Asia.

The genus *Phoenix* is one of the most widely cultivated groups of palms, its species being extensively used for bold landscape planting, as individual specimens, for avenue planting and, to a lesser extent, as potted plants. The edible Date Palm, *P. dactylifera*, with its selected forms, has been cultivated since biblical times and is of considerable economic importance, particularly in the Middle East and Africa. Since about 1900 this species has been cultivated commercially in the hot dry valleys of southern California with considerable success, but attemps to establish plantations in climatically similar areas of Australia have not been profitable. *P. sylvestris* is cultivated in India for the production of palm wine from the inflorescences.

As well as being ornamental, *Phoenix* species are among the hardiest of palms in cultivation. They will grow in soils of poor quality and in dry areas, larger species being more tolerant of hot drying winds than most other palms. All species prefer full sun, but will grow quite happily in moderately shaded positions, though seldom flowering and fruiting under such conditions. When grown as pot plants, roots of *Phoenix* species quickly grow through the holes in the bottom of containers and should be cut off as they appear. An objection sometimes raised against the use of *Phoenix* species is that the sharp spiny lower leaflets may be a nuisance in some situations.

When grown together under cultivation, the different species tend to hybridize freely and plants raised from seed may not remain true to type, varying considerably in their appearance. The species most affected in this manner seem to be *P. reclinata*, *P. sylvestris* and *P. roebelenii*. Perpetuation of hybrids should be discouraged, otherwise in the long term there will be no possibility of identifying species of any cultivated *Phoenix*.

Propagation is generally from seed which germinates within 2 to 3 months of sowing. The selected fruiting forms of *P. dactylifera* are grown from the suckers which form at the base of established specimens. Seedlings should be potted promptly into a deep container. The smaller species *P. roebelenii*, with finer roots, is more adaptable to containers than any of the larger growing types.

P. canariensis Canary Island Date Palm

A large, spreading palm, with a solitary trunk to about 20 m high and 70 cm in diameter, bears a diamond pattern of leaf scars. Leaves are dull, deep green, about 6 m long, and over one hundred form the massive, dense crown; leaf stalks are short; leaflets are numerous, closely arranged along the midribs and directed upwards and forward, with the lowest ones being particularly spiny.

The many densely branched inflorescences are produced among the leaf bases and bear masses of creamy-yellow flowers. On female plants they become pale orange and are often heavily laden with orange fruits about 2 cm long and 1 cm in diameter.
Distribution: Canary Islands.

P. dactylifera Date Palm

The Date Palm is a tall suckering species with a patterned trunk to about 20 m or more high and 30 to 40 cm in diameter;

Phoenix canariensis

Phoenix dactylifera

older plants form several stems if allowed to do so. Leaves are 6 to 7 m long, forming a loose crown of erect and spreading fronds; leaflets are greyish-green, crowded and evenly spaced along the midribs; they are forward-pointing and spreading.

The much-branched inflorescences are freely produced among the leaf bases; the male plants have cream flowers and female plants yellow flowers. Fruits are large, yellow to deep orange, oblong to ovoid in shape, 5 to 7 cm long and 2 to 3 cm in diameter. Fruit does not form readily in cooler, moist areas and for free fruiting hot dry conditions are necessary, in addition to the presence nearby of a male tree.

Distribution: The Date Palm of commerce is believed to have originated in North Africa, but is now so widespread its precise origin is obscure.

Phoenix loureirii

P. loureirii

A clump-forming tropical palm not unlike *P. pusilla*, with several stems 2 to 3 m high and 20 to 30 cm in diameter arising from the ground with the old leaf bases attached. Leaves are carried in a twisted and reflexed manner. The bright green leaflets are narrow, stiff and well spaced and arise in different planes. Inflorescences are short; flowers are cream on male and female plants. Fruits are small, egg-shaped and reddish to bluish-black in colour.
Distribution: eastern India to southern China.

P. pusilla

A clump-forming palm with several closely placed stems from 30 cm to 3 m high and 15 to 20 cm in diameter. Stems are densely covered with rather erect, old leaf bases. The bright green leaves, about 2 m long, arising from several closely spaced stems, present a dense crowded appearance. Leaflets are light green, stiff and sharply pointed and arise from the leaf stalk in different planes, giving the leaf a somewhat plumose appearance. The small numerous cream flowers on male and female plants are produced on short, branched inflorescences among the leaf bases. Fruits are small, about 12 mm long and purplish-black in colour.
Distribution: southern India and Sri Lanka, on seashores.

P. reclinata African Wild Date

An ornamental clustering feather palm with a number of slender trunks up to 15 m high and 10 to 12 cm in diameter, commonly growing in an outward inclined manner and covered with overlapping leaf bases. Suckering commences at an early stage and continues throughout the life of the palms with 20 or more stems developing in the cluster.

The recurved, bright green leaves, 2 to 3 m long form a much less dense crown than most *Phoenix* species. The shiny leaflets are crowded along the midrib and at first the two ranks are directed inwards and become spreading as they age.

The slender, much-branched inflorescences, with distinctive boat-shaped bracts and cream to yellow flowers are produced among the leaf bases. Fruits are bright orange-yellow, egg-shaped, about 15 to 20 mm long and are produced freely on female plants.
Distribution: tropical and southern Africa.

Phoenix reclinata

P. roebelenii Roebelen Date

A slender graceful palm with the solitary trunk rarely exceeding 3 m high and covered with old peg-like, projecting leaf bases, rounded on the ends; the trunk of the Roebelen Date is commonly narrowest at the base. The leaves, about 1.5 m long, are crowded in the crown, with the lower ones pendulous; leaf stalks and midribs are slender with narrow, glossy green leaflets evenly spaced and curved downwards.

The inflorescences are short with cream flowers on both male and female plants; the latter produce numerous small black ellipsoid fruits.
Distribution: Laos, along the lowlands of the Mekong River.

P. rupicola Cliff Date

A slender, beautiful palm with a solitary trunk, about 5 to 7 m high and 15 to 20 cm in diameter. Unlike other *Phoenix* species, the trunk of the Cliff Date is often free of attached old leaf bases or has only a few. The base of the crown is swollen,

Phoenix roebelenii

Phoenix sylvestris

Phoenix rupicola

similar to *P. roebelenii*, and also has matted brownish fibres. The light green leaves about 3 m long are commonly twisted and pendulous. The leaflets are numerous, stiff, thin textured and bright green and are crowded along the midrib, arising in more or less the one plane, giving the leaf a flat appearance.

The inflorescences among the leaf bases are short, much branched and pendulous, with cream flowers on both male and female plants. The attractive fruits are oblong, about 20 mm long, shiny, and a deep purplish-red colour when ripe. Distribution: India.

P. sylvestris Indian Wild Date
The Indian Wild Date is a large palm closely resembling *P. canariensis*, but with the trunk about 8 to 12 m high and less robust. Leaves are shorter, about 3 to 4 m, and the crown is more compact. The leaflets are bluish-green and evenly spaced along the midrib. They tend to be arranged in a criss-cross manner. The much-branched inflorescences with yellow stalks are produced among the leaf bases in a similar fashion to *P. canariensis* with purplish-red fruits being profusely produced.
Distribution: India.

P. zeylanica
A slender palm with a solitary trunk about 6 m or less high and 20 to 30 cm in diameter, densely covered with old, crowded leaf bases. It has a compact crown with somewhat pendulous, sharp leaves, about 2 m long; leaf stalks are short, and the leaflets numerous, light green, stiff and sharply

pointed, particularly on the lower part. They are well spaced along the midrib and arise in different planes, giving the blades a rather spikily plumose appearance.

Inflorescences are much branched and spreading; flowers are cream to yellow. The reddish to purplish-black fruits are oblong to obovoid, about 12 mm long.

Distribution: southern India and Sri Lanka, near the sea.

Pholidocarpus

Tall fan palms make up this genus of 5 species occurring in the Malay Peninsula, Borneo, Sumatra, Celebes and the Moluccas. The genus is closely allied to *Livistona*. The palms have a solitary, rough ringed trunk and a dense crown, globular in shape, without a crownshaft, and consisting of many large leaves. The leaf stalks are long and armed along the margins with strong spines. The leaf blades are broad, almost circular in outline, undulate and shortly costapalmate, being divided into a number of segments, the primary divisions sometimes extending to the leaf stalk. The segments are further subdivided into 2 tapered segments.

The inflorescences which are produced among the leaf bases are large and much branched, with a number of short branchlets; the stalk or peduncle is covered with several leathery bracts which persist, and each main branch has a thin membranous bract which gradually disintegrates as the branch grows. The bracts enclosing the flowers are very small. Flowers are small, numerous and bisexual, commonly arranged in groups of 3 towards the base of the branchlet and in pairs or singly on the upper part. The calyx is bell to tube-shaped with 3 small teeth; the 3 petals, with their edges touching in bud, are free to the base or urn-shaped in the lower parts, the 6 stamens have the bases of the filaments joined into a tubular or urn-shaped ring. The ovary is 3-celled, the cells separate but united at their apexes, each with a single ovule. The style is tapered and terminates in a somewhat small, pointed stigma. The fruits are round to egg-shaped with a tessellated corky surface, and fibrous mesocarp. The seed has a cavity on the side of attachment which is filled with brown material from the intrusion of the case; the endosperm is ruminate.

This genus differs from *Livistona* chiefly in the large fruit with a corky layer and in the stamen filaments being united into a tube.

HABITAT, USES, CULTIVATION   These palms grow in tropical low coastal areas near the sea and in forests where there is a plentiful supply of moisture; frequently they occur in swampy areas. They have not been cultivated to any great extent outside their tropical habitat, species of *Livistona* and *Washingtonia* being used when tall fan palms are needed.

Propagation is from seed which requires heat for satisfactory germination.

P. macrocarpus

A tall fan palm with a solitary grey, ringed, smooth to rough trunk about 15 to 20 m high and 30 to 40 cm in diameter; the trunk is covered with leaf bases in younger plants. The dense crown is globular in outline and has numerous leaves 3 m or more long; leaf stalks are straight, bent towards the base, about 2 to 2.5 m long with spines along the margins; blades are about 2 m broad, almost circular in outline, divided almost to the leaf stalk into broad segments which are further divided

Pholidocarpus macrocarpus

Pholidocarpus mucronatus

into 2 tapered segments, often with the tips drooping. The inflorescences arise among the leaf bases, and are long and much branched; the cream flowers have their petals united in the lower part to form a cup shape. Fruits are very large, egg-shaped, 10 to 11 cm long, brown, with a corky cracked surface.

Distribution: Malay Peninsula.

P. mucronatus

A tall fan palm with a solitary ringed smooth to rough trunk about 15 to 20 m high and 30 to 40 cm in diameter. The dense crown is globular with a number of leaves 2 to 3 m long; leaf stalks are 1.5 to 2 m long, straight for most of their length but bent towards the base and toothed on the margins; blades are 1 to 1.5 m broad, circular in outline, and divided into broad segments to about a third or more of their depth, each further divided into 2 stiff, tapered segments.

Inflorescences are among the leaf bases, long and branched; flowers are cream with petals divided to the base. There are numerous fruit, ovoid, 8 to 9 cm long, brown, with a cracked corky surface; seed case has spiny projections.

Distribution: Sumatra.

Pigafetta

A genus of 1 tropical species of very rapid growth, occurring in the Celebes, Moluccas and possibly western New Guinea, this is a very tall, robust feather palm with a solitary grey-ringed trunk. The trunk is smooth and green except for the prominent rings, though on older parts it may go grey. It grows to 50 m or higher and 25 to 40 cm in diameter. The crown is dense, without a crownshaft, and with very large arching leaves about 6 m long with stout leaf stalks about 2 m long, channelled above, their broad sheathing bases armed with small spines arranged in comb-like transverse rows. The blades have numerous long, fairly broad, linear leaflets tapered to a fine point and spaced evenly along the midrib. The upper and lower surfaces of the midrib and upper parts of the leaflets near the apex are armed with spines.

The inflorescences, male and female on different plants, are similar in appearance and arise among the leaf bases, always inclined to the left in relation to the trunk; 1.5 to 2 m long, each consists of a long, steeply ascending main axis, tightly sheathed in overlapping bracts, with a number of pendulous lateral branches from which arise numerous pendulous flower-bearing branchlets. The white flowers are each enclosed in bracts and immersed in tufts of hairs. Male flowers have 3 sepals fused into a bell shape, 3 petals united into a tube at the base, and 6 stamens, their filaments also united into a tube at the base. Female flowers have sepals united into a cup shape which is at first entire, but soon splitting, 3 petals separate almost to the base, 6 sterile stamens united at the base. The ovary is 1-celled but with 3 ovules, only one of which develops into a seed, and has a 3-lobed stigma at its apex. The creamy-yellow fruits are small and round, 10 to 12 mm in diameter, and covered with scales, with a thin, dry wall. The seed is covered by a fleshy aril and has a non-ruminate endosperm.

HABITAT, USES, CULTIVATION   This large tropical feather palm has a rather specialized habitat. Occurring in high-rainfall regions between about 300 and 1500 m altitude, it is absent from undisturbed rainforest: seedlings germinating on the forest floor use up their food reserves and then die. However, growth is very abundant and rapid in newly opened-up habitats, such as edges of man-made clearings, gravel bars in rivers, recent landslips, and old lava flows.

In its native regions *Pigafetta* is valued for its timber, used extensively for construction purposes. Its extremely rapid growth has created interest in its potential use in areas of similar climate as a timber tree. Its fruits are reported to be eaten in the Celebes.

With suitably hot moist conditions and high rainfall this palm grows very rapidly and makes a most impressive specimen, but will not withstand cold or dry conditions. Its habitat preferences suggest that it requires strong light and deep, open-textured soil of high mineral content for optimum growth.

Propagation is from seed, which must be fresh; germination is rapid, sometimes taking under a month. Seedlings must not be too heavily shaded.

P. filaris Wanga Palm
For description see above under genus.

Pinanga
Beautiful, shade-loving feather palms from the humid tropics, many of the 100 or more species of *Pinanga* have the potential to become spectacular indoor plants. They occur from India (Sikkim and Assam with a few outlying species in the hills of South India) to Sri Lanka, South-East Asia to South China, and the islands of the Malay Archipelago, eastward to New Guinea. The greatest number of species occur in the Malay Peninsula, Sumatra, Borneo and the Philippines.

They are chiefly small, slender stemmed, undergrowth palms with a few tall and moderately robust species. The smooth often bamboo-like stems usually have prominent rings and may be solitary or multiple, or in some species there may be no above ground stem. The crownshaft is well developed, except for some slender, very rapid-growing species, where the growth of the stem results in the leaves being widely spaced along it. The leaf stalks are short, slender and smooth; the blades are very variable, even within the same species; they may be undivided except for the cleft apex, or divided into a relatively few broad leaflets each with a number of veins and forward-curved apex, or narrow leaflets with pointed apexes, to broad and truncated with toothed apex. On the same leaf there are frequently pointed leaflets on the lower part of the blade and upper leaflets with toothed apexes. This variability in the leaves led early botanists, with limited material available for examination, to give frequently a number of different names to the one species.

The short inflorescences have a few fleshy branches or may be reduced to a single spike. Borne mostly below the leaves, in a few species they are between the leaf bases. In bud the inflorescences are sheathed by a thin-textured bract (the prophyll) which is shed early. An interesting feature of the inflorescence is the change of colour from green, when the flowers open, to deep pink to purple when in fruit.

The flowers are separate male and female on the same inflorescence and are in groups of 3, with 1 female between 2 male in close, regularly arranged groups in 2 rows and somewhat sunken into the zigzagging, fleshy, floral branchlets, or in some species they may be arranged spirally. Male flowers are asymmetrical with 3 sepals slightly overlapping and 3 pointed petals with edges touching in bud; there are a minimum of 9 stamens, and usually there is no sterile pistil. The female flowers have 3 sepals which are overlapping and united; the 3 petals are overlapping except the tips which touch in bud; sterile stamens are absent. The ovary is 1-celled with 1 ovule and an entire stigma at the apex.

Fruits are small, ellipsoid to egg-shaped, or elongate and cylindrical, sometimes curved and with the old stigma attached at the apex; the mesocarp is fleshy to fibrous and the outer skin pink to black; the seed endosperm is ruminate or rarely non-ruminate.

A striking feature of many species is the purplish to orange mottled or variegated juvenile foliage which is best developed in heavy shade.

HABITAT, USES, CULTIVATION   These palms are virtually all undergrowth species, occurring in dense tropical rainforests at low to medium altitudes; they are found chiefly on hillsides or valleys, or on the banks of streams which sometimes become flooded, but not on swampy ground.

These palms are grown chiefly in moist tropical areas in protected, shaded to partly shaded positions, to which they are particularly suited; they will not tolerate cold or dry conditions. Most species adapt well to cultivation in containers, often making very fast growth under hothouse conditions in more temperate climates. Their interesting and elegant leaf shapes and varied coloration in the young stages make them highly ornamental container subjects, but they have yet to be proven hardy enough for general indoor decoration. Seed of many species, often unidentified, has been available in recent years from seed collectors and traders.

Propagation is usually from seed, which germinates freely within 2 to 3 months; no doubt in moist tropical areas of high rainfall, vegetative division of clump-forming types would be satisfactory.

Pinanga densiflora

P. densiflora

A dense, clump-forming palm often producing roots above ground; stems are 2.5 to 4 m high and 2.5 cm in diameter. Individual crowns are small. Leaves are about 1.5 m long; leaf stalks are short; leaf blades have broad leaflets crowded on the midrib, lower ones with forward curved points, upper 2 truncate and toothed. Inflorescences arise below the crownshaft and are pendulous, becoming pinkish-red; fruits are small, ellipsoid, about 12 mm long, black.
Distribution: Sumatra.

P. disticha

A tiny, clump-forming palm with very slender bamboo-like stems, 1 to 2 m high. Individual crowns are very small, with widely spaced leaves, each about 30 cm long; leaf stalks are very slender with the blade having 2 entire, broad lobes forming a V shape or sometimes divided into narrow leaflets, dark green, often mottled with pale yellow-green. Inflorescences are in slender spikes, 5 to 10 cm long. Fruits are oblong, narrowed to both ends, about 12 mm long, orange-red.
Distribution: Malay Peninsula

Pinanga disticha

146

P. javana

A solitary stemmed palm with a trunk to about 10 m high and 8 to 10 cm in diameter, distinctly ringed. The crown has spreading leaves 1.5 to 2 m long, and a prominent crownshaft. The leaf stalks are short and the blades have a number of leaflets of even width, each tapering to a point and evenly arranged along the midrib. Inflorescences are short and arise below the crownshaft. They are pendulous and have zigzag floral branchlets. Fruits are small.

Distribution: Western Java at about 1500 m altitude.

P. kuhlii

A cluster-forming palm with green, smooth stems to 8 m high (often much less in cultivation) and 3 to 5 cm in diameter. Individual crowns are small with leaves about 1 m long; leaf stalks are slender with brown scales; the blades have a few broad leaflets of variable width, each with several main veins, lower leaflets with forward curved points and upper ones with truncated, toothed apexes. Inflorescences arise below the crownshaft, branched and about 30 cm or less long; flowers are cream to pinkish; fruits are egg-shaped, about 12 mm long, dark red.

Distribution: Java, Sumatra, South Andaman Islands.

Polyandrococos

This is an attractive and unusual feather palm for warm areas. The genus consists of 1 species occurring in eastern Brazil, in the coastal areas of Bahia and Sergipe. It has a rough, ringed, solitary brown or grey trunk which grows to 5 or 6 m high and 20 cm or more in diameter. The dense crown consists of a number of erect leaves 3 to 4 m long, and is without a crownshaft. The leaf stalks are about 60 cm long, stout, ribbed below, expanded into a broad base carried close against the trunk. The blades, about 2 m long, have numerous, long, narrow, stiff, pointed leaflets, each with a conspicuous midvein and tapering to a sharp point, crowded along the midrib and often grouped into clusters.

Inflorescences arise among the leaf bases; they are up to 1 m or longer and form dense unbranched spikes of yellowish flowers, at first erect, becoming pendulous in fruit; the whole inflorescence is enclosed in the bud stage by 2 bracts, the lower outer one short and tubular, the upper one large, with longitudinal grooving, woody, club-shaped and tapering to a pointed apex. The outer bract splits down one side and remains on the plant after the flowers open. The flowers are separate male and female and are densely crowded along the spike with the male flowers opening first. Flowers are arranged in the lower part of the spike in groups of 3 with 1 female between 2 male, but with male flowers only on the upper part. Male flowers have 3 sepals joined at the base and 3 larger petals with edges touching in bud, stamens from 90 to 120. Female flowers have 3 overlapping sepals, 3 larger overlapping petals except for the tips touching, sterile stamens joined forming a cup shape, ovary with 3 cells and 3 ovules, and 3 stigmas. The crowded fruits are round to slightly conical, about 3 cm in diameter, yellow with a fleshy but strongly fibrous mesocarp, and very thick, woody endocarp with a smooth inner surface. The endosperm is ruminate.

HABITAT, USES, CULTIVATION   This palm grows in undulating open country or woodlands, close to the sea, in dry, very sandy soil.

Pinanga kuhlii

The inhabitants of its native region feed its fruits to their livestock and use its trunks for building.

As a cultivated palm, *Polyandrococos* makes an interesting but not especially ornamental specimen. It should grow well in tropical and subtropical areas of highly seasonal rainfall, and on poor coastal sands.

Propagation is from seed which may take quite a few months to germinate.

P. caudescens (syn. *Cocos caudescens, Diplothemium caudescens*), Buri Palm.
For description see above under genus.

Pritchardia

These beautiful, medium to fairly tall fan palms make up a genus of 36 species. They occur in some island groups of the Pacific, with the greatest number of species being confined to the Hawaiian Islands. The solitary, smooth to rough, ringed trunk, often has vertical markings. The light to dense crown, without a crownshaft, has leaves with an unarmed leaf stalk and costapalmate, almost circular to narrowly fan-shaped blades, cupped upwards, undulate and often distinctly pleated. They are divided to about a quarter to half their depth into tapered segments, each of which is further subdivided into 2 pointed lobes.

The long-stalked inflorescences arise among the leaf bases, each having a number of short, stiff branches. In bud stage the inflorescence is enclosed in a number of tightly overlapping, tubular bracts, which remain on the plant when flowers open. Flowers are bisexual, cream to yellow or orange and scattered singly along the branchlets. The sepals are joined into a tube, often bell-shaped, which is shortly 3-toothed; the longer petals also form a tube which falls off when flowers open. The ovary is conical to turbinate (top-shaped) with the 3 cells partly free but united at top into an elongated style, only 1 ovule usually developing into a seed. Fruits are round to egg-shaped with the old style at the apex and persistent calyx at the base. The mesocarp layer is slightly fleshy with longitudinal fibres; the seed coat is thickened on one side but does not intrude into the non-ruminate endosperm.

HABITAT, USES, CULTIVATION   On their native islands, *Pritchardia* species occur in elevated regions of high rainfall, on hillsides and in valleys in rainforest on volcanic soils.

The leaves of *Pritchardia* are used for weaving into various articles such as hats, and the seeds are eaten in their immature state.

These attractive fan palms require moist, tropical or subtropical, protected coastal positions with a plentiful supply of moisture. They are sun-loving palms but may burn readily when in exposed positions, and will not withstand cold. Propagation is from seed which germinates within 2 to 3 months.

P. affinis Loulu Palm
A variable species with a brown, rough-ringed trunk to about 10 m high and 20 to 30 cm in diameter. The crown is fairly open; the leaf stalks are 1 m or more in length; blades are mid-green, fan-shaped, undulate, about 1 m broad, divided to about a quarter of their depth into tapered segments which are further subdivided.

Inflorescences have a long stalk with one main panicle of numerous flowers which are cream to yellow in colour. Fruits are spherical, about 25 mm in diameter.
Distribution: island of Hawaii.

P. beccariana Loulu Palm

A slender palm with a brown closely ringed trunk with vertical striations, 15 to 18 m high and 20 to 30 cm in diameter. The open crown is spherical in shape; leaf stalks are 1 to 1.5 m long, greyish-green with greyish-brown fibres at the base; blades are mid-green, divided to about one-quarter of their depth into tapered segments which are further subdivided and somewhat drooping.

Fruits are ovoid to spherical, 2.5 to 3.5 cm long, shiny black with the remains of the old stigma attached.
Distribution: island of Hawaii.

P. hillebrandii Loulu Palm

A medium-sized palm, with a solitary, rough, ringed trunk, 6 to 7 m high and 15 to 25 cm in diameter. The dense crown is greyish-green; leaf stalks are broad, 1 m long. The blades are greyish-green, undulate, divided to about half their depth into tapered segments which are further subdivided into slender points.

Inflorescences are much branched, on long stalks; the numerous flowers are cream coloured. Fruits are globular, brownish-black, about 15 to 20 mm in diameter.
Distribution: Hawaiian Islands.

P. kaalae Loulu Palm

A palm with a solitary, rough, ringed trunk with vertical

Pritchardia hillebrandii

Pritchardia kaalae

Pritchardia martii

fissures, about 10 m high and 15 to 25 cm in diameter. The crown is dense, the light green leaves have stalks about 1 m long; blades are fan-shaped, about 1 m broad, divided to about a third of their depth into tapered, divided segments.

Inflorescences are small, branched, on long stalks; flowers are yellow. Fruits are spherical, brownish-black in colour.

Distribution: island of Oahu.

P. maideniana

A medium-sized palm, with trunk about 5 m tall, gradually flared out toward the base, about 12 cm in diameter higher up, with a rough texture and brown in colour. The crown is small and dense; leaves are very stiff and erect, yellowish-green, with short, thick leaf stalks; blades are wedge-shaped at the base, divided to slightly more than half their depth into stiff segments which are deeply divided again into two fine points; leaf stalks and centres of blades are densely coated with pale brown wool. Inflorescences are erect, shorter than the leaves, with woolly bracts. The large flowers are densely clustered, orange in colour. Fruits are round, 12 to 14 mm in diameter, and brownish-black.

Distribution: wild origin unknown, named in 1913 from plants cultivated in the Sydney Botanic Gardens, presumably introduced from somewhere in the Pacific as were many other plants in these gardens last century. It is a distinctive species, unlikely to be confused with any other. Two old plants still survive in Sydney.

P. martii Loulu Hiwa Palm

A low-growing palm with a solitary brown, rough, ringed trunk, 3 to 5 m high and 20 to 25 cm in diameter. The crown is dense and the erect leaves have stalks 1 m long; the blades are about 1 m broad, fan-shaped, shiny mid-green, distinctly pleated, divided to about one-third of their depth into tapered segments, each further subdivided.

Inflorescences are on long stalks, much branched; flowers are yellow. Fruits are egg-shaped, shiny greenish-brown, 25 to 30 mm long and 25 mm broad.

Distribution: Hawaiian Islands.

Pritchardia maideniana

Pritchardia pacifica

P. pacifica Fiji Fan Palm

A large fan palm with a solitary ringed, brown, corky trunk to 10 m or more high and 25 to 30 cm in diameter. The crown is medium to dense; leaf stalks are 1 m or more long; blades 1 m or more broad, fan-shaped, divided to about a quarter of their depth into tapered, divided, stiff-pointed segments. Inflorescences do not extend beyond the leaves and are about 1 m long, much branched; flowers are yellow. The round black fruits are about 12 mm in diameter.

Distribution: Tonga, though introduced to Fiji before European discovery and formerly considered native there.

P. thurstonii

A slender palm with a solitary, brown, ringed trunk about 8 m high and 20 cm in diameter, with distinct vertical fissures. The crown is medium-sized; leaf stalks are about 1 m; blades 1 m or more broad, fan-shaped, divided into tapered segments almost to the middle in the central portion.

Inflorescences are up to 2 m long extending beyond the leaves, with yellow flowers. Fruits are spherical, deep red, 6 to 7 mm in diameter.

Distribution: Fiji, growing on limestone.

Ptychosperma

Tropical feather palms comprise this genus of 28 species occurring chiefly in New Guinea, though with species also in the Solomon Islands, the Bismarck Archipelago, and northern Australia. These slender palms have a smooth, ringed trunk, solitary or with several forming a cluster. The trunk is surmounted by a distinct crownshaft, the surface of which is usually scaly to woolly, formed by the leaf bases which usually have an appendage (often triangular) on the upper edge, mostly opposite the leaf stalk. The crown is open, with the leaf stalks slender, scaly to woolly; the leaf blades are oblong, elliptical in outline with a number of narrow to broad, linear to wedge-shaped leaflets each with a prominent midvein and thickened marginal veins. The leaflet apexes are oblique to concave, notched or toothed to varying degrees; leaflets are regularly or irregularly arranged along the midrib.

Inflorescences are below the crownshaft, branched, with the stalks generally thick, short, and fleshy, and green, yellow to red in colour. The whole inflorescence is enclosed in bud by 2 large overlapping bracts flattened at the sides, tapered towards the apex and attached near the base of the stalk, falling off before flowering. Flowers are few to numerous towards the lower parts of the branchlets in groups of 3, 1 female flower between 2 male, but with only male flowers in pairs or singly on the upper part. Male flowers are ovoid with 3 overlapping sepals and 3 petals with edges touching in bud; stamens number 9 to 100 or more, and the sterile pistil is elongate. Female flowers are smaller than the males; they have 3 sepals and 3 petals, overlapping except that the petal tips touch in bud, minute sterile stamens and a 1-celled ovary with 1 ovule and 3 stigmas. Fruits are spherical to ellipsoid with the old stigma remaining attached, and are red, orange or purplish-black when ripe. The mesocarp is thin, fleshy and fibrous. Seeds are longitudinally 5-grooved or 5-angled; the endosperm is ruminate or non-ruminate.

HABITAT, USES, CULTIVATION   These tropical feather palms are inhabitants of moist forests, from lowland coastal

Ptychosperma macarthurii

forests to rainforests in mountain valleys. Sometimes they grow around the margins of freshwater swampy areas, and they mostly occur as understorey plants.

Several species of *Ptychosperma*, in particular *P. elegans* and *P. macarthurii*, have been widely cultivated in warm moist coastal areas in many parts of the world where they are used in landscaping. Their colourful fruit, profusely borne, add to their decorative qualities. Under cultivation, a warm location with a plentiful supply of water and protection from drying winds give best results. Some species can make attractive container subjects for indoor use, but temperature and humidity must be maintained at adequate levels for them.

Propagation is usually by seed which should be fresh; germination takes about 2 to 3 months. Cluster-forming types may be propagated by division of suckers from existing plants under nursery conditions.

P. elegans Solitaire Palm
A slender feather palm with a solitary greyish ringed trunk about 12 m high and 6 to 8 cm in diameter. The crown is compact with 7 to 11 leaves 1.5 to 2.5 m long; the distinct crownshaft is woolly and somewhat whitish or brownish; leaf stalks are about 20 to 30 cm long and scaly; the blades have many broad leaflets, evenly spaced and crowded along the midrib, each tapering to an oblique notched apex.

Inflorescences are below the crownshaft, about 60 cm long with numerous branches; flowers are greenish-white. Fruits are egg-shaped, about 15 mm long and bright red.
Distribution: Australia: north-eastern Queensland (south to about the Tropic of Capricorn).

P. macarthurii Macarthur Palm
A slender, clump-forming feather palm with a number of smooth grey ringed stems to about 7 m high and 4 to 5 cm in diameter. The crowns have about 8 to 10 spreading arched leaves up to about 2 m long; the crownshafts are smooth and green, woolly and whitish in colour when young; the leaf stalks are about 20 cm long; the blades have a number of broad leaflets crowded along the midrib, each with an oblique, toothed apex.

Inflorescences are below the crownshaft, 30 to 40 cm long, branched, with cream flowers. Fruits are bright red, egg-shaped, about 14 mm long.
Distribution: north-eastern Australia (Cape York Peninsula), New Guinea.

P. propinquum
A slender feather palm with a smooth, distinctly ringed trunk to about 8 m long and 2 m in diameter, solitary or with a number of stems in a cluster. The spreading crown has several leaves about 1 m long; the crownshaft is green, brownish in the upper part; leaf stalks are about 30 cm long with brownish coloured scales; the blades have a number of broad leaflets with concave, notched apexes and are arranged in clusters of 2 to 3 on the midrib.

Inflorescences arise from below the crownshaft and are about 20 to 40 cm long; stalks are dark and woolly. The flowers are cream. Fruits are egg-shaped, about 15 cm long, and red in colour.
Distribution: eastern Indonesia: Moluccas and other islands adjacent to West Irian.

P. sanderianum

A slender clump-forming feather palm with several greyish, distinctly ringed trunks about 4 m tall and 4 to 5 cm in diameter. The crowns have about 8 to 10 arched, spreading leaves; crownshafts are greenish-brown with a distinct appendage; leaf-stalks are about 20 cm long; the blades have a number of long narrow leaflets with apexes deeply concave with long toothing.

Inflorescences arise below the crownshaft and are about 30 cm long and branched; flowers are cream. Fruits are red, egg-shaped, about 15 mm long.

Distribution: not definitely known, but probably New Guinea.

Raphia

Massive, erect leaves distinguish these large, moisture loving tropical feather palms. The genus of about 30 species occurs in most of Africa south of the Sahara and in Madagascar, and there is 1 species in Central America and Brazil. They are either with or without an above-ground trunk which may be solitary or multiple, and mostly covered in the upper part with old leaf bases and long, tough, blackish, spiny fibres from the leaf sheaths, the trunk dying after flowering and fruiting. The large crown is formed of straight or arched leaves up to about 20 m in length in one species, these being the largest known leaves of any type of plant; in the stemless species, the large leaves arise from ground level. The leaf stalks are long and smooth and are unarmed on the margins; the blades have numerous, very long leaflets, each tapering to a pointed apex, with a single midvein and spiny along the upper midvein and margins.

The terminal inflorescences are very large, with a number of separate pendulous branches, each of which is branched several times, finally into small branchlets carrying male and female flowers. The inflorescences, including primary stalk and secondary stalks, are clothed with numerous sheathing bracts. Each branch or branchlet also has a bract at its base, and there are innumerable smaller bracts, each enclosing a flower, with bracteoles below the calyx. The male and female flowers look similar, with the female flowers situated on the lower parts of the branchlets and the males on the upper parts. Male flowers have 3 sepals joined at the base with a double-keeled bracteole below; the 3 petals have pointed apexes and the 6 to 20 stamens are joined at the base. Female flowers are similar, but have a further thin bracteole enclosing the calyx and petals. The sterile stamens are joined into a ring, and the ovary is 1-celled with 3 short stigmas.

Fruits are large and egg to top-shaped, with a small pointed apex; the outer surface is covered with hard, shiny, brown, overlapping scales, and the mesocarp layer is oily. The large seed has a ruminate endosperm.

HABITAT, USES, CULTIVATION   This group of large palms grows in a range of habitats, but the greater number of species grow in wet areas such as swamps, along the banks of streams, and in other situations where there is a plentiful supply of water.

In Africa these palms are most important to the inhabitants as they are used for many different purposes. The large midribs of the leaves and the leaf stalks are widely used for constructing the framework of houses, as poles for various uses and for making into furniture; they are also split into

Ptychosperma sanderianum

strips for weaving into mats, baskets etc; the well known raffia is also obtained from the leaflets. The tough, blackish fibre (piassava) obtained from the leaf sheaths is used for making brooms and is exported for this purpose; tough ropes are also made from the fibre. Palm wine is made by fermenting the sap from the trunk. The sap is obtained by either cutting down the trunk and allowing the sap to drain out, after which the trunk is used for construction purposes, or by boring a hole in the stem near the apex. Oil is obtained from the oily mesocarp layer of the fruit, which in some regions is boiled and eaten.

These large palms, as well as being useful, make interesting specimens where there is ample space, warmth and a plentiful supply of water. Cultivation of them is unlikely to succeed except in the tropics.

Raphia hookeri

Propagation is from seed which requires several months to germinate.

R. hookeri

A large feather palm with a solitary trunk or several trunks to about 10 m high and 30 cm in diameter, covered in the upper part by leaf bases and masses of blackish spiny fibres. The crown dies after flowering and fruiting. The dense crown bears massive, arching, shiny, light green leaves about 12 m long; the leaf stalks are also long; the blades have a plume-like appearance, with numerous leaflets each about 1.5 m long and tapered to a point arising in different planes and drooping.

Inflorescences are terminal, to about 2.5 m long, with large, pendulous, densely flowered branches; flowers are brownish in colour. Fruits are large, top-shaped to ellipsoid, about 6 to 12 cm long and 4 to 5 cm in diameter, with a sharp point and covered with light brown, hard, shiny, overlapping scales.

Distribution: tropical West Africa.

Reinhardtia (syn. *Malortiea*)

Delicate, slender rainforest feather palms with some unusual features make up this genus of 5 species. The palms are very small to medium-sized and are found only in Central America, from southern Mexico to northern Colombia. They are solitary or form few-stemmed clumps, the thin stems closely or distantly ringed. Sometimes the stems are partially covered in the fibrous remains of old leaf sheaths, which do not form a crownshaft. The leaves may be crowded at the top of the trunk or distributed along it. Each leaf consists of a very slender leaf stalk, almost equal in length to, or longer than the blade, which may be undivided with toothed margins and either cleft or pointed at the apex, or divided into few to many leaflets. In all but one species the leaflets are few and broad, many-ribbed and toothed, oblong to wedge-shaped, the uppermost pair fused together.

Inflorescences arise among the leaves, each consisting of a long stalk and a usually short portion with flower-bearing branchlets which turn bright orange or red after flowering. Two tubular papery bracts on the peduncle enclose the whole inflorescence in early bud. The whitish flowers are separate male and female, mostly in groups of 3 enclosed by a pointed bract, with 1 female between 2 male flowers, or in pairs or solitary towards the ends of branchlets. Male flowers have 3 sepals, 3 larger pointed petals with edges touching in bud, 8 to 40 stamens and no sterile pistil. Female flowers have 3 sepals sometimes joined at the base, 3 petals overlapping in bud except at the tips, sterile stamens fused into a toothed ring which is attached to the petals, and an egg-shaped or ellipsoid ovary which has 3 cells each with 1 ovule and is terminated by a fleshy 3-lobed stigma. Normally only 1 ovule develops into a seed.

Fruits are egg-shaped or ellipsoid, blackish when ripe, 1-seeded with the remains of stigma prominent and often spine-like at the apex. The mesocarp is thin, containing flattened fibres, and the endocarp is very thin and papery. The seed surface is often grooved by sunken veins, and the endosperm is ruminate or non-ruminate depending on the species.

HABITAT, USES, CULTIVATION   *Reinhardtia* species are all inhabitants of tropical rainforest undergrowth, mostly near sea level, though one species is found at altitudes of up to 1600 m. They grow on mountain slopes and valley floors, often on the banks of streams but apparently not in poorly drained situations.

Cultivation of these delicate small palms is possible outdoors only in warm climates, in a very sheltered position where a high level of moisture and humidity can be maintained. Exposure to direct sun should be avoided, and soil should have a high humus content. Including as they do some of the smallest known palms, with very graceful and curious foliage, members of this genus have considerable value as indoor plants. However, they seem fussy about levels of light, temperature and humidity (as compared with, say, *Chamae-dorea* species), as well as potting medium, which should be very open and freely draining.

Reinhardtia are readily grown from seed, which germinates readily in as little as six weeks with sufficient warmth.

R. gracilis (syn. *Malortiea gracilis*) Window Palm
The Window Palm is a variable species within which 4 fairly distinct geographical varieties are recognized. Stems are clustering or sometimes solitary, to 2.5 m tall and 14 mm diameter, with much of the upper part sheathed closely by the brown fibrous bases of the leaves which arise at fairly wide intervals on the stem. Leaf stalks are very thin, from as little as 7 to as much as 60 cm long; blades are 15 to 30 cm long, often wider than long, with 2 to 4 pairs of leaflets positioned opposite one another. The leaflets are broadly wedge-shaped, coarsely toothed at the apex, and with small holes or "windows" at their bases between the main veins. Inflorescences are equal to or slightly longer than the leaves, with a varying number of short branchlets. Fruits are green ripening to black, ellipsoid to obovoid, 8 to 16 mm long, with a protuberance at the apex which may be small or large.
Distribution: southern Mexico, and Central America as far as Costa Rica.

The plant pictured above is *R. gracilis* var. *gracilior*, found in southern Mexico, Honduras, Guatemala and Belize and distinguished by its small size (under 1 m tall, stems 4 to 7 mm in diameter), its short, broad leaflets, and fruit 12 to 14 mm long with small apical protuberance.

Rhapidophyllum

Consisting of a single species which is low-growing and very cold-tolerant, this genus is native to south-eastern U.S.A., from South Carolina to Florida and westward to Mississippi. It is a small clump-forming fan palm with the stem erect or creeping and freely producing roots and suckers from its base. The prostrate to upright stems are covered with leaf-bases from which arise dark fibres mixed with black erect spines. At the top the sheath apexes are shredded into brown ribbons. The medium-sized crown consists of erect leaves with slender leaf stalks 60 to 100 cm long, toothed along the margins; the metre-wide palmate blades are glossy green above and covered by silvery-white scales beneath; they are fan shaped and divided almost to the base into tapered, stiffly spreading segments, varying in width, each with one to several main veins and jaggedly toothed at the apex.

The irregularly produced inflorescences are short, not elongating much beyond the leaf bases, each with very short, crowded branches and a number of overlapping bracts enclosing it in bud. Flowers are tiny, yellow or orange to purple. Usually the male and female are borne on separate plants, but sometimes bisexual flowers or separate male and female flowers appear on the same plant. The two are fairly similar in appearance; the 3 sepals and 3 petals are free; the ovary is divided to the base into 3 segments, each egg-shaped with the apex tapering into a short stigma; the stamens of the male flowers are similar to but usually longer than those of the female flowers. The fruits are egg-shaped to spherical, brown, about 2.5 cm long, often with a small spine near the apex, and with a thin fleshy mesocarp layer.

HABITAT, USES, CULTIVATION   This species grows chiefly in wooded, often swampy areas in rich, moist, sandy, chalky or clay soils in shaded positions. In its natural habitat this palm is becoming rare.

Growth is slow and as a result this palm has received limited attention for cultivation. Germination of seed takes from 6 months to 2 years or more; generally, most plants cultivated in the United States have been obtained from the wild, an undesirable practice.

For landscaping purposes this palm has a similar use to that of the clump-forming *Serenoa* but can withstand lower temperatures, and more shade. It is unsuited to tropical climates.

R. hystrix Needle Palm
For description see above under genus.

Rhapis

These are most decorative, small, clump-forming fan palms. The genus of about 12 species occurs on the mainland of eastern Asia, from southern China to Thailand with the greatest number of species in Indo-China. Most are poorly known, even to botanists. The palms have numerous slender, cane-like stems which arise closely together from underground rhizomes and are covered with matted brown fibres from the leaf sheaths, weathering to a greyish colour. The small leaves are widely spaced along the stem, or rarely crowded at the apex. The leaf stalks are very slender and either smooth or minutely toothed along the margins; the blades are small and palmate, divided right to the leaf stalk into rather few radiating segments. Each segment is contracted at the apex, has several main veins and is finely pleated, with minute toothing along the edges and small irregular teeth at the tip.

The inflorescences, which arise from the upper leaf sheaths, are male and female on separate plants and usually pinkish at flowering stage. Each consists of a slender stalk, a short rhachis and a varying number of flower-bearing branchlets. Each inflorescence is covered in early bud by 2 thin papery bracts, the lower outer one long and tubular in the lower part and spreading above, and the upper one with a shorter tubular part. The small flowers are arranged spirally and singly along the branchlets. Male flowers have 3 sepals joined into a cup shape in the lower part, 3 petals joined at the base into a tube with the edges of the broader upper ends touching in bud, 6 stamens arranged in 2 rows, and a minute sterile ovary which may consist of 3 separate segments. The female flowers have similar petals and sepals to the male, except that the calyx (sepals) has a fleshy elongated base, 6 small sterile stamens, and 3 1-celled ovaries, joined only at the very base and each with a small style and stigma. Fruits are 1 to 3-seeded, globose to egg-shaped when single-seeded, but deeply lobed when 2 or 3-seeded, each lobe containing a seed and appearing like a separate fruit. The remains of the tiny style is found at the apex. The mesocarp of the fruit is fleshy with some fibres; the outer seed case is thin and the seed is intruded from the base by spongy seed coat; the endosperm is not ruminate.

HABITAT, USES, CULTIVATION   These palms are forest-dwellers from subtropical and tropical areas of better rainfall; the 2 widely cultivated species were brought many years ago from China where they were already in cultivation. *Rhapis* species are most decorative small palms being useful for planting in many situations, for example adjoining buildings (with ample space for them to spread as they can grow into quite large clumps). They are particularly suited for use as potted specimens as they have a graceful shape and may be used both outdoors and indoors, growing happily in low light conditions. Pots should be large enough to allow additional stems to develop and plants should be repotted when they fill their containers.

Although *Rhapis* species will grow in full sun, the leaves tend to become yellow and ends of segments often become brown, except in very humid climates. When grown in a partly shaded, protected position with ample soil moisture, the leaves are a rich green colour. They are particularly useful palms for warm shaded areas. Seed is not usually available, but when obtainable it is germinated in the usual manner and takes 2 to 3 months or more, depending upon temperature. Being clump-forming plants which continue to form new stems, they may be propagated by the division of older plants; the divided plants are often slow in re-establishing themselves.

R. excelsa (syn. *R. flabelliformis*) Lady Palm
A dense, clump-forming palm, growing to several metres across with up to several hundred slender, crowded stems to around 2.5 m tall, and 15 to 25 mm diameter. Most new stems are produced from the outer edges of the clump in the manner of bamboo, hence the common name Bamboo Palm which is sometimes applied to this species as an alternative to Lady Palm. The stems are covered between the leaf stalks with matted, ragged brown fibres which weather to grey. Leaves are about 60 to 70 cm long, spaced widely along the stems; leaf stalks are 30 to 35 cm long; blades 30 to 35 cm across, divided to the base into 4 to 10 radiating, dark glossy green segments usually unequal in width, truncate and toothed at the apex. Flowers are pinkish-cream, on stiff, short, branched inflorescences among the upper leaf bases. Fruits are small, spherical, white, with juicy flesh, about 7 mm in diameter.
Distribution: uncertain; believed to be somewhere in southern China but never found growing wild.

R. humilis Slender Lady Palm
A clump-forming palm closely resembling *R. excelsa*, growing 2 to 3 m across at the base with stems more closely

Rhapis excelsa

158

crowded, 2 to 6 m high and 15 to 25 mm in diameter. Fibres covering the stems are paler, more closely woven and less ragged in appearance than in *R. excelsa*. Leaves are similar in size to *R. excelsa* but with mostly 15 to 20 segments which are slightly drooping, narrow, mid-green and less glossy, tapered almost to a point at the apex. Inflorescences are larger with more numerous branches and longer stalks slightly woolly. Female flowers, and fruits, are unknown, hence all cultivated plants in the world are the result of vegetative propagation from the one clone.

Distribution: uncertain; introduced from plants cultivated in China.

Rhapis humilis

159

Rhopalostylis

These small to medium feather palms make interesting and unusual specimens. There are 2 species in this South Pacific genus, one native in New Zealand, the other represented by one variety in Norfolk Island and another in the Kermadec Islands. They have solitary, smooth, grey to greenish trunks which are prominently and closely ringed. The sheathing bases of the strongly ascending leaves form a short rather bulbous green crownshaft. The leaves have very short stalks, a strong, stout midrib and crowded, evenly spaced, forward-pointing leaflets with acute tips. Small brown scales are found on the undersides of the leaflets and midribs.

Inflorescences are produced freely from below the crownshaft once a trunk height of about 1.5 m is reached. Each has a short thick stalk from which arise two interlocking bracts of equal size, rather short and broad, which sheath the whole inflorescence in bud and are cast off together just as the flowers begin opening. The thick fleshy angular branches of the inflorescence and the crowded flowers are a pale mauve colour. Flowers are in groups of two male and one female arranged spirally on the branches or paired or solitary males only on the upper parts. Male flowers are asymmetric, with 3 very narrow sepals, 3 keeled petals, their edges touching in bud, 6 stamens, and a cylindrical sterile pistil. Female flowers are shorter with 3 sepals, 3 petals, their edges overlapping in the lower part but touching in bud at tips, no sterile stamens, and a 1-celled ovary with 1 ovule and a 3-lobed stigma. Fruits are small, red, spherical to slightly conical or ovoid, with fleshy and fibrous mesocarp and an ellipsoid seed with non-ruminate endosperm. The embryo is at the base of the seed.

HABITAT, USES, CULTIVATION   *Rhopalostylis* species grow chiefly in protected dense lowland forest areas, usually not very far from the sea. They need a mild, warm-temperate climate and a plentiful supply of moisture.

The leaves of the New Zealand species were used extensively by the Maoris for covering the walls and roofs of their dwellings, and the leaflets were used for basket weaving; the soft growing apex of the palm was used as a source of food.

Cultivation is easy in a suitably moist climate without extremes of temperature, though growth is slow. Exposure to hot dry winds will result in burning of the leaves. The very erect growth of their deep green leaves, and the dense crowding of the leaflets make these palms interesting subjects for cultivation. They are readily propagated from fresh seed which is freely produced and normally takes 2 to 3 months to germinate.

R. sapida Nikau Palm

The Nikau Palm is slender, with a trunk rarely exceeding 8 m in height and about 10 cm in diameter, dark grey and very closely and prominently ringed. The very narrow crown has a smooth green crownshaft about 30 cm long and about 12 to 16 very straight, erect leaves about 1.5 to 2 m long, crowded together, giving the palm a feather-duster-like appearance. The midrib of the leaf is often slightly twisted. Inflorescences are 25 to 40 cm long, stiff and spreading in flower, somewhat drooping in fruit. Fruits are almost spherical to ovoid, 8 to 12 mm long and 7 to 8 mm in diameter.
Distribution: New Zealand.

Rhopalostylis sapida

R. baueri

A fairly robust palm with greyish, closely ringed trunk to 10 or 12 m high, 15 to 20 cm in diameter. The crown is somewhat spreading, with a green crownshaft about 50 cm long, its surface thinly coated with brown scurfy material. The leaves are up to 3 or 4 m long, straight and ascending or somewhat arching; leaflets are also slightly arching. Inflorescences are 50 cm or more long with drooping branches, pendulous in fruit. Fruits are almost spherical, slightly conical, about 12 mm in diameter.

Distribution: Norfolk Island (var. *baueri*); Kermadec Islands (var. *cheesemanii*).

Roystonea (syn. *Oreodoxa*)

Stately, very tall feather palms make up this genus of about 6 species which occurs mainly in the West Indies, but also the southern tip of Florida, south-eastern Mexico, and along the central northern coastline of South America. They are robust palms with a smooth, solitary, ringed trunk, commonly swollen towards the midpoint or in the lower section to varying degrees, or of even width throughout. The trunk is surmounted by a long smooth crownshaft formed from the sheathing leaf bases. The crown is dense with long arching leaves; the leaf stalks are short and stout and the blades have numerous long, narrow leaflets, tapered to a pointed apex. In one species the 2 ranks of leaflets arise from the midrib in the same plane, giving the leaf a flattened appearance, while in the remainder the leaflets arise in different planes, giving the leaf a plume-like appearance.

The inflorescences are below the crownshaft and are long and branched. In bud they are are enclosed in 2 bracts, the lower, outer one short and the upper, inner one large with a pointed apex, the inflorescences in bud growing in an erect manner and presenting a horn-like appearance before opening. The bracts are later shed.

The small flowers, which are white to yellow, are male or female and are arranged in groups of 3 in the lower part of the branchlets with 1 female flower between 2 male and, in the upper part, male flowers only. Male flowers have 3 overlapping sepals and 3 petals with edges touching in bud; there are usually 6 stamens and a small sterile pistil. Female flowers have 3 overlapping sepals and 3 petals joined in the lower part with the edges touching towards the apex; the ovary is 1-celled with 1 ovule, the stigma is sessile with 3 thickened points.

The fruits are almost spherical to ellipsoid with the old stigma attached near the base on one side. The mesocarp layer is thin and fleshy with weak fibres; seed endosperm is ruminate. Fruits are small and produced in large numbers.

HABITAT, USES, CULTIVATION   These palms occur chiefly in lowland areas, often in patches of rainforest, in swampy places, often with brackish water, and along streams; also in tropical regions of high rainfall, often close to the sea.

Cultivation of *Roystonea* species is widely carried out in lowland tropical areas, their imposing appearance making them suitable for individual specimen planting, or in avenue and feature groupings. In warm tropical areas with a plentiful supply of water, growth is fairly rapid; however, outside the tropics, although they may be successful in warmer protected

positions, their growth is usually slow and not always satisfactory.

Propagation is from seed which takes about 2 months to germinate.

R. oleracea (syn. *Oreodoxa oleracea*) Caribbean Royal Palm
A very tall palm with a robust, smooth, ringed, greyish to greyish-green trunk about 30 to 40 m high and 40 to 60 cm in diameter, of fairly even diameter though tapering slightly to the long, smooth, shiny green crownshaft, about 2 m long. The leaves are large, about 5 to 7 m long, with a stout, short leaf stalk about 60 cm long; leaflets are light green, crowded along the midrib with the 2 ranks in the same plane or presenting a slightly plume-like appearance.

Inflorescences are below the crownshaft, 1 m or more long, much branched with undulate branches and branchlets and numerous small cream flowers. Fruits are small, oblong, slightly flattened, 15 to 20 mm long and 8 to 10 mm in diameter. They are purplish-black and produced in large numbers.
Distribution: Venezuela and islands of the southern Caribbean.

R. regia (syn. *Oreodoxa regia*) Cuban Royal Palm
A tall robust palm with a greyish to greyish-green trunk to about 25 m high and about 60 cm diameter, swollen in the midpoint, often tapering in the lower part but enlarging again close to the ground. The crownshaft is shiny green, about 2 m or more, and often partly obscured by the lower drooping leaves. The leaves are about 3 to 4 m long with stout leaf stalks, about 60 cm in length. Leaflets are light green, crowded along the midrib and arising in different planes, and thus giving the leaves a plume-like appearance.

Inflorescences are about 1 m long, with branches and branchlets relatively straight. Fruits are almost spherical, small, about 8 to 12 mm long, reddish-brown to purplish and borne in large numbers.
Distribution: Cuba.

Sabal

Sun-loving, very hardy fan palms which grow well in sandy or swampy soil. Most *Sabal* species have a useful place in landscape planting. There are approximately 15 species in the genus which includes a large proportion of the palms native to the U.S.A. and extends from North Carolina to Florida, Texas, Mexico, Guatemala, Venezuela and the West Indies.

The solitary trunks of these palms may be almost a metre in diameter and 25 m or more high, or subterranean and branched, or very short. The trunk, without a crownshaft, may be smooth to rough and ringed or with the persistent, split, interlaced leaf bases remaining attached. The crown has numerous large leaves, deep green to greyish, with stout leaf stalks, smooth margins and a broad base which is split into a distinct Y shape where it joins the trunk. The leaf blades are broad and mostly costapalmate, often curved, undulate and with the costa arched downward, and divided to about half their depth into broad segments, each of which is further subdivided into 2 slender, often drooping, pointed lobes, often with thread-like fibres adhering to the margins.

The large inflorescences arising among the leaf bases are much branched and have a number of tightly overlapping, smooth, greenish bracts. The flowers are small and bisexual;

Roystonea regia

the 3 sepals are fused into a cup; the 3 petals are fused into a tube in the lower part with the upper free parts often long and narrow. There are 6 stamens, a 3-angled ovary with 3 cells, a single column-shaped style and small circular stigma.

The fruits are spherical or almost spherical, the mesocarp thin and dry; frequently 2 or 3-lobed fruits occur where more than 1 ovule has developed. The seed has a shiny brown coat and is spherical to flattened and slightly hollowed out at the base.

The endosperm is not ruminate.

HABITAT, USES, CULTIVATION   *Sabal* species grow chiefly in low-lying or swampy areas where they may occur in large stands with other forest vegetation. They are inhabitants of subtropical to tropical regions and often occur in areas subject to seasonal rainfall, frequently with long dry seasons.

These fan palms which, apart from *S. minor*, are tall growing plants with large fan-shaped leaves, require ample space to be shown to advantage. The United States species at least are hardy and will grow under a range of conditions. As with most other fan palms, growth is slow, particularly in the younger stages. For best results a deep soil with a plentiful supply of moisture is required. *S. minor* is suited to cultivation in containers.

Propagation is carried out from seed which germinates readily, usually taking from 2 to 3 months from the time of sowing. As plants are deep rooted, potting on should be carried out while the palms are still small.

S. causiarum Puerto Rican Hat Palm
A large palm with a massive trunk, smooth and ringed, 10 to 20 m high, 60 to 100 cm in diameter. The dense crown has numerous large leaves 3 to 4 m long. Leaf stalks are 1.5 to 2.5 m in length, blades are light green, folded inwards, to 2 m across, strongly costapalmate and arched downwards, divided to about half their depth into numerous segments with drooping tips. White flowers are borne on large, much-branched inflorescences which arise among the leaf bases, equal to or exceeding the length of the leaves. Fruits are spherical to slightly pear-shaped, about 10 to 12 mm in diameter, dark brown to almost black.
Distribution: Puerto Rico.

S. mauritiiformis Savannah Palm
The Savannah Palm is a tall-growing palm with a fairly smooth, brownish, ringed, solitary trunk to about 20 m high and 20 to 25 cm in diameter, usually with a few dead leaf bases persisting below the crown. The crown is dense with numerous mid-green leaves, shiny above and bluish-greyish beneath; leaf stalks are 1 to 1.5 m long; leaf blades 1 to 1.5 m across, strongly costapalmate, deeply folded, evenly divided to about two-thirds to three-quarters their depth into long, drooping, tapered segments.

Flowers are cream on much-branched inflorescences, almost as long as the leaves. Fruits are spherical or taper slightly towards the base, 8 to 12 mm in diameter, brown to black.
Distribution: Central America, South America (only in Colombia and Venezuela), Trinidad.

S. mexicana (syn. S. texana) Mexican Palmetto
The Mexican Palmetto or Texas Palmetto is a large robust palm with a rough trunk, commonly with persistent leaf

Sabal causiarum

Sabal mauritiiformis

Sabal mexicana

bases, at least on the upper part, to about 20 m high and 60 cm in diameter. The crown is dense; leaves are large and greyish-green, 2 to 3 m long. The leaf stalks are stiff, 1 to 1.5 m in length; leaf blades are 1 m or more, strongly costapalmate, undulate and divided to about three-quarters their depth into numerous drooping segments.

Flowers are white. Inflorescences are sometimes equal to or longer than the leaf stalks. The dark brown or black fruits are rounded, somewhat flattened at the base, about 12 to 20 mm in diameter, often twinned.

Distribution: Mexico, Texas (only on the Rio Grande), Guatemala.

S. minor Dwarf or Blue Palmetto

A small palm with an underground or short rough trunk with persistent leaf bases 25 to 30 cm diameter. Leaves are palmate to slightly costapalmate, bluish grey to glossy green, about 2 m long; petiole about 1 m, blade flat to slightly inward-folded, 60 to 100 cm broad, divided to about half way into stiff, pointed segments, collapsing at base and hanging downwards as they age. Flowers white on much-branched inflorescences above leaves. Inflorescences erect on long peduncles, up to twice as tall as the leaves. Fruit globular to 12 mm diameter, dark brown.

Distribution: south-eastern U.S.A. over an extensive area.

S. palmetto Palmetto, Cabbage Palm

A tall robust palm, the Palmetto has a trunk 6 to 25 m or more tall and 30 to 45 cm in diameter. The trunk may be smooth, ringed and greyish or rough, covered with interlaced,

Sabal palmetto

Sabal minor

persistent leaf bases. The crown is dense and compact. Leaves are large, light green with stout leaf stalks 1 to 1.5 m long. Leaf blades are strongly costapalmate, arched downwards, distinctly undulate and divided into numerous stiff or drooping segments to about half the depth of the blades.

Flowers are white to cream on a much-branched inflorescence, carried on a long stalk and arising amongst the leaf bases. The inflorescences are generally about as long as the leaves. Fruits are round with a somewhat tapering base, about 8 to 12 mm in diameter, brown to black in colour.
Distribution: south-eastern U.S.A.

S. princeps

A large robust palm with a rough, brown ringed trunk or with interlaced leaf bases attached, 20 m or more high and 40 to 50 cm in diameter. The crown is open to fairly dense with very large leaves; leaf stalks are stout, 2 m or more long; blades 2 m or more broad, undulate and divided into numerous segments with the divided sections drooping.

White flowers on long, branched, drooping inflorescences arise among the leaf bases. Fruits are globulose, tapered towards the stalk, about 15 mm in diameter, brown to black.
Distribution: West Indies, exact origin unknown.

S. yapa

A medium-sized palm, with trunk to 10 m tall, usually less, about 20 to 25 cm in diameter, roughly ringed, sometimes with persistent leaf bases on the upper part. The crown is moderately open. The stalks of the erect to drooping leaves are over 1 m long, usually longer than the leaf blades. The blades are bright green and divided nearly to the base into many stiff, narrow segments, these each apparently divided and then divided again into narrow, fine-pointed lobes. Inflorescences are usually much longer than the leaves, profusely branched. The flowers are white; fruits are spherical to slightly pear-shaped, 9 to 11 mm in diameter, sometimes 2 or 3-seeded.
Distribution: Cuba.

Salacca

Spiny, clump-forming feather palms comprise this genus of 14 species, occurring in tropical South-East Asia, Sumatra, Java, Borneo and the Philippines. The palms are stemless, or almost so; their crowns consist of a number of long, arched leaves, crowded at their base. The leaf stalks are long and spiny; the blades have numerous broad to narrow, lance-shaped to oblong, several-veined leaflets, which taper to a curved apex (or in a few species leaves are completely undivided). The leaflets are variably arranged, often in groups of 2 or 3, and may arise in 1 or more than 1 plane.

Inflorescences arise among the leaf bases with separate male and female flowers on different plants. The inflorescences are covered by several incomplete papery bracts which become lacerated and divided to the base into a number of ragged sections. The male inflorescences have several branches on which are crowded numerous small flowers arranged in pairs and enclosed by bracts, with an additional hairy to woolly bracteole beneath the 3 thin sepals which are round at the base. The 3 petals are longer than the sepals. They are united into a fleshy tube at the base and are thin in

Sabal yapa

the upper part. There are 6 stamens and the sterile pistil is minute. Female inflorescences have fewer branches than the male with few flowers which are solitary or in pairs, often with 1 flower sterile, and are subtended by bracts. The female flowers are larger than the male and have 3 thin sepals; the 3 petals, longer than the sepals, are united at the base into an urn-like shape, the upper part with edges touching in bud. There are 6 sterile stamens; the ovary is 3-celled with 3 ovules and its surface is covered with scales which may be prolonged into bristles; the style is short with 3 lobed stigmas. Fruits are spherical, egg to top-shaped with 1 to 3 seeds, each covered with a fleshy, edible layer, or aril; the outer surface is covered with overlapping scales, sometimes extended into long flexible spines or bristles.

HABITAT, USES, CULTIVATION   These tropical palms grow in rich soils in moist shaded forests, often occurring in swampy areas and along streams where they may form impenetrable thickets.

Apart from *S. zalacca*, which is commonly grown for the acid-tasting fruit, these prickly palms are little cultivated, except in tropical botanic gardens.

Propagation is by seed which has to be fresh and takes 2 to 3 months to germinate.

S. zalacca (syn. *S. edulis*)

A variable clump-forming palm; leaves are about 4 to 5 m long, with the leaf stalks about 2 m, armed with large, flattened spines. The leaf blades have a number of broad leaflets, tapered to the apex, shiny green above, greyish beneath. They are irregularly arranged along the midrib, often in pairs.

Inflorescences are branched, without spines. Male inflorescences are drooping, about 50 to 100 cm long. Female inflorescences, 20 to 30 cm long, have crowded, stout, erect spikes. Fruits are egg-shaped or almost spherical, reddish-brown to purplish-brown, covered with scales, sometimes with bristly extensions.

Distribution: Malay Archipelago; exact origin uncertain.

Scheelea

There are 28 species of these feather palms which commonly grow to a great size. The genus is widely distributed in tropical America, from Paraguay to southern Mexico. Some botanists have combined with it closely allied genera such as *Attalea, Orbignya* and others.

These robust palms have a tall, solitary, smooth trunk, ringed or wholly or partly covered with old leaf bases, or with a short or almost no trunk. There is no crownshaft; the dense crown consists of leaves 5 to 10 m long with conspicuous broad bases pressed close against the trunk, and flexible fibres extending along the margins and on to the short leaf stalks when present. The blades have numerous long, linear leaflets crowded along the midrib, arranged singly, or commonly in clusters, frequently becoming brown and pendulous in the upper part.

Inflorescences arise among the leaf bases; they are once-branched only, with numerous slender branchlets, and are enclosed in bud stage by 2 bracts, the lower one tubular and the upper, inner one large and spindle-shaped with vertical furrows and extended into a long pointed apex, splitting down one side to release the flowers and remaining on the tree. There are separate male and female flowers; the few female (rarely up to 20) are clustered toward the base of each branchlet usually with 1 between 2 male; the remainder of each branchlet carries only male flowers, which are frequently sterile (sometimes whole plants have only functional male or female flowers). Male flowers are numerous and usually spirally arranged, or sometimes confined to one side of the branchlet; each has 3 tiny sepals and 3 elongated club-shaped to cylindrical petals with edges touching in bud; the 6 stamens are short and straight; sterile pistil is absent or very minute. Female flowers are large, each subtended by 2 bracts, with 3 large overlapping sepals and 3 petals overlapped in a rolled manner, becoming larger as they open; sterile stamens are united in a ring around the ovary which has 3 or sometimes more cells, each with 1 ovule; the style is very short or absent and stigmas are 3 to 6-branched.

The fruits are large, ovoid, 4 to 10 cm long, with perianth and ring of sterile stamens remaining attached at the base; the fruits consist of a fibrous outer layer and a fleshy and fibrous inner mesocarp layer. The 1 to 5 seeds are enclosed in a very thick, dense, woody endocarp, each seed in its own cavity. Seed endosperm is non-ruminate.

HABITAT, USES, CULTIVATION   These palms occur on coastal plains, valleys, or foothills up to about 1000 m or more in altitude. They grow in woodlands, forests or grasslands, sometimes in large stands, frequently in flat areas along streams. Often they are found in regions of strongly seasonal rainfall, and their bases may be inundated throughout the wet season; some species grow in permanently swampy ground.

In their native regions the leaves are used for thatching, or for weaving into various articles; the trunks are used for constructional purposes, the young apex is eaten and sap which collects in the cavity left by its removal is fermented to yield an alcoholic beverage. Fruits and seeds are eaten by cattle and oil is extracted from the seed endosperm and used in soap and toiletries.

These large feather palms are sometimes used in warmer areas for avenue planting and as large specimen plants. The great size of the palms and the habit of the leaf ends commonly turning brown may not appeal to many growers. They are for tropical areas with a plentiful supply of moisture. Propagation is from seed, which germinates in 2 to 3 months.

S. butyracea

A large robust palm, with solitary grey, smooth, ringed trunk 10 to 30 m tall and 40 cm or more in diameter. The crown is very dense with large erect leaves 5 m or more long; leaf stalks are absent, leaf bases broad and erect; blades have numerous broad leaflets crowded along the midrib, not clustered, with both ranks directed inwards. Inflorescences are among the leaf bases, each with a large fluted bract. Fruits are egg-shaped, 4 to 5 cm long, 2 to 5 cm broad.
Distribution: Colombia, Venezuela.

Schippia

This genus with only a single species occurs in Guatemala and Belize and is a slender fan palm with a ringed solitary trunk. The crown is of open growth; leaf stalks are slender and flexible, without spines on the margins and with brown fibres at the base, which is split into a Y shape; the blades are palmate, circular in outline, and cupped upwards, being

Scheelea butyracea

divided almost to the petiole into radiating tapering segments, which are further divided at the apex.

Inflorescences arise among the leaf bases with several branches, enclosed by tubular bracts and with a number of branchlets. The single flowers are spirally arranged. Flowers are male and female on the one plant with bisexual flowers towards the base of the branchlet and flowers in the upper part which appear similar but are functionally male only. Each flower is on a slender stalk and has 3 sepals and 3 petals with edges touching in bud. There are 6 stamens; the ovary is 1-celled. The distinct style expands into a 1-sided stigma. Fruits are round, with the remains of the stigma at the apex and a thin, fleshy mesocarp. The seed endosperm is slightly hollowed out at the base and not ruminate.

HABITAT, USES, CULTIVATION   This palm occurs as an understorey plant in wet, moist lowland forest at about 200 m or less above sea-level.

In cultivation it is a slender, attractive fan palm suitable as a small specimen in a warm, moist, protected position or as a pot plant. Propagation is from seed.

S. concolor

A small, slender fan palm with a ringed trunk about 10 m high and 10 cm in diameter. The crown is open; leaf stalks are slender, flexible, 2 m long; blades are palmate, about 1 m broad, light green, circular, cupped upwards, densely divided into radiating, tapered segments.

Inflorescences are 60 cm long, branched, with numerous small flowers. Fruits are globular, 25 mm in diameter, white in colour
Distribution: Belize (formerly British Honduras), Guatemala.

Serenoa

A single species, *S. repens*, comprises this genus, occurring in south-eastern U.S.A. from South Carolina to the Florida Keys and westward to Alabama and Mississippi. A low-growing, clump-forming fan palm, it often has stems entirely underground or sometimes with erect to oblique or over-arching rough, shaggy trunks to 3 m long. The crown of each stem is small but together they may form a large cluster. The bluish-green to yellowish-green leaves are erect to spreading, with slender leaf stalks about 1 m long and distinctly toothed along the margins. The leaf blades are palmate with a waxy coating, 50 to 100 cm across, erect, undulate and deeply divided into stiff segments, each of which is further subdivided at the apex.

The short, much-branched inflorescences arise among the leaf bases and are sheathed in bud in a series of narrow, overlapping, tubular bracts, persisting on the rhachis. The branchlets bear numerous white flowers which are bisexual and quite conspicuous; each has 3 sepals joined into a tube which is 3-lobed at the apex, 3 free petals much longer than the sepals and becoming recurved, 6 stamens joined into a ring at the base, and an ovary of 3 separate lobes, joined at the top into a single elongated style with minute stigma at the apex. Each ovary-lobe has 1 cell with 1 ovule, but only 1 of the 3 ovules develops into a seed. Fruits are ovoid, bluish to bluish-black, 20 mm long and 12 mm broad with thick, oily mesocarp which becomes unpleasant-smelling with age. Seeds are ovoid, somewhat flattened and sculptured on one side; the endosperm is non-ruminate.

HABITAT, USES, CULTIVATION   This palm occurs in low-growing scrub on flat land, often near the sea and in its natural habitat may form dense thickets.

The fruits were eaten by the Indians of its native region. They are now used as a health-food or herbal medicine, being thought by some to have therapeutic properties.

This low-growing fan palm is an attractive dwarf clustering palm for warm-temperate and subtropical conditions in coastal areas. It will withstand occasional quite heavy frosts.

Another dwarf fan palm *Sabal minor* occurs naturally in the same areas, but *Serenoa* is easily distinguished from it by the spiny edges of the leaf stalks and the shorter inflorescences of conspicuous white flowers. Both palms require similar conditions for cultivation. Seed germinates within 2 to 3 months of sowing. Clumps are not easily transplanted or divided.

S. repens (syn. *Sabal serrulata*) Saw Palmetto
For description see above under genus.

Syagrus

Low-growing to quite tall and very slender to robust feather palms form this genus of about 34 species closely related to *Butia* and *Arecastrum*. They usually have a solitary trunk, sometimes multiple or below ground; the trunk is smooth and ringed or covered with leaf bases particularly on the upper part. The crown, without a crownshaft, may be open to dense, with spreading leaves; the bases of the leaf stalks are expanded and extended down the trunk with fibres from the leaf sheaths amongst the bases and extending along the margins to varying degrees; the blades have a number of narrow, tapered leaflets evenly or unevenly distributed along the midrib, sometimes in clusters and directed outwards in different planes giving the leaf a plume-like appearance.

The inflorescences arise from the leaf bases with one main branch (rarely unbranched) with a few to a number of branchlets. They are enclosed in bud stage in 2 bracts, a lower outer, tubular, flattened bract and a large, woody, spindle-shaped inner bract with distinct vertical fluting, splitting down one side to release the flowers. Flowers are separate male and female, with the latter commonly on the lower part of the branchlets between 2 male flowers and with male flowers only on the upper part. Male flowers have sepals much shorter than petals, with edges touching in bud, 6 stamens and a small sterile pistil. Female flowers are ovoid to elongate-pyramidal with sepals and petals rolled together; the sterile stamens are in a small ring and the ovary is 3-celled with a single pistil and 3 stigmas. Fruits are spherical to egg-shaped with a fibrous, dry or fleshy mesocarp; the seed is enclosed in a woody endocarp with 3 pores near the base and 3 shiny dark brown bands extending from the pores to the apex on the inner surface; the endosperm is white, non-ruminate, with a central cavity.

HABITAT, USES, CULTIVATION   Species of *Syagrus* grow chiefly among shrubby vegetation to woodland, often on rocky ridges in tropical and subtropical areas with highly seasonal rainfall.

Leaves of larger species are used for thatching and the trunk for constructional purposes, spears etc. The fruit is used for feeding cattle in some areas and sometimes some of the more fleshy fruits are eaten by humans.

Some workers have included *Butia*, *Arecastrum*, and *Microcoelum* under *Syagrus*, which increases the number of species; however, this view is not accepted by other authorities.

Generally these feather palms are not widely cultivated as they are not highly ornamental and require warm conditions, and plants such as *Arecastrum* and *Butia* can provide similar effects and are more adaptable.

Propagation is from seed which is said to take from 3 to 12 months to germinate.

S. sancona (syn. *S. tessmannii*, *Cocos sancona*)

A tall, slender feather palm. It has a smooth grey ringed solitary trunk to about 20 m tall and 15 to 20 cm in diameter with an enlarged base. Crown without a crownshaft, fairly dense, with erect to spreading leaves; leaf stalks are broader at the base with brown fibres among the bases and extending along the margins; blades have mid-green leaflets crowded along the midrib in groups of 3 to 4, extending outwards in various planes, giving the leaf a plume-like appearance.

Inflorescences are among the leaf bases, about 1 m long, with one main branch and numerous branchlets, enclosed in bud stage by a large, ribbed, spindle-shaped woody bract splitting down one side to release yellow flowers; fruits are ovoid, yellowish.

Distribution: Peru.

Thrinax

Thrinax species are attractive, small to medium-sized fan palms. This genus was formerly regarded as having 12 species, but a recent review has reduced the number to 4, one with 2 subspecies; they occur in the West Indies, Central America and the Florida Keys. The palms have a slender, solitary trunk, ringed with leaf scars and old, split leaf bases just below the crown; the trunk is often enlarged at ground level by the formation of numerous tough roots. The crown is of rather open growth, without a crownshaft. The leaves have slender flexible leaf stalks with smooth margins and the expanded bases split into a Y shape where they join the trunk, with ragged brownish-grey fibres from the old leaf sheaths amongst the bases. Leaf sheaths have a velvety covering in younger stages. Leaf blades are distinctly palmate, rather circular in outline, undulate to flat and divided to varying depths into broad segments which are further divided at the apex.

The inflorescences which arise amongst the leaf bases are erect to arched, with a number of branches, each with numerous flower-bearing branchlets; there are a number of overlapping tubular bracts, each branch being subtended by a bract. The flowers are bisexual on a slender to very short stalk, and are unlike those of most palms in that there are no separate sepals and petals, only 6 lobes on the rim of a cup-shaped perianth. There are generally 5 to 12 stamens, usually with straight, slender filaments. The ovary is single-celled, with 1 ovule and the stigma is short and funnel-shaped.

Fruits are small, globular or somewhat flattened, smooth and white when ripe, with the remains of the stigma attached at the apex. The flesh is thin and mealy; the seed is flattened at the base and intruded by the seed coat from the base, the intrusion sometimes penetrating completely through the endosperm which is not ruminate.

HABITAT, USES, CULTIVATION   Species of *Thrinax* grow in forest areas, often in thickets, frequently in well-drained soils on limestone and other alkaline types from sea level to 1200 metres; some grow in areas with distinct seasonal rainfall and long dry periods, while others are in areas of continued high rainfall, and some in positions exposed to salt-laden winds. *Thrinax* species are attractive, small fan palms for specimen planting in warmer tropical areas, being particularly suitable for cultivation in alkaline soils. *T. radiata* grows well in coastal areas where it withstands the sea spray well. As with other fan palms, growth is slow, particularly in the early stages.

Various common names are applied to different species, "Thatch Palm" being the one most frequently met with.

Propagation is from seed germination of which takes 2 to 3 months before the first lance-shaped seed leaf appears.

T. morrisii (syn. T. microcarpa) Peaberry Palm

A palm of variable size, from as little as 1 m up to occasionally 10 m tall. The trunk of the Peaberry Palm is smooth but closely and prominently ringed, pale grey, 10 to 20 cm in diameter, sometimes swollen at the base. The crown is rather open and spherical; the leaf stalks are under 1 m long, their bases covered with thin brown fibres from the sheaths, the apexes of which project upward as fibrous tongues, though not very prominent. The blades about equal the leaf stalks in length. They are circular, strongly undulate, shiny green above, silvery beneath to varying degrees. Inflorescences are erect or arching, equalling or markedly exceeding the leaves in length, with silvery-white to tan bracts and white flowers ageing quickly to orange-yellow. The white fruits are spherical, mostly 4 to 5 mm in diameter, rarely to 8 mm.
Distribution: West Indies (Leeward Islands to Cuba and Bahamas), Florida Keys.

T. radiata (syn. T. floridana) Florida Thatch Palm

A palm of variable stature, the Florida Thatch Palm is sometimes only 2 m tall but usually 5 to 10 m; the trunk is 8 to 12 cm in diameter, broadened at the base and sheathed in fibrous, old leaf bases on the upper part, smooth and ringed lower down. The crown is moderately dense, spherical or somewhat elongated, usually with a mass of dead leaves at the base. Leaf stalk bases are covered in a loose mass of fibres from leaf sheaths, the apexes of which are notched into V shapes instead of projecting as tongues as in other species. The leaf stalks are shorter than or equal to the blades, which are circular, not strongly undulate, 1.2 to 1.6 m in diameter, shiny green above, slightly paler and duller green beneath. Inflorescences are erect or slightly arching, shorter than the leaves, with white flowers. Fruits are white, spherical, 7 to 8 mm in diameter.
Distribution: West Indies (Cuba, Haiti, Jamaica), Florida (Keys and coast south-west of Miami), Central America (Honduras, Belize, far south-east Mexico).

Thrinax morrisii

Thrinax radiata

Trachycarpus

Slender, compact fan palms comprise this genus of about 6 species, occurring in China and the Himalayas. They have solitary trunks or rarely are multistemmed. The trunks are either smooth and ringed, or covered with persistent old leaf bases with densely matted fibres from the old leaf sheaths. The leaves have a slender stalk with inconspicuous toothing along the margins. Leaf blades are palmate, relatively flat and frequently divided to about half their depth into tapered, pointed segments, which are shortly and closely divided at the tips.

The inflorescences are among the leaf bases with male and female on separate plants. Both are sheathed with overlapping, whitish to brown bowl-shaped bracts. The male flowers have 3 overlapping sepals and 3 larger petals with edges touching in the upper part; there are 6 stamens and the sterile pistil consists of 3 small separate segments. The female flowers have sepals and petals similar to the male flowers, with 6 small sterile stamens and a pistil with 3 separate ovaries, each with a separate style and a minute stigma.

Fruits are either spherical, oblong or kidney-shaped and grooved slightly on the inner side with 2 small knobs towards the base representing the undeveloped ovaries. The outer skin is tough and covered with small dots, the mesocarp is thin, dryish or fleshy with numerous small gritty bodies, as in the flesh of some pears. The seed endosperm is not ruminate and is intruded on one side by the seed coat.

HABITAT, USES, CULTIVATION   These palms grow in high mountain forests, where there may be snow during the winter, and in various types of soil.

There are several species of *Trachycarpus* in cultivation although some are uncommon. *Trachycarpus fortunei*, the most widely cultivated species, is sometimes mistaken for the European palm *Chamaerops humilis*. Their compact growth makes them suitable for small gardens and they differ from most other palms in that they are able to withstand severe frosts. *Trachycarpus fortunei* is virtually the only palm which will grow successfully in cool-temperate climates, such as the British Isles; the other species are also suitable for cooler climates. These plants make attractive potted specimens grown in well-drained soil. Propagation is from seeds which germinate readily within about 2 months.

T. fortunei (syn. *Chamaerops excelsa*) Chusan Palm, Chinese Windmill Palm

Commonly known as the Chusan or Chinese Windmill Palm, this is a compact palm with a solitary, slender, brownish-grey trunk, often covered with old leaf bases, with broken-off, recurved leaf stalks at least on the upper part, and with masses of greyish-brown, loose, matted fibres. The leaves are about 1.5 m long, with a stalk 50 to 100 cm long with small toothing along the margins; the palmate blades are circular in outline and about 1 m broad, dark green above and greyish beneath, divided to more than half their depth, and at irregular intervals more deeply divided, almost to the top of the leaf stalk. The segments are stiff or frequently drooping at the tip.

The inflorescences arising among the leaves are about 70 to 80 cm long, densely flowered with yellow flowers. Fruits are kidney-shaped, 9 to 12 mm broad, pale bluish-white in colour.

Trachycarpus fortunei

Distribution: China, where it has been cultivated for centuries.

T. martianus

A slender palm with a solitary trunk about 10 to 12 m high and 15 cm in diameter. The trunk is smooth, greyish and closely ringed, usually with leaf bases persisting immediately below the crown with closely matted, greyish-brown fibres. Leaves are about 1.5 m long with a slender stalk 60 to 100 cm in length; the palmate blades are regularly divided to over half their depth into segments, each clearly divided at the apex.

Inflorescences are among the leaf bases; the male inflorescences are about 1 m long with cream flowers and the female are 1.5 m long with more widely spaced, greenish-yellow flowers. The fruits are oblong, flattened, grooved, about 12 mm long and 7 to 8 mm broad, orange coloured, with a bluish bloom.

Distribution: Eastern Himalayas from Nepal to northern Burma.

T. wagnerianus

A small fan palm with a solitary trunk growing to about 7 m high and 15 cm in diameter, somewhat resembling the trunk of *T. fortunei* but with the matted fibres closely attached. The small leaves are about 1 m long, with a short leaf stalk; the leaf blades are about 40 to 45 cm broad, stiff and leathery, with the segments irregularly divided. In young plants the tips of the segments are edged with white hairs.

Flowers are white and are carried on short branches of the inflorescences which arise among the bases of the leaves. The fruits are oblong.

This species is commonly misnamed *T. takil* and is less widely grown than other species.

Distribution: The native habitat of this palm is unknown.

Trithrinax

A genus of 5 species of unusual, attractive smallish fan palms occurring in Brazil, Uruguay, Paraguay, northern Argentina and Chile. The trunks are solitary or sometimes clump-forming, always clothed in old leaf bases with the sheaths of greyish-brown, woven, very thick fibres which project as stiff spines from the sheath margins. The compact crown consists of leaves with stiff, broad, unarmed leaf stalks; the palmate blades are divided to about half their depth or more into broad, stiff, tapered segments, in turn divided to varying degrees at their apexes into 2 stiff points which are usually pressed closely against one another.

The inflorescences which arise among the leaf bases are short and much branched and in the bud stage are covered with large cream cup-shaped bracts, which become brown and are shed progressively as flowers open. Flowers are bisexual, with the sepals joined to form a 3-lobed cup, the 3 longer petals separate and overlapping in bud. There are 6 stamens, and 3 ovaries which are quite separate, each containing 1 ovule with elongate styles terminated by small stigmas; only 1 ovary usually develops into a fruit.

Fruits are globular, cream to yellowish-green, with a thick whitish mesocarp; seed is smooth and the seed coat has a plug-like intrusion into the endosperm which is not ruminate.

HABITAT, USES, CULTIVATION   These palms are found on coastal and higher plains along the banks of streams and

Trachycarpus wagneranus

swamps or in grassland or low woodland, where they normally grow in full sunlight.

In their native habitat, hats and cloth are made from the fibres of the leaf sheath, and the fruit is frequently fermented to make an alcoholic drink. A type of cooking oil is extracted from the seeds and a reddish sago obtained from the trunk.

These small fan palms are usually cultivated in warm temperate areas and are tolerant of fairly low temperatures. They make attractive small specimen palms, though in confined spaces the spines projecting from the old leaf sheaths on the trunks may be a deterrent to their use. However, the curious patterning of these spines and their associated fibres, together with the stiff symmetry of the crowns, attracts attention and interest.

Propagation is from seed which usually takes 2 to 3 months to germinate.

T. acanthocoma

A small stiff palm with a solitary rough trunk to about 4 m high and 20 cm in diameter, covered with old leaf bases with greyish-brown coarsely woven fibres and numerous stiff, often recurved spines. The crown has about 20 leaves, each about 2 m long; the stiff leaf stalks are about 1 m in length and the palmate blades 1 m or more long, dull mid-green in colour above and with a waxy bloom beneath, divided to about half their depth into broad, pointed, sometimes drooping segments, each segment shortly bifurcated. Inflorescences are much branched, 60 to 80 cm long, with fleshy branches and cream bracts, which quickly turn brown and fall off. The flowers and branches are white. The spherical fruits are greenish-yellow to creamy-white, 2.5 mm in diameter.
Distribution: southern Brazil, possibly also Paraguay and northern Argentina.
Note: We are not completely certain as to the identification of the palm pictured here as there is some doubt as to the correct application of the name *T. acanthocoma*, the literature available being somewhat confusing on this subject.

Veitchia (syn. *Adonidia*)

Tall, slender feather palms make up this genus of about 18 species occurring in the Philippine Islands, New Hebrides, New Caledonia and Fijian Islands. The distinctly ringed, solitary trunks are surmounted by a conspicuous long tubular crownshaft formed from the bases of the leaves. The medium crowns of spreading to somewhat erect leaves are graceful and feather-like; leaflets are numerous, broad, and erect to drooping; the apex of each leaflet is toothed, obliquely-truncate to tapered and sometimes presents a ragged appearance; the leaf stalks are short and without spines.

The inflorescences are produced below the crownshaft on a stiff, thick leaf stalk and the panicles are much branched. Prior to opening, the inflorescences are enclosed in 2 stiff, papery bracts, the outer one 2-edged and tapering to a pointed apex and the inner similar but shorter in length. Both bracts are shed when flowers open. Flowers are male or female and are spirally arranged on the branchlets in groups of 3, 2 male and 1 female, the latter with 2 bracteoles. There are 3 sepals and 3 petals, the edges of both overlapping in bud in female flowers. Stamens are numerous in male flowers and

Veitchia arecina

174

the bottle-shaped sterile pistil is as long as the stamens. Female flowers have 3 to 6 sterile stamens; the ovary is 1-celled with 1 ovule and the style is thickened with 3 short stigmas. Fruits are egg-shaped, orange to red, with the remains of stigmas on the apex and with a fleshy, fibrous mesocarp layer. The seed is ellipsoid to ovoid in shape, and non-ruminate.

HABITAT, USES, CULTIVATION   Palms of this genus occur in tropical rainforests from sea level to elevations of about 650 m. In areas where *Veitchia* species occur naturally use is made of the leaves for thatching walls and buildings; the trunk is used for construction purposes, for making ribs for canoes and for spears and arrows.

These graceful palms grow fairly rapidly and are cultivated in moist tropical areas, making attractive specimen palms for locations protected from drying winds.

Propagation is from seed, germination of which takes from 1 to 2 months when fresh seed is used.

V. arecina

A slender feather palm with a closely ringed, rough greyish solitary trunk about 6 to 10 m high and 15 to 20 cm in diameter. It has an open, spreading, crown; the leaves, about 2 m long, are slightly arched. The crownshaft is creamish-green and the leaf stalks creamy coloured. The blades have broad, drooping leaflets well spaced along the midrib. The apex of each leaflet is toothed with an obliquely cut-off appearance.

Inflorescences are much branched, spreading, with smooth branchlets; flowers are greenish-cream. The red fruits are egg-shaped, 4 to 5 cm long, 3 cm in diameter.
Distribution: New Caledonia.

V. joannis

A tall feather palm with a greyish-brown ringed solitary trunk to 32 m high and 35 cm in diameter. The compact crown has arched leaves 2 to 3 m long; the crownshaft is greyish-green with leaf stalks 10 to 30 cm long. The blades have broad leaflets tapering to both ends and with a toothed apex, more or less pendulous.

Inflorescences are 50 to 60 cm long with greenish-white soft hairs on the branchlets, and somewhat pendulous panicles. Flowers are greenish to white, with stamens very numerous on male flowers. Fruits are ovoid, 5 to 6 cm long, 2 to 3 cm wide, red to crimson in colour.
Distribution: Fiji (on several islands).

V. mcdanielsii

A slender feather palm with a whitish-green, ringed, solitary trunk 25 m high and 15 cm in diameter, enlarged at the base. The crown is compact with spreading leaves to 3 m or more long. The crownshaft is whitish-green and the leaf stalks are short, creamy green in colour. The drooping blades have broad leaflets spaced along the midrib, tapered to a toothed apex.

Inflorescences are 1 m or more in length, much branched, with whitish flowers. Fruits are ovoid, about 3 to 3.5 cm long and 1.5 to 2 cm broad, bright red.
Distribution: New Caledonia.

Veitchia mcdanielsii

V. merrillii (syn. *Adonidia merrillii*)

A slender palm with a closely ringed, greyish, solitary trunk about 5 m or more high and 15 cm in diameter with an enlarged base. The crown is compact and the leaves distinctly arched; the green crownshaft has close, fine scales; and the leaf stalks are 10 to 15 cm long; the blades have broad leaflets crowded along the midrib and a toothed apex with an oblique cut-off appearance.

Inflorescences are stiff, 40 to 50 cm long, and broad on a short stalk; flowers are greenish to white. Fruits are egg-shaped, about 2.5 to 3 cm long and 1.5 to 2 cm broad, and bright crimson.
Distribution: Philippine Islands.

V. montgomeryana

A slender palm with a greyish, ringed, solitary trunk 12 m or more high and 20 cm in diameter, often enlarged at the base. The erect crown has leaves 2 to 3 m long, directed upwards. Crownshaft is bright green with a covering of greyish to rusty fine scales; leaf stalks are 20 to 26 cm long, greyish; blades have dark green rather stiff leaflets, fairly evenly spaced along the midrib, held almost horizontally on the lower part and drooping towards the upper part, tapered to both ends, with an oblique, toothed, narrow apex. Inflorescences are about 60 cm long with a thick stalk; flowers are greenish-white. The red, smooth fruits are oblong-obovate, about 4 to 5 cm long and 2 to 4 cm broad. This species was formerly included with *V. joannis*.
Distribution: Described from cultivated specimens, the origin not known but possibly the New Hebrides.

Veitchia merrillii

176

V. pedionoma

A slender palm with a brown, smooth, distinctly ringed solitary trunk 6 to 10 m high and 20 cm in diameter. The crown is light and erect; leaves are 3 to 4 m long, arched towards the apex; crownshaft is brownish-green; leaf stalks are 40 to 60 cm long and the blades have broad leaflets spaced along the midrib and crowded towards the top; leaflets are tapered to both ends with an oblique-toothed apex.

Inflorescences are 60 cm long and broad, branches and branchlets smooth, flowers white to cream. Fruits are ovoid, 13 to 15 mm long and 6 to 7 mm broad, bright orange to red. Distribution: Fiji: Vanua Levu.

V. sessilifolia

A slender palm resembling *V. pedionoma*, with a smooth, distinctly ringed greenish-brown solitary trunk 11 m high and 20 cm in diameter. The crown is light, leaves are erect and gently curved, 3 to 3.5 m long. Crownshaft is brownish-green; leaf stalks 10 to 26 cm long; blades have broad, erect to spreading leaflets tapered to both ends and an oblique-toothed apex.

Inflorescences are about 1 m long, branches and branchlets with a brown scaly covering; flowers are white to cream. Fruits are oblong-ellipsoid, 16 to 22 mm long, 8 to 11 mm in diameter, dull orange to red. Distribution: Fiji: Vanua Levu.

V. winin

A tall, slender palm with a greyish to brown, ringed, solitary trunk to 20 m or more high, 17 cm in diameter, enlarged at the base. The crown is light and spreading; the leaves are 3 to

Veitchia sessilifolia

Veitchia winin

4 m long, fairly straight; the crownshaft is long, greenish-cream; leaf stalks are 23 to 28 cm long, reddish-brown; the blades have leaflets evenly spaced along the midrib, spreading to drooping, broad, tapering to both ends, with an oblique-toothed apex.

Inflorescences are about 45 cm long with whitish branches and branchlets; flowers are white to cream. The smooth red fruits are ovoid-oblong, 18 to 19 mm long, and 9 to 10 mm in diameter.

Distribution: New Hebrides: Malekula Island.

Verschaffeltia

The 1 species of this genus, *V. splendida*, is native to the tiny Seychelles Islands, between Madagascar and Sri Lanka. It is a slender feather palm with a tall (up to 25 m but usually much less), solitary, distinctly ringed trunk with needle-like spines emerging from the trunk rings, these spines becoming fewer in number in mature palms. Stilt roots arise from the trunk about 1 m or more above the ground and grow outwards and downwards into the ground, forming a narrowly conical cluster. The compact crown has broad leaves which are distinctly curved downwards; the crownshaft is smooth in mature plants, but in younger specimens both the crownshaft and leaf stalks are spiny. The leaf stalks are short, about 25 cm; the blades are broad and undivided or irregularly and shallowly divided into broad segments in younger palms. In mature plants the blades are sometimes divided almost to the base, with the apexes of segments ragged.

The 1 to 2 m long inflorescences which arise among the leaves are much branched and each is enclosed in bud by 2 to 3 thin, overlapping bracts. The yellow flowers are separate male and female on the same plant, generally with a female flower between and below 2 male; male flowers have 3 overlapping sepals and 3 petals with edges touching in bud, 6 stamens and a short, sterile pistil. Female flowers are larger and have 3 overlapping sepals and 3 petals with edges touching in bud, 6 sterile stamens and an ovary which is 1-celled with 1 ovule.

Fruits are round, 20 to 25 mm in diameter, with remains of the stigma in a lateral position, green to brown in colour; seed endosperm is ruminate.

HABITAT, USES, CULTIVATION   This tropical palm naturally occurs on the sides of steep hills in protected rainforest areas at elevations of about 300 to 600 metres, often in rocky soils.

In the Seychelles the trunks were split and used for the walls of small buildings and for water gutters. Under cultivation this attractive palm requires humid tropical conditions with high rainfall and preferably a protected position. In cooler climates it can make a spectacular tub specimen in a hot house, but is probably unsuitable for general indoor growing in houses.

Propagation is from seed which germinates readily within 2 to 3 months under warm, humid conditions.

V. splendida

For description see above under genus.

Washingtonia

Large, vigorous, rather fast-growing and very hardy fan palms

Verschaffeltia splendida

make up this genus of 2 species which occurs naturally in north-western Mexico, 1 species extending just over the border into south-western U.S.A. They have solitary robust trunks which are swollen at the base and may be very tall and covered with a dense, close skirt or thatch of old leaves, or are grey, rough and closely ringed. The crown is fairly dense, without a crownshaft, and the leaves have broad, flattened stalks which are toothed along the margins; the costapalmate blades are divided to about half their depth into numerous finely pointed drooping segments, often with white thread-like fibres between; each segment is deeply divided into two long, fine-pointed lobes.

The long slender inflorescences which arise among the leaf bases consist of a long, arching rhachis from which arise several long slender branches, each in turn with a number of branches which bear many short stiff branchlets; in the bud stage the inflorescence is completely enclosed in close-fitting tubular bracts, each of the main side branches as well as the central axis having its own series of bracts. These bracts persist when flowers open, becoming papery and straw-coloured.

Flowers are bisexual. Each has 3 sepals fused at the base into a bell-shaped tube, the tips overlapping in bud. The 3 petals have bases fused into a narrow tube, the free upper parts being long and narrow. The petals fall at an early stage taking with them the 6 long stamens which are attached to the tube. The ovary has 3 cells which are free from each other at the base but united above into a single, long slender style, terminated by a minute stigma. Only 1 of the 3 ovules develops into a seed.

Fruits are small, egg-shaped and brownish with the base of the style remaining attached. Their thin dry flesh encloses a small, glossy brown seed flattened or slightly concave on one side; the endosperm is not ruminate.

HABITAT, USES, CULTIVATION *Washingtonia* species are found in rocky arid areas among other vegetation, commonly in gullies and canyons where there are permanent springs or soaks.

These hardy fan palms are widely cultivated in the southern states of the U.S.A., also in Australia where they may be confused with the native *Livistona australis*, from which they are readily separated by the long slender inflorescences, the thick robust trunk in *W. filifera* and the trunk swollen at the base and tapering in *W. robusta*. Except in very tall specimens, the old leaves, unless disturbed, remain attached to the trunk indefinitely, forming a thick, close-fitting, skirt-like thatch which can be a very striking feature, but unfortunately is nearly always removed by over-enthusiastic gardeners or vandals setting it on fire. Underneath the thatch the trunk is clean, greyish, closely ringed and furrowed.

Both species of *Washingtonia* make attractive specimen palms for landscaping in various situations in warmer temperate areas or in drier tropical situations (for which *W. robusta* is the better suited species), a sunny position giving the best results. They tolerate transplanting remarkably well at almost any size. They also make attractive potted specimens.

Propagation is from seed, which takes about 2 months to germinate. Subsequent seedling growth is fast, provided adequate room is available for the deep-running roots.

W. filifera Cotton Palm, Californian Washingtonia
The Californian Washingtonia is a striking robust fan palm with thick solitary trunk to about 15 m high and 60 to 80 cm in diameter, slightly swollen at the base. The trunk may be covered in a dense skirt of old dead leaves or may be clean and grey, slightly rough with fine vertical fissures, and closely ringed. The crown is fairly open with long greyish-green leaves; leaf stalks are 1.5 to 2 m long, toothed along the margins towards the base; blades are costapalmate, 1.5 to 2 m long, divided to at least half their depth into fine-pointed, 2-lobed segments with long white threads between segments. Inflorescences are 3 to 5 m long, arising among leaf bases and projecting beyond and below the crown, with branches pendulous, flowers white. Fruits are ovoid, brownish-black, to 6 mm long, 3.5 to 4.5 mm broad.
Distribution: southern California, south-western Arizona, north-western Mexico (states of Sonora and Baja California).

W. robusta Mexican Washingtonia
A tall fan palm with long, tapered trunk to about 25 m or more high, considerably enlarged at the base, about 25 cm in diameter at mid-point; old leaves usually remain attached in smaller specimens, or trunk is greyish-brown and slightly rough. Leaves form a compact head; leaf stalks are about 1 m long with toothing all along the margins; blades shiny mid-green, about 1 m long, divided to about half their depth into pointed, drooping segments; white threads are usually only present between segments in younger plants. Inflorescences are about 2 to 3 m long, arising among the leaf bases and hanging below the crown, covered with pale brown tubular bracts; flowers are flesh-coloured. Fruits are almost spherical, dark brown, pea-sized and produced in very large numbers.
Distribution: north-western Mexico: southern Sonora and Baja California.

Washingtonia robusta

APPENDIX I: PALM CLASSIFICATION

Historically various workers have arranged the palms into families, subfamilies, tribes and subtribes. There is now agreement between botanists that palms represent a single family. The very natural scheme published by the late Professor Harold E. Moore has been adopted here. Under this scheme the palm family is first divided into 15 Major Groups each of these being denoted by the name of a genus followed by the suffix "oid", e.g. the genus *Areca* gives its name to the Arecoid Palms. Within each Major Group, alliances of genera are recognized, though some of the Major Groups contain only one alliance, indeed only one genus; e.g. the Phoenicoid Palms include the genus *Phoenix* only. In contrast the Arecoid Palms consist of 18 alliances with 88 genera.

Those Major Groups which include genera described in this book are outlined below in alphabetical order.

Arecoid Palms 88 genera, 760 species

Feather palms, solitary or multiple trunks usually smooth, ringed, rarely with prickles or spines; crownshaft mostly present; leaves pinnate or simple and pinnately ribbed, leaflets reduplicate (with fold downwards); inflorescence never terminal, usually below the leaves at maturity and usually enclosed in bud by 1 or 2 non-woody bracts consisting of the prophyll only or the prophyll and 1 (rarely 2) sterile peduncular bract; flowers always male or female, commonly arranged in groups (triads) on floral branchlets, with 1 female flower between 2 earlier-opening males or on some parts of branches single or paired male flowers only. Ovary with 1 cell and 1 ovule except in a few genera. Fruit usually smooth, 1-seeded, rarely 2 or 3-seeded, mesocarp fleshy or dry with included fibres; endocarp usually thin. Germination adjacent except in *Orania*; first leaf usually 2-lobed, rarely linear.

Triovulate Genera
Reinhardtia Alliance: (1 gen./5 spp.) *Reinhardtia*
Orania Alliance: (2 gen./17 spp.) *Orania*

Uniovulate Genera
Euterpe Alliance: (6 gen./90 spp.) *Euterpe*
Roystonea Alliance: (1 gen./6 spp.) *Roystonea*
Dypsis Alliance: (7 gen./91 spp.) *Chrysalidocarpus*
Archontophoenix Alliance: (6 gen./11 spp.) *Archonto-phoenix, Chambeyronia, Rhopalostylis*
Cyrtostachys Alliance: (1 gen./8 spp.) *Cyrtostachys*
Linospadix Alliance: (4 gen./54 spp.) *Linospadix, Laccospadix, Howea*
Ptychosperma Alliance: (8 gen./106 spp.) *Drymophloeus, Carpentaria, Veitchia, Normanbya, Ptychosperma, Brassiophoenix*
Areca Alliance: (10 gen./227 spp.) *Gronophyllum, Hydriastele, Pinanga, Areca*
Clinostigma Alliance: (27 gen./117 spp.) *Dictyosperma, Pelagodoxa*
Oncosperma Alliance: (8 gen./13 spp.) *Oncosperma, Verschaffeltia, Phoenicophorium, Nephrosperma*

Borassoid Palms 7 genera, 56 species

Large fan palms with solitary or dichotomously branched or multiple trunks, usually with persistent leaf bases or marked with leaf scars; crownshaft lacking, leaves costapalmate; inflorescences among leaf bases, male and female on separate plants; peduncle long with several tubular, sterile bracts, first-order branches subtended by sheathing, fertile bracts; floral branchlets in clusters, with male flowers in sunken pits formed by united bracts, female flowers often larger than male, not sunken; fruit 1 to 3-seeded, mesocarp fibrous, endocarp surrounding each seed, endosperm often hollow.

Germination remote, cotyledon stalk often thick and long; first leaves undivided or palmate.

Genera
Borassus Alliance: (4 gen./13 spp.) *Borassodendron, Borassus, Latania*
Hyphaene Alliance: (3 gen./43 spp.) *Hyphaene*

Caryotoid Palms 3 genera, 75 species

Feather or bipinnate-leaved palms with solitary or multiple trunks, commonly covered with old leaf bases or fibres from leaf sheaths, or bare and ringed; crownshaft lacking; leaves pinnate or bipinnate, leaflets shallowly induplicate (with V upright), leaflets always with upper margins toothed; first inflorescence usually occurring among leaf bases near stem apex with further inflorescences occurring successively lower down on the stem which ultimately dies; inflorescence enclosed in several overlapping peduncular bracts in bud; flowers in triads, as in the Arecoid Group, or less commonly male and female flowers on different inflorescences from the same leaf axil; fruit with flesh containing irritant crystals; mostly 3-seeded, the seeds with hard coat.

Germination remote; first leaves entire or 2-lobed.

Genera
Arenga, Caryota, Wallichia

Ceroxyloid Palms* 4 genera, 30 species

Dioecious feather palms, often very tall, with solitary, smooth, ringed trunk; leaves pinnate, rarely forming a crownshaft, reduplicate (with fold downwards); inflorescences below leaves, sometimes several from one ring, long-peduncled, enclosed in bud by several sterile bracts; flowers stalked, male and female on separate plants and borne singly along branchlets. Fruit globose or irregularly angled or lobed, 1 to 3-seeded.

Germination adjacent; first leaves narrow, undivided or 2-lobed.

Only Genus
Ceroxylon

Chamaedoreoid Palms 6 genera, 146 species

Small to medium-sized feather palms with solitary or multiple trunks, smooth and ringed; crownshaft present or absent, leaves pinnate or simple and pinnately ribbed, frequently with old leaflets abscissing from the rhachis, leaflets shallowly reduplicate to flat at the base; inflorescences among or below the leaf bases, enclosed in early bud by a series of overlapping bracts, consisting of a prophyll and usually 3 or more sterile peduncular bracts; flowers male or female on the same or different plants; if on the same plant, they are in rows with the lowest 1 or 2 female and the upper ones male; if on different plants, the female usually solitary and the male in short rows or solitary; ovary with 3 cells and 3 ovules, only 1 developing into a seed; fruit normally 1-seeded, with a fleshy, often irritant mesocarp; endocarp thin.

Germination adjacent; first leaves 2-lobed or pinnate.

Genera
Gaussia, Opsiandra, Hyophorbe, Chamaedorea

Cocosoid Palms 28 genera, 583 species

Small to large feather palms with solitary or multiple trunks, sometimes scrambling, clothed in persistent leaf bases or bare and marked with leaf scars, sometimes spiny on all parts; crownshaft lacking; leaves pinnate or simple and pinnately ribbed; inflorescences among leaf bases, the peduncle with a usually short prophyll and a single large, often woody sterile peduncular bract enclosing the inflorescence in bud; rhachis bearing only first-order side branches or sometimes unbranched; flowers always male or female, spirally arranged in triads, usually with male flowers only toward ends of branches, sometimes with solitary females toward bases; fruits 1-7-seeded with mesocarp fleshy or dry, usually fibrous, endocarp usually hard and woody, each seed in a separate cavity, usually with a corresponding pore; endosperm often hollow.

Germination remote or adjacent; first leaves narrow and undivided or 2-lobed.

Genera
Cocos Alliance: (20 gen./122 spp.) *Cocos, Butia, Jubaea, Jubaeopsis, Syagrus, Arecastrum, Microcoelum, Parajubaea, Allagoptera, Polyandrococos, Scheelea, Orbignya*
Elaeis Alliance: (2 gen./3 spp.) *Elaeis*
Bactris Alliance: (6 gen./415 spp.) *Aiphanes, Acrocomia, Bactris, Astrocaryum*

Coryphoid Palms 32 genera, 322 species

Dwarf or creeping to large fan palms with solitary or multiple trunks covered with persistent leaf bases or bare and marked with leaf scars; crownshaft lacking; leaves palmate or costapalmate divided to base into segments or deeply lobed or simple with toothed margins; inflorescences among the leaves or rarely terminal, usually with a succession of sterile and fertile, tubular, non-woody bracts; flowers bisexual or male and female flowers on separate plants; fruit spherical to ovoid with mesocarp fleshy or dry, usually non-fibrous, endocarp usually thin; seed commonly intruded from one side or base by the seed coat.

Germination remote; first leaves undivided, linear to elliptical, rarely toothed or 2-lobed.

Genera
Trithrinax Alliance: (14 gen./68 spp.) *Trithrinax, Rhapidophyllum, Trachycarpus, Chamaerops, Schippia, Rhapis, Thrinax, Coccothrinax*
Livistona Alliance: (13 gen./226 spp.) *Livistona, Pholidocarpus, Licuala, Pritchardia, Acoelorrhaphe, Serenoa, Brahea, Copernicia, Washingtonia*
Corypha Alliance: (3 gen./14 spp.) *Corypha*
Sabal Alliance: (1 gen./14 spp.) *Sabal*

Lepidocaryoid Palms 22 genera, 664 species

Dwarf to large, usually prickly feather palms, with solitary or multiple stems, prostrate, erect or climbing, ringed, sometimes armed with root spines; crownshaft absent, leaves pinnate or simple and pinnately ribbed; usually spiny, often with rhachis modified into a climbing organ (cirrus), rarely palmate. Inflorescences among leaves or sometimes terminal, frequently with some modified into climbing organs (flagella), with a prophyll only or with several tubular, sheathing bracts; flowers bisexual or separate male and female (plants monoecious, dioecious or polygamous), in pairs or solitary, few to numerous. Fruits usually 1-seeded, skin covered with overlapping scales; mesocarp usually thin, rarely thick and fleshy or spongy; endocarp rarely woody, seed often with enveloping fleshy aril.

Germination adjacent or remote; first seed leaves undivided, 2-lobed or compound.

Hermaphrodite Genera
Korthalsia Alliance: *Korthalsia*

Polygamous Genera
Eugeissona Alliance: (1 gen./7 spp.) *Eugeissona*
Metroxylon Alliance: (1 gen./8 spp.) *Metroxylon*

Monoecious Genera
Raphia Alliance: (1 gen./28 spp.) *Raphia*

Dioecious Genera
Salacca Alliance: (4 gen./18 spp.) *Salacca, Pigafetta*
Calamus Alliance (9 gen./518 spp.) *Calamus*

Nypoid Palms 1 genus, 1 species

Feather palms with a prostrate, stout, underground stem, often branching dichotomously, rooting from lower side; crownshaft lacking; leaves erect, pinnate, reduplicate; inflorescences among leaf bases, erect with long peduncle, enclosed in bud by a short lower prophyll and a large papery sterile bract, floral branches subtended by bracts; flowers male or female, the male flowers in short dense spikes on branches arising from below the dense head of female flowers which terminates the rhachis; fruiting head more or less globular, with tightly packed irregularly angled fruits, with pyramidal old stigmas; seed large, intruded on one side by a ridge of thick endocarp.

Germination often commencing on fruiting head, plumule extending, pushing fruit away; first leaves with several leaflets.

Only Genus
Nypa

Phoenicoid Palms 1 genus, 17 species

Dioecious dwarf or prostrate to large feather palms with solitary or multiple trunks with persistent petiole bases in spiral patterns; crownshaft lacking, leaves pinnate, differing from all other feather palms in having deeply induplicate leaflets (V fold upwards) and lower leaflets modified into stiff, sharp spines; inflorescences among leaves, usually enclosed in bud by a 2-lobed bract (prophyll); flowers male and female on separate plants, arranged singly in spirals; fruit ovoid to oblong, mesocarp fleshy and fibrous, endocarp membranous; seed cylindrical, deeply intruded by seed coat along a groove running its whole length.

Germination remote; first leaves narrow-elliptical.

Only Genus
Phoenix

APPENDIX II:

MAJOR PALM COLLECTIONS OF THE WORLD

There are a number of collectors throughout the world who grow many different kinds of palms and large numbers of botanical gardens have collections of at least a few species, often in glasshouses. There are only a few public collections in the world with extensive representation of the many genera of palms; naturally, most of these are in tropical and subtropical regions.

The following are some of the more notable collections: Fairchild Tropical Gardens, Coconut Grove, near Miami, Florida, U.S.A., probably has the largest collection of palms in the world. The Bogor Botanic Gardens (Kebun Raya) near Jakarta in Java and its high altitude annex at Cibodas offer ideal growing conditions for palms of the wet tropics. The Botanic Gardens in Singapore have a large collection growing under conditions similar to those at Bogor, but at present limited numbers are being added to the collection; the same applies to the Peradineya Botanic Gardens in Sri Lanka. In India there is a large collection in the National Botanic Gardens, Howrah, near Calcutta. Huntington Gardens, in the Los Angeles area, U.S.A., has a very good representation of palms suited to more temperate climates. The Royal Botanic Gardens, Sydney, Australia, have a similar collection. In northern Australia, there are good collections in the Botanic Gardens at Cairns, Townsville and Rockhampton in Queensland and at Darwin in the Northern Territory.

In cool-temperate climates there are several good palm collections in heated glasshouses. Notable amongst these are the Royal Botanic Gardens, Kew, England, Longwood Gardens in Pennsylvania and The Bailey Hortorium at Cornell University, Ithaca, New York, U.S.A., which has a large research collection.

APPENDIX III:

PALMS FOR DIFFERENT CLIMATIC ZONES AND SPECIFIC PURPOSES

In the following listings all the palms mentioned in this book are allocated to one or more climatic zones. These are the zones in which those species could be expected to grow well outdoors without special protection except shading and shelter from wind where appropriate, and without constant irrigation. Obviously, when special measures such as protection from cold, irrigation, and maintenance of localized high humidity are put into effect, the cultivation of many species can be extended into both cooler and drier zones. However, it should be noted that the reverse does not generally apply, and thus it is not always possible to successfully grow palms from cooler climates in the tropics, or palms from semi-arid inland areas in moist coastal areas.

Note that many palms are listed under two or more climatic zones, reflecting a high degree of adaptability. If a genus is listed for one zone only it may not necessarily mean that it will not grow in other zones, but that it simply has never been tried in them. Of course for a commonly cultivated genus, such as *Cocos* or *Trachycarpus*, the climatic limits will have been fairly well established by trial and error over a long period.

In addition to the climatic zone lists there are several lists of palms adapted to specific environmental conditions, e.g. seashores, deep shade.

Where the genus name only is listed it is intended to mean that all species covered in this book are included; otherwise the particular species adapted to that zone or environment are given.

1. Palms for moist tropical climates:

Extreme minimum temperature 10°C or higher; average annual rainfall 1500 mm or higher; rainfall of driest month 25 mm or higher.

Acoelorrhaphe
Acrocomia
Aiphanes
Allagoptera
Archontophoenix alexandrae
Areca
Arenga
Astrocaryum
Bactris
Borassodendron
Borassus
Calamus australis
Calamus caryotoides
Carpentaria
Caryota
Chamaedorea
Chrysalidocarpus
Coccothrinax
Cocos
Copernicia
Corypha
Cyrtostachys
Dictyosperma
Drymophloeus
Elaeis
Eugeissona
Euterpe
Gaussia
Gronophyllum
Hydriastele
Hyophorbe
Hyphaene
Korthalsia

Latania
Licuala
Livistona (except *L. australis*)
Metroxylon
Nephrosperma
Normanbya
Nypa
Oncosperma
Opsiandra
Orania
Orbignya
Pelagodoxa
Phoenicophorium
Phoenix (except *P. canariensis*, *P. dactylifera*)
Pholidocarpus
Pigafetta
Pinanga
Polyandrococos
Pritchardia
Ptychosperma
Raphia
Reinhardtia
Rhapis
Roystonea
Sabal
Salacca
Scheelea
Schippia
Syagrus
Thrinax
Veitchia
Verschaffeltia

2. Palms for dry tropical climates:

Extreme minimum temperature 10°C or higher; average annual rainfall 250 to 1500 mm; one or more months with rainfall under 25 mm.

Allagoptera
Arecastrum
Borassus
Butia
Caryota urens
Chrysalidocarpus lutescens
Copernicia
Corypha
Hyophorbe
Hyphaene

Latania
Livistona alfredii
Livistona mariae
Phoenix reclinata
Phoenix sylvestris
Polyandrococos
Roystonea
Sabal mexicana

(Note: nearly all palms adapted to such semi-arid climates require permanent subsoil moisture.)

3. Palms for moist subtropical and frost-free warm-temperate climates:

Extreme minimum temperature 3° to 10°C; average annual rainfall 1200 mm or higher; rainfall of driest month 25 mm or higher.

Acoelorrhaphe
Acrocomia
Allagoptera
Archontophoenix
Arecastrum
Arenga
Butia
Calamus
Carpentaria
Caryota
Chamaedorea
Chamaerops
Chambeyronia
Chrysalidocarpus
Copernicia alba
Dictyosperma
Euterpe
Gaussia
Jubaeopsis
Laccospadix
Licuala ramsayi

Linospadix
Livistona
Microcoelum
Normanbya
Opsiandra
Parajubaea
Phoenix
Pritchardia
Ptychosperma
Reinhardtia
Rhapidophyllum
Rhapis
Rhopalostylis
Roystonea regia
Sabal
Schippia
Serenoa
Syagrus
Trithrinax
Washingtonia

4. Palms for cooler temperate but almost frost-free moist climates:

Extreme minimum temperature −2°C to 3°C; average annual rainfall 1000 mm or higher.

Archontophoenix cunninghamiana
Arecastrum
Arenga engleri
Brahea
Butia
Calamus muelleri
Caryota mitis
Ceroxylon alpinum
Chamaerops
Hedyscepe
Howea
Jubaea
Livistona australis
Livistona chinensis

Parajubaea
Phoenix canariensis
Phoenix dactylifera
Phoenix sylvestris
Rhapidophyllum
Rhapis
Rhopalostylis
Sabal minor
Sabal palmetto
Serenoa
Trachycarpus
Trithrinax acanthocoma
Washingtonia

5. Frost-tolerant palms:

Most of the following palms will survive winter temperatures down to about −5°C. Some, such as *Rhapidophyllum* and *Trachycarpus*, may survive temperatures of −8°C.

Brahea
Butia
Chamaerops
Jubaea
Livistona australis
Parajubaea
Phoenix canariensis
Phoenix dactylifera

Rhapidophyllum
Rhopalostylis sapida
Sabal minor
Sabal palmetto
Trachycarpus fortunei
Washingtonia filifera

6. Palms for dry temperate climates:

Extreme minimum temperature −2°C to 10°C; average annual rainfall 250 to 800 mm (or to 1200 mm in summer-rainfall subtropical areas).

Brahea
Butia
Chamaerops
Jubaea
Livistona mariae

Phoenix canariensis
Phoenix dactylifera
Phoenix sylvestris
Washingtonia

7. Palms which will tolerate deep shade:

Note: no palm will grow in shade deeper than that found on the floor of evergreen rainforest, that is, forest in which the tree crowns all overlap. In many parts of the interiors of houses and other buildings light levels are well below this level and will not support plant growth.

Archontophoenix
Arecastrum
Calamus
Caryota mitis
Chamaedorea
Chrysalidocarpus
Drymophloeus
Howea
Hydriastele
Laccospadix

Licuala
Linospadix
Microcoelum
Normanbya
Phoenix reclinata
Phoenix roebelenii
Pinanga
Ptychosperma
Reinhardtia
Rhapis

8. Palms which will tolerate full sun from an early age:

Note: the adult crowns of most taller palms will tolerate full sun, even though the younger stages may require shade or partial shade. Also, many palms which tolerate full sun in very humid tropical conditions will burn in cooler and drier conditions. Only palms which are sun-hardy at all stages are listed here.

Acoelorrhaphe
Allagoptera
Arecastrum
Arenga pinnata
Borassodendron
Borassus
Brahea
Butia
Caryota urens
Chamaedorea glaucifolia
Chamaedorea seifrizii
Chamaerops
Cocos
Copernicia
Corypha
Elaeis
Gronophyllum

Hyophorbe
Hyphaene
Jubaea
Latania
Livistona
Metroxylon
Oncosperma
Parajubaea
Phoenix
Pigafetta
Pritchardia
Roystonea
Sabal
Serenoa
Trachycarpus
Trithrinax
Washingtonia

9. Palms suitable for planting near the sea:

Exposed to occasional salt spray and somewhat saline soil conditions.

Acoelorrhaphe
Allagoptera
Arecastrum
Butia
Chamaerops
Cocos
Howea
Hyophorbe

Livistona australis
Livistona decipiens
Oncosperma tigillarium
Phoenix canariensis
Phoenix sylvestris
Roystonea
Sabal

10. Palms suitable for indoor decorative use under normal domestic conditions:

These palms, apart from being decorative in their younger stages, must tolerate low light levels and sudden changes in temperature and humidity. They must also be adaptable to growth in containers.

Arecastrum
Arenga engleri
Arenga porphyrocarpa
Calamus caryotoides
Calamus muelleri
Caryota
Chamaedorea
Chamaerops
Chrysalidocarpus lutescens
*Dictyosperma
Howea
Laccospadix

*Licuala
Linospadix
Microcoelum
*Phoenicophorium
Phoenix roebelenii
*Pinanga
*Reinhardtia
Rhapis
Sabal minor
Washingtonia

*These palms are likely to be more fussy than the others about warmth and humidity.

APPENDIX IV:
NOTES ON RECENT NAME CHANGES

Arecastrum romanzoffianum (p. 52) — in an important paper titled "An Outline of a Classification of Palms" by Dransfield and Uhl (*Principes* vol. 30, pp. 3—11 (1986)), presented as a precursor to the forthcoming book *Genera Palmarum*, *Arecastrum* is included in the genus *Syagrus*. This is hardly a surprise, as its status as a distinct genus has always been somewhat controversial. The species name under this classification would be *Syagrus romanzoffia.*

Gaussia — this genus is the subject of a recent botanical revision (Quero & Read, *Systematic Botany*, vol. 11, pp. 145—154 (1986)), in which, in addition to the two previously known species, two species are transferred from *Opsiandra*, not now regarded as a distinct genus. One of these is pictured and described on p. 132 as *Opsiandra maya*, and should now be called *Gaussia maya*; its range is extended to the Mexican state of Quintana Roo. The other was newly described in *Opsiandra* only in 1982, and occurs in the Mexican states of Oaxaca and Tabasco.

Microcoelum (p. 126) — in the revised classification of palms cited above under *Arecastrum*, this genus is treated as a synonym of *Lytocaryum*. The correct name under this classification for the species pictured would presumably be *Lytocaryum weddellianum*.

Opsiandra (p. 132) — this name disappears into synonymy under *Gaussia* (see note above).

Orania appendiculata (p. 133) — in a recent paper by Dransfield, Irvine and Uhl (*Principes* vol. 29, pp. 56—63 (1985)), this Australian species is shown to be out of place in *Orania*, and a new genus *Oraniopsis* is described to accommodate it. Most fascinating is the discussion of its relationships, with the conclusion that its strongest affinities are with the isolated Ceroxyloid Palms, *Ceroxylon* (northern S. America), *Juania* (Juan Fernandez Islands off Chile) and the Madagascan *Ravenea* and *Louvelia*. Appendix I, Palm Classification, should be amended accordingly (p. 182) with the Ceroxyloid Palms expanded to include *Oraniopsis*.

GLOSSARY

Acuminate: tapering suddenly to a slender point.

Acute: ending in a point.

Albumen: the substance stored within the seed endosperm.

Alternate: alternately placed; as when the leaflets are not opposite one another on the opposite sides of the rhachis.

Anther: that part of the stamen which contains the pollen.

Aril: an outgrowth of the stalk or funicle of the ovary which forms a fleshy layer over the seed testa in fruits of the Lepidocaryoid palms.

Auricle: an ear-shaped lobe at the base of a leaflet as in the genus *Arenga*.

Axil: the point or angle between the trunk or branch and a leaf.

Axillary: arising from an axil.

Axis: the central portion or longitudinal support on which other organs or parts are arranged, e.g. the rhachis.

Beaked: having an extended point or appendage.

Bifid: dividing into 2, e.g. the division of a segment into 2, as in many fan palm segments.

Bipinnate: leaves, pinnately divided with the leaflets again divided in a pinnate manner.

Bisexual: having both fertile male (stamen) and female (pistil) parts in the same flower.

Blade: the lamina; expanded portion of the leaf distinct from the petiole. May be entire or divided into separate leaflets or part divided into segments.

Bract: a specialized leaf associated with an inflorescence. Bracts may be of greatly differing shape, size, arrangement and texture. Large bracts may completely enclose an inflorescence as in Cocosoid palms, splitting down one side, spreading and persisting; some authors use the older terminology of spathe for this type of bract, or spathel when smaller. Bracts are common on the peduncle or stalk of the inflorescence, frequently being tubular; the first bract is known as a prophyll; those which do not subtend a branch are said to be sterile; some inflorescences have a number of bracts on the floral branches and each may subtend one or several flowers.

Bracteole: a small bract within and additional to the bract subtending a flower.

Caducous: falling off early, as with the bracts of some inflorescences.

Callus: a growth of or thickened tissue.

Calyx: the outer ring of floral organs, each of which is known as a sepal.

Campanulate: bell-shaped.

Carpel: the organ enclosing and protecting the ovules.

Caudex: the stem or axis of a plant; when tall and robust known as the trunk.

Cell: the cavity of the ovary containing the ovule or ovules; in its more basic botanical sense, it refers to the structural unit (usually microscopic in size) of most plant tissues.

Clavate: club-shaped.

Compound: referring to the blade, with two or more completely separate leaflets.

Corolla: the inner series or whorl of floral organs, each of its parts being known as a petal.

Costa: a rib of the leaf, especially the midrib.

Costapalmate: a fan-shaped or palmate leaf in which the petiole is extended as a midrib or rhachis into the blade.

Cotyledon: the seed leaf with one end embedded in the endosperm and with the plumule and radicle at the other end.

Crown: the head or cluster of leaves surmounting the top of the trunk or stem.

Crownshaft: the usually conspicuous collective leaf sheaths which retain an encircling cylindrical shape until the leaf becomes older and splits down the side opposite the petiole and with the petiole and blade falls off, leaving an encircling scar and a similar sheathing leaf base beneath. This arrangement of leaf sheaths is best developed amongst the Arecoid feather palms.

Cuneate: wedge-shaped, with the narrow end towards the point of attachment.

Deciduous: falling off, as in the bracts of inflorescences.

Dioecious: plants that have unisexual flowers, the male flowers being on one plant and the female flower on another.

Drupe: a succulent, indehiscent fruit in which the fruit wall consists of 2 distinct layers, an outer fleshy or fibrous layer called the mesocarp and an inner usually hard endocarp which encloses one or more seeds; the endocarp may be divided into separate parts each enclosing a seed.

Ebracteate: without bracts.

Ellipsoid: an elliptic solid body.

Elliptical: having an outline the shape of an ellipse.

Embryo: the young plant enclosed by the seed wall and embedded in the endosperm.

Endocarp: the inner layer of the fruit enclosing the seed, often but not necessarily hard and woody.

Endosperm: the nutritive tissue or albumen of the seed, providing food for the embryo and later the developing plant.

Entire: with unbroken margin, i.e. without teeth or lobes.

Exocarp: the outer skin of the fruit.

Fertile: of flowers, producing seed; of anthers, containing pollen; of fruit, containing seed; of seed, containing a fertile embryo.

Fertilization: the action of the pollen on the ovule that results in the production of seed.

Filament: the stalk of a stamen at the apex of which the anther is situated.

Free: not united or joined with any other part.

Fruit: the mature ovary and whatever parts of the flower may be attached to it after the ovules have developed into seeds.

Funicle: the stalk of the ovary.

Fused: joined and growing together.

Genus: a group of species that resemble one another; the first word in a botanical name denotes the genus, e.g. *Phoenix rupicola* belongs to the genus *Phoenix.*

Germination: when the embryo of the seed begins to grow and emerges from the seed coat.

Glabrous: without hairs.

Glaucous: covered with a bloom of wax, giving an ashy to greyish appearance.

Hair: an outgrowth from the epidermis; a single elongated cell, or may consist of several or many cells.

Hastula: the terminal outgrowth of the petiole in fan palms, also called a ligule.

Hermaphrodite: a flower containing both functional male and female parts (bisexual).

Hoary: densely covered with hairs or bristles, giving a white or greyish appearance.

Homogeneous: of seed endosperm, uninterrupted by repeated penetrations of the seed coat (testa).

Hybrid: the progeny of two plants of different species.

Imbricate: with edges overlapping.

Indehiscent: not splitting when mature.

Irregular: of leaves, with leaflets not arranged in a uniform manner; of flowers, having one or more segments of different shape or size to the others in the same whorl; of fruits, of uneven shape.

Lamina: see blade.

Lanceolate: narrowly elliptical, tapering equally to both ends, generally used for leaves and other organs more than 3 times but less than 8 times as long as broad.

Leaflet: each separate portion of a compound leaf as in feather palms.

Linear: long and narrow with more or less parallel sides, with length more than 8 times breadth.

Lobe: any projection or division, especially of a rounded form, such as the division of a leaf; the free portion of united sepals or petals.

Locule: a compartment within an ovary, also known as a cell.

Membranous: thin, semi-transparent.

Mesocarp: the fleshy or fibrous layer of the fruit between the exocarp and the endocarp.

Midrib: the central nerve or vein of a leaf.

Monocotyledon: a member of 1 of the 2 great divisions of the flowering plants, characterized by having only 1 cotyledon or seed leaf, mostly parallel leaf venation, and no true cambium layer allowing subsequent growth in stem.

Monoecious: having organs of both sexes on the one plant, whether or not in separate flowers.

Mucronate: terminating abruptly in a sharp stiff point called a mucro.

Nerve: a vein; generally applied to the larger, more conspicuous veins in a leaf or leaflet.

Node: the part of the stem from which a leaf arises.

Nut: a 1-celled dry fruit that contains 1 seed and does not open when mature.

Ob-: a prefix signifying the reverse or opposite direction, e.g. obovate, an egg-shape with the narrow end towards the base.

Oblong: longer than broad, with nearly parallel sides and usually rounded ends.

Obovate: egg-shaped with the narrow end at the point of attachment.

Obtuse: blunt.

Opposite: of leaflets of feather palms, arranged in pairs on the rhachis, opposite to one another.

Orbicular: Circular or nearly circular in outline.

Ovary: the swollen basal part of the pistil that contains the ovules or immature seed; may be part of a single carpel, or of 2 or more fused carpels.

Ovate: egg-shaped, with the broad end towards the base.

Ovoid: egg-shaped and of a solid form, such as an ovoid fruit.

Ovule: the immature seed before fertilization.

Palmate: of leaves, with ribs, veins or segments radiating from a central point in the manner of a hand or fan.

Panicle: a much branched inflorescence, each branch bearing flowers arranged in a racemose or spicate manner.

Pedicel: the flower-stalk of a single flower.

Pedicellate: stalked (of flowers).

Peduncle: the stalk of an inflorescence.

Pedunculate: having a peduncle.

Perennial: a plant that lives for a number of years.

Perianth: the floral organs; sepals and petals (calyx and corolla) collectively, particularly when they are similar.

Persistent: applied to the leaves which remain attached to the trunk after they are spent; the bracts which remain after flowering; the sepals or petals which remain after flowering; the stigma which remains attached to the ripened fruit.

Petal: one of the organs forming the corolla.

Petiole: the stalk of the leaf; in palms that part between the sheathing base and the lowest part of the blade.

Pinna: a leaflet; the primary division of a pinnate leaf.

Pinnae: plural of pinna.

Pinnate: a compound leaf having the leaflets arranged in a feather-like manner, i.e. arranged along each side of a central stalk or rhachis.

Pinnule: a secondary leaflet of a bipinnate leaf.

Pistil: the female organ of the flower, usually consisting of a stigma, a style or stalk and an ovary or seed box; in palms, usually containing 1 to 3 cells and ovules.

Plicate: pleated or folded like a fan.

Plumule: the first leaf emerging from the growing apex of the embryo in a newly germinated seed.

Pollen: the dust-like grains contained in the anthers, carrying the male genetic material.

Prostrate: applied to palms, where the trunk grows horizontally along the ground.

Raceme: an inflorescence with pedicellate flowers arranged along an axis or rhachis, the lowest usually opening first.

Radicle: the first root from the embryo in a germinating seed.

Rainforest: a dense, usually layered forest, with a closed canopy, dominated by soft-leaved trees, generally characterized by the presence of lianas and epiphytes.

Recurved: curved backwards or downwards.

Reflexed: bent sharply backwards and downwards.

Rhachis or rachis: the axis of an inflorescence; the axis or stalk of a pinnate leaf to which the leaflets are attached.

Rhomboid: quadrangular, with an acute angle at each end and the lateral angles obtuse.

Ruminate: of seed endosperm, penetrated by many uneven infoldings of the seed coat (testa).

Seed: the fertilized or mature ovule, containing the embryo and endosperm within an outer coat or testa.

Segment: each subdivision of a deeply divided leaf.

Serrate: toothed like a saw.

Sessile: without a stalk.

Shoot: a new growth.

Simple: of leaves, not compound; of an inflorescence, not branched.

Solitary: single, only one from the same place.

Spadix: a spicate inflorescence in which the axis is fleshy or succulent; but formerly used to denote any palm inflorescence.

Spathe: a large sheathing bract or pair of bracts enclosing a spadix; formerly used for the large peduncular bract(s) of palms.

Species: a unit in classification.

Spicate: consisting of a spike.

Spike: an inflorescence of sessile flowers along an undivided axis or stalk.

Spine: a stiff, sharp-pointed outgrowth from a surface or margin of any organ.

Spinous: having the form of a spine: used of various organs that are modified in this way, e.g. lower leaflets of *Phoenix*.

Spiny: bearing spines.

Stamen: the male organ of the flower, which produces the pollen, usually consisting of a filament or stalk and an anther containing the pollen; the stamens collectively are termed the androecium.

Staminode: an infertile rudimentary stamen.

Sterile: infertile, unable to reproduce or contribute to reproduction; of bracts, those that do not subtend flower-bearing branches.

Stigma: the upper part of the pistil which receives the pollen; in palms this is commonly 3-lobed.

Style: the slender part of the pistil between the ovary and the stigma; when this is absent the stigma is termed sessile.

Testa: the seed coat, covering the embryo and endosperm.

Trunk: in palms, the main axis or stem from which the roots, leaves and inflorescence arise; it may be slender as a pencil to massive in diameter, short to very tall, or grow completely underground.

Undulate: wavy — of leaves, applied to the up and down appearance of the margins of the leaflets in some feather palms; of fan palms, the manner in which the blade may be distinctly waved up and down in addition to the normal segment pleating; of the inflorescence, the wavy floral branchlets of some species.

Unisexual: of a flower, having only functional male or female parts; of an inflorescence, having functionally all male or all female flowers.

Valvate: with the edges touching but not overlapping, as the petals of male flowers in most palms.

Variety: a subdivision of a species.

Vein: a thickened part of a leaf or leaflet, through which runs conducting or fibuous tissues; the larger veins are often referred to as ribs or nerves.

BIBLIOGRAPHY

Backer, C.A. & Bakhuizen van den Brink, R.C., *Flora of Java*: Arecaceae — vol. 3, pp. 165-199 (1968).

Bailey, F.M., *Queensland Flora*: Palmae Part 5 — pp. 1670-1691 (1902).

Bailey, L.H., Palms, and their Characteristics. *Gentes Herbarum*, vol. 3, fasc. 1, pp. 3-29, fig. 1-19 (1933).

Bailey, L.H., Certain Palms of Panama. *Gentes Herbarum*, vol. 3, fasc. 2, pp. 33-116, fig. 20-88 (1933).

Bailey, L.H., American Palmettoes. *Gentes Herbarum*, vol. 3, fasc. 6, pp. 275-339, fig. 145-190 (1934).

Bailey, L.H., The Royal Palms — Preliminary Survey. *Gentes Herbarum*, vol. 3, fasc. 7, pp. 343-387, fig. 191-226 (1935).

Bailey, L.H., The King Palms of Australia — Archontophoenix. *Gentes Herbarum*, vol. 3, fasc. 8, pp. 391-409, fig. 227-238 (1935).

Bailey, L.H., Certain Ptychospermate Palms of Horticulturists. *Gentes Herbarum*, vol. 3, fasc. 8, pp. 410-437, fig. 239-254 (1935).

Bailey, L.H., Arecastrum — the Queen Palms. *Gentes Herbarum*, vol. 4, fasc. 1, pp. 3-14, fig. 1-7A (1936).

Bailey, L.H., The Butias. *Gentes Herbarum*, vol. 4, fasc. 1, pp. 16-50, fig. 8-27 (1936).

Bailey, L.H., Washingtonia. *Gentes Herbarum*, vol. 4, fasc. 2, pp. 53-81, fig. 28-45 (1936).

Bailey, L.H., Erythea — the Hesper Palms. *Gentes Herbarum*, vol. 4, fasc. 3, pp. 85-118, fig. 46-71 (1937).

Bailey, L.H., Notes on Brahea. *Gentes Herbarum*, vol. 4, fasc. 3, pp. 119-125, fig. 72-74 (1937).

Bailey, L.H., Native Bactrids of the Greater Antilles. *Gentes Herbarum*, vol. 4, fasc. 5, pp. 173-184, fig. 101-110 (1938).

Bailey, L.H., Coccothrinax in the Southern Greater Antilles. *Gentes Herbarum*, vol. 4, fasc. 7, pp. 247-259, fig. 158-164 (1939).

Bailey, L.H., Howea in Cultivation — the Sentry Palms. *Gentes Herbarum*, vol. 4, fasc. 6, pp. 189-198, fig. 111-118 (1939).

Bailey, L.H., Lucuba Palm in the New World. *Gentes Herbarum*, vol. 4, fasc. 6, pp. 218-219, fig. 138-139 (1939).

Bailey, L.H., Ptychospermate Palms — Supplement. *Gentes Herbarum*, vol. 4, fasc. 6, pp. 209-217, fig. 128-136 (1939).

Bailey, L.H., Species of Rhapis in Cultivation — the Lady Palms. *Gentes Herbarum*, vol. 4, fasc. 6, pp. 199-208, fig. 119-127 (1939).

Bailey, L.H., Acoelorraphe vs. Paurotis — Silversaw Palm. *Gentes Herbarum*, vol. 4, fasc. 10, pp. 361-365, fig. 228-229 (1940).

Bailey, L.H., Acrocomia — Preliminary Paper. *Gentes Herbarum*, vol. 4, fasc. 12, pp. 421-476, fig. 254-298 (1941).

Bailey, L.H., Palms of the Seychelles Islands. *Gentes Herbarum*, vol. 6, fasc. 1, pp. 3-44, fig. 1-29 (1942).

Bailey, L.H., Palms of the Mascarenes. *Gentes Herbarum*, vol. 6, fasc. 2, pp. 51-104, fig. 30-73 (1942).

Bailey, L.H., Studies in Palms 4. Brahea and one Erythea. *Gentes Herbarum*, vol. 6, fasc. 4, pp. 177-197, fig. 87-100 (1943).

Bailey, L.H., Revision of the American Palmettoes. *Gentes Herbarum*, vol. 6, fasc. 7, pp. 367-459, fig. 186-251 (1944).

Bailey, L.H. assisted by Moore, H.E., Palms Uncertain and New. *Gentes Herbarum*, vol. 8, fasc. 2, pp. 93-205, fig. 4-87 (1949).

Basu, S.K., The Indian Botanic Garden, Calcutta. *Principes*, vol. 13, No. 4, pp. 115-119 (1969).

Beccari, O., Asiatic Palms — Lepidocaryeae: Part 1. The Species of Calamus. *Annals of the Royal Botanic Garden, Calcutta*, vol. 11, pp. 1-518, plates 1-238 (1908).

Beccari, O., La "Copernicia cerifera" in Riviera ed una nuova specie di Livistona. *Webbia*, vol. 3, pp. 295-305 (1910).

Beccari, O., Contributi alla cognoscenza delle Palme I — Del Genere Kentia; II — Del Genera Howea; III — Una nuova "Cocoina" affricana: Jubaeopsis caffra; IV — Di una nuova varieta di Cocos nucifera...; V — Le Palme de genere Eugeissona...; VI — Nuova revisione del Genere Pritchardia. *Webbia*, vol. 4, part 1a, pp. 143-240 (1913).

Beccari, O. Asiatic Palms — Lepidocaryeae: Part 3. The Species of the Genera Ceratolobus, Calospatha, Plectocomia, Plectocomiopsis, Myrialepis, Zalacca, Pigafetta, Korthalsia, Metroxylon, Eugeissona. *Annals of the Royal Botanic Garden, Calcutta* vol. 12, part 3, pp. 1-231, plates 1-120 (1918)

Beccari, O., Recensione delle Palme del Vecchia Mondo Appartenenti alla Tribu delle Corypheae. *Webbia* vol. 5, part 1, pp. 5-70 (1921).

Beccari, O., Le Palme della Nuova Caledonia. *Webbia* vol. 5, part 1, pp. 71-146, Plate I — XIII (1921).

Beccari, O., Asiatic Palms — Corypheae, *Annals of the Royal Botanic Garden, Calcutta* vol. 13, pp. 1-356, plates 1-99 (1933).

Beccari O. & Rock, J.F., A Monographic Study of the Genus Pritchardia, *Memoirs of the Bernice Pauahi Bishop Museum* vol. 8, no. 1, pp. 1-77, plates I-XXIV (1921).

Beccari, O. & Hooker, J.D., Palmeae, in Hooker, J.D., *Flora of British India*, vol. 6, pp. 402-483 (1892-3).

Bentham, G. & Hooker, J.D., *Genera Plantarum*: Ordo 187. Palmae, vol. 3, pp. 870-948 (1883).

Blombery, A.M., Australian Native Plants, p. 149, fig. 82, pp. 284-5, 447-456, Angus and Robertson, Sydney (1979).

Bondar, G., *Palmeiras do Brasil* (Boletim N. 2, Instituto de Botanica, Sao Paulo, Brasil), pp. 1-159, fig. 1-57 (1964).

Brown, F.B.H., *Flora of Southeastern Polynesia. I. Monocotyledons*. Bernice P. Bishop Museum Bulletin 84, Family 4 Palmae, pp. 117-121, plates 25, 26 (1931).

Buhler, T., Notes on Marcottage of Certain Palms, *Principes*, vol. 18, no. 3, pp. 111-112 (1974).

Burret, M., Eine neue Palmengattung aus Sudamerika. *Notizblatt des Botanischen Gartens und Museums zu Berlin-Dahlem*, Band 11, Nr. 101, pp. 48-51 (1930).

Burret, M., Die Palmengattungen Martinezia und Aiphanes. *Notizblatt des Botanischen Gartens und Museums zu Berlin-Dahlem*, Band 11, Nr. 107, pp. 557-577 (1932).

Burret, M., Die Palmengattung Gronophyllum Scheff. *Notizblatt des Botanischen Gartens und Museums zu Berlin-Dahlem*, Band 13, Nr. 117, pp. 200-205 (1936).

Burret, M., Palmae neogeae XI. *Notizblatt des Botanischen Gartens und Museums zu Berlin-Dahlem*, Band 13, Nr. 119, pp. 478-481 (1937).

Burret, M., Die Palmengattung Hydriastele Wendl et Drude und

Adelonenga Becc. *Notizblatt des Botanischen Gartens und Museums zu Berlin-Dahlem* Band 13, Nr. 119, pp. 482-487 (1937).

Burret, M., Palmae chinenses. *Notizblatt des Botanischen Gartens und Museums zu Berlin-Dahlem*, Band 13, Nr. 120, pp. 582-606 (1937).

Burret, M., Die Palmengattung Syagrus Mart. *Notizblatt des Botanischen Gartens und Museums zu Berlin-Dahlem*, Band 13, Nr. 120, pp. 677-696 (1937).

Burret, M., Systematische Ubersicht uber die Gruppen der Palmen. *Willdenowia*, Band 1, Heft 1, pp. 59-74 (1953).

Burret, M., & Potztal, E., Microcoelum, eine neue Palmengattung (Cocoideae). *Willdenowia*, Band 1, Heft 3, pp. 386-388 (1956).

Burret, M., & Potztal, E., Systematische Ubersicht uber die Palmen (Fortsetzung). *Willdenowia*, Band 1, Heft 3, pp. 350-385 (1956).

Corner, E.V.H., *The Natural History of Palms*, pp. 1-393, figs. 1-133, plates 1-24. Weidenfeld and Nicolson, London (1966).

Dahlgren, B.E. & Glassman, S.F., A Revision of the genus Copernicia. *Gentes Herbarum*, vol. 9, fasc. 1-2, pp. 1-232. Fig. 1-190 (1961-63).

Dale, I.R., & Greenway, P.J., *Kenya Trees & Shrubs* — Palmae: pp. 10-13, Plates 14-16 (1961).

Dransfield, J., New Light on Areca langloisiana. *Principes*, vol. 18, no. 2, pp. 51-57 (1974).

Dransfield, J., The Genus Borassodendron (Palmae) in Malesia. *Reinwardtia*, vol. 8, part 2, pp. 351-63, fig. 1-6 (1972).

Dransfield, J., Notes on Caryota no Becc. and Other Malesian Caryota Species. *Principes*, vol. 18, no. 3, pp. 87-93 (1974).

Dransfield, J., Palms in the Everyday Life of West Indonesia. *Principes*, vol. 20, no. 2, pp. 39-47 (1976).

Dransfield, J., A Note on the Habitat of Pigafetta filaris in North Celebes. *Principes*,

vol. 20, no. 2, p. 48 (1976).

Dransfield, J., A Synopsis of the Genus Korthalsia (Palmae: Lepidocaryoideae). *Kew Bulletin*, vol. 36, no. 1, pp. 163-194 (1981).

Essig, F.B., Ptychosperma in Cultivation. *Principes*, vol. 21, no. 1, pp. 3-11 (1977).

Essig, F.B., A Revision of the Genus Ptychosperma. *Allertonia*, vol. 1, no. 7, pp. 415-478, fig. 1-9 (1978).

Essig, F.B., The Genus Orania Zipp. (Arecaceae) in New Guinea. *Lyonia* vol. 1, no. 5, pp. 211-233 (1980).

Furtado, C., The Identity of Hyphaene natalensis Kuntze. *Gardens' Bulletin, Singapore*, vol. 25, part 2, pp. 283-297 (1970).

Furtado, C., Asian Species of Hyphaene. *Gardens' Bulletin, Singapore*, pp. 299-309 (1970).

Furtado, C., A New Search for Hyphaene guineensis Thonn. *Gardens' Bulletin, Singapore*, pp. 311-334 (1970).

Glassman, S.F., Studies in the Palm Genus Syagrus Mart.. *Fieldiana: Botany*, vol. 31, no. 15, pp. 363-397 (1968).

Glassman, S.F., Studies in the Palm Genus Syagrus Mart. II. *Fieldiana: Botany*, vol. 32, no. 8, pp. 77-103 (1969).

Glassman, S.F., A Conspectus of the Palm Genus Butia Becc. *Fieldiana: Botany*, vol. 32, No. 10, pp. 127-172 (1970).

Glassman, S.F., A synopsis of the Palm Genus Syagrus Mart. *Fieldiana: Botany*, vol. 32, no. 15 pp. 215-240 (1970).

Glassman, S.F., Preliminary Taxonomic Studies in the Palm Genus Scheelea Karsten. *Phytologia*, vol. 37, no. 3, pp. 219-250 (1977).

Glassman, S.F., Re-evaluation of the Genus Butia With a Description of a New Species. *Principes*, vol. 23, no. 2, pp. 65-79 (1979).

Gooding, E.G.C., Loveless, A.E. & Proctor, G.R., *Flora of Barbados* — Palmae: pp. 83-88. Her Majesty's Stationery Office, London (1965).

Hodge, W.H., Oil-Producing Palms of the World — a Review. *Principes*, vol. 19, no.

4, pp. 119-136 (1975).

Kellett, J., Looking Back on the Florida Freeze of 1962. *Principes*, vol. 13, part 1, pp. 23-35 (1969).

Kimnach, M., The Species of Trachycarpus. *Principes*, vol. 21, no. 4, pp. 155-160 (1977).

Kitzke, E.D. & Johnson, D., Commercial Palm Products Other Than Oils. *Principes*, vol. 19, no. 1, pp. 3-26 (1975).

Langlois, A.C., *Supplement to Palms of the World*, pp. 1-252, fig. 1-264. The University Presses of Florida, Gainesville (1976).

Li, H.-L.L., *Woody Flora of Taiwan* — Palmae: pp. 915-920, fig. 365-368, Livingston Publishing Company, Narberth, Pennsylvania (1963).

Little, E.L., & Wadsworth, F.H., *Common Trees of Puerto Rico and the Virgin Islands* — Palm Family (Palmae): vol. 1, pp. 34-47, fig. 4-10 (1964); vol. 2, pp. 68-79, fig. 265-271 (1974). U.S. Department of Agriculture, Forest Service, Washington D.C.

MacBride, J.F., Flora of Peru — 16. Palmae. *Botanical Series, Field Museum of Natural History* (later *Fieldiana: Botany*), vol. 13, part 1, no. 2, pp. 321-418 (1960).

McCurrach, J.C., *Palms of the World*, pp. i-xxxv, 1-290. Harper & Brothers, New York (1960) (reprinted by Horticultural Books Inc., Stuart, Florida (1976)).

McFadden, L.A., Palm Diseases. *Principes*, vol. 3, no. 2, pp. 69-75 (1959).

Marloth, R., *The Flora of South Africa* — Fam. 9. Palmae: vol. 4, pp. 46-50, fig. 8, plates 11-12. Darter Bros. & Co., Capetown & William Wesley & Son, London (1915).

Martelli, U., "Pelagodoxa henryana" Becc., Palma delle Isole Marquesas. *Nuovo Giornale Botanico Italiano*, n.s. vol. 39, n. 2, pp. 243-250, plates 7-9 (1932).

Martius, K.F.P. von, *Historia Naturalis Palmarum*, vol. 1, pp. i-clxiv (1831-1849); vol. 2, pp. 1-152 (1823-1837); vol. 3, pp. 153-350

(1837-1850).

Merrill, E.D., *Enumeration of Philippine Plants* — Palmae: vol. 1, pp. 142-172. Bureau of Science, Manila (1922).

Moore, H.E., Exotic Palms in the Western World. *Gentes Herbarum*, vol. 8, fasc. 4, pp. 295-315, fig. 111-120 (1953).

Moore, H.E., Synopses of Various Genera of Arecoideae. Veitchia. *Gentes Herbarum*, vol. 8, fasc. 7, pp. 481-536, fig. 139-155 (1957).

Moore, H.E., Synopses of Various Genera of Arecoideae. Reinhardtia. *Gentes Herbarum*, vol. 8, fasc. 7, pp. 541-576, fig. 157-168 (1957).

Moore, H.E., An Annotated Checklist of Cultivated Palms. *Principes*, vol. 7, no. 4, pp. 119-182 (1963).

Moore, H.E., New Palms from the Pacific II. *Principes*, vol. 13, no. 2, pp. 67-76 (1969).

Moore, H.E., Additions and Corrections to "An Annotated Checklist of Cultivated Palms". *Principes*, vol. 15, No. 4, pp. 102-106 (1971).

Moore, H.E., The Major Groups of Palms and Their Distribution. *Gentes Herbarum*, vol. 11, fasc. 2, pp. 27-141, fig. 1-60 (1973).

Moore, H.E., New Genera and Species of Palmae from New Caledonia. *Gentes Herbarum*, vol. 11, fasc. 4, pp. 291-309, fig. 1-10 (1978).

Moore, H.E., The Genus Hyophorbe (Palmae). *Gentes Herbarum*, vol. 11, fasc. 4, pp. 212-245, fig. 1-19 (1978).

Moore, H.E., Family 39. Arecaceae, in Smith, A.C., *Flora Vitiensis Nova*, vol. 1, pp. 392-438, fig. 81-86, Pacific Tropical Botanical Garden, Lawai, Kauai, Hawaii (1979).

Moore, H.E., Endangerment at the Specific and Generic Level in Palms. *Principes*, vol. 23, no. 2, pp. 47-64 (1979).

Moore, H.E. & Anderson, A.B., Ceroxylon alpinum and Ceroxylon quindiuense (Palmae) *Gentes Herbarum*, vol. 11, pp. 168-185 (1976).

Moore, H.E. & Fosberg, F.R., The Palms of Micronesia and the Bonin Islands. *Gentes Herbarum*, vol. 8, fasc. 6, pp. 423-478, fig. 129-138 (1956).

Moore, H.E. & Guého, L.J., Acanthophoenix and Dictyosperma (Palmae) in the Mascarene Islands. *Gentes Herbarum,* vol. 12, fasc. 1, pp. 1-16, fig. 1-7 (1980).

Muirhead, D., *Palms* pp. 1-140. Dale Stuart King, Six Shooter Canyon, Globe, Arizona (1961).

National Academy of Sciences, *Underexploited Tropical Plants with Promising Economic Value,* pp. i-ix, 1-189. National Academy of Sciences, Washington, D.C. (1975).

Read, R.A., The Genus Thrinax (Palmae: Coryphoideae). *Smithsonian Contributions to Botany,* no. 19, pp. 1-98, fig. 1-57 (1975).

Reitz, P.R. (ed.), *Flora Illustrada Catarinense,* Fasciculo PALM by P.R. Reitz, pp. 1-189, fig. 1-67, Itajai — Santa Catarina — Brazil (1974).

Robertson, B.L., Aspects of the Morphology of Jubaeopsis caffra Becc. *Principes,* vol. 21, no. 4, pp. 169-175 (1977).

Robertson, B.L., The Inflorescence of Jubaeopsis caffra Becc. *Journal of South African Botany,* vol. 43, No. 3, pp. 223-230 (1977).

Russell, T.A., The Raphia Palms of West Africa. *Kew Bulletin,* vol. 19, no. 2, pp. 173-196 (1965).

Russell, T.A., 193. Palmae, in Hepper, N., *Flora of West Tropical Africa,* vol. 3, part 1, pp. 159-169, fig. 373-5. Her Majesty's Stationery Office, London (1968).

Sastrapradja, S., Mogea, J.P., Sangat, H.M., & Afriastini, J.J., *Palem Indonesia* pp. 1-119, Lembaga Biologi Nasional, Bogor, Indonesia (1978).

Shuey, A.G. & Wunderlin, R.P., The Needle Palm: Rhapidophyllum hystrix. *Principes,* vol. 21, no. 2, pp. 47-59 (1977).

Staff of the L.H. Bailey Hortorium, Cornell University, *Hortus Third, A Concise Dictionary of Plants Cultivated in the United States and Canada,* pp. xiv + 1290. Macmillan Publishing Co., Inc., New York and Collier Macmillan Publishers, London (1976).

Standley, P.C., Trees and Shrubs of Mexico — 8. Phoenicaceae. Palm Family. *Contributions from the United States National Herbarium,* vol. 23, part 1, pp. 70-84 (1920).

Standley, P.C., & Steyermark, J.A., Flora of Guatemala — Palmae, *Fieldiana: Botany,* vol. 24, part 1, pp. 196-299, fig. 35-51 (1958).

Stevenson, G.B., *Palms of Southern Florida,* pp. 1-25, published by the author (1974).

Tomlinson, P.B., Systematics and Ecology of the Palmae. *Annual Review of Ecology and Systematics,* vol. 10, pp. 85-107 (1979).

Tomlinson, P.B., & Soderholm, P.K., The Flowering and Fruiting of Corypha elata in South Florida. *Principes,* vol. 19, no. 3, pp. 83-99 (1975).

Tralau, H., The Gènus Nypa van Wurmb., *Kungl. Svenska Vetenskapsakademiens Handlingarm Fjärde Serien,* Band 10, Nr. 1, pp. 5-29, plates I-V (1964).

Wallace, A.R., *Palm Trees of the Amazon and their Uses,* pp. i-viii, 1-129, plates I-XLVIII. John van Voorst. London (1853).

Wessels Boer, J.G., Palmae, in Lanjouw, J. (ed.), *Flora of Suriname,* vol. 5, part 1, pp. 1-172, plates I-XVII, fig. 1-10. E.J. Brill, Leiden (1965).

Wessels Boer, J.G., *The Geonomoid Palms.* pp. 1-202, plates 1-10. N.V. Noord-Hollandsche Uitgevers Maatschappij, Amsterdam (1968).

Whitmore, T.C., *Palms of Malaya,* pp. i-xv, 1-132, fig. 1-106, plates 1-16, Oxford University Press, Kuala Lumpur (1973).

INDEX

Notes

1. Common names of the palms are cross-referenced to their botanical names.
2. Where there is more than one page reference, the main entry for genus and species is indicated by bold type.
3. Illustrations (photographic) are indicated by 'pl'.